Case Studies in Sport Development

Other titles in the Sport & Global Cultures Series

Long Run to Freedom: Sport, Cultures and Identities in South Africa
John Nauright

Reading Baseball: Books, Biographies, and the Business of the Game
Braham Dabscheck

Rethinking the Olympics: Cultural Histories of the Modern Games
Robert K. Barney, Ed.

Sport, Race, and Ethnicity: Narratives of Difference and Diversity
Daryl Adair, Ed.

Sport for Development, Peace, and Social Justice
Robert J. Schinke and Stephanie J. Hanrahan, Eds.

Case Studies in Sport Development: Contemporary Stories Promoting Health, Peace, and Social Justice

Robert J. Schinke, EdD
Laurentian University

Ronnie Lidor, PhD
The Zinman College of Physical Education and Sport Sciences
Wingate Institue

Editors

Fitness Information Technology
A DIVISION OF THE INTERNATIONAL CENTER FOR PERFORMANCE EXCELLENCE

262 Coliseum, WVU-CPASS
PO Box 6116
Morgantown, WV 26506-6116

Library of Congress Card Catalog Number: 2013942574

ISBN: 978-1-935412-62-5

Cover Design: 40 West Studios

Cover Photo: Courtesy Big Stock Photo

Typesetter: 40 West Studios

Production Editor: Matt Brann

Copyeditor: Geoffrey Fuller

Proofreader: Matt Brann

Indexer: Matt Brann

Printed by: Data Reproductions Corp.

10 9 8 7 6 5 4 3 2 1

Fitness Information Technology
A Division of the International Center for Performance Excellence
West Virginia University
262 Coliseum, WVU-CPASS
PO Box 6116
Morgantown, WV 26506-6116

800.477.4348 (toll free)
304.293.6888 (phone)
304.293.6658 (fax)
Email: fitcustomerservice@mail.wvu.edu
Website: www.fitinfotech.com

Contents

Preface

Sport for peace is quickly becoming a popular topic within the global organizations. Groups such as Right to Play feature positive interventions for populations at risk, through sport. Sport is more than competition and the opportunity to become physically fit and active in one's own life. As you will find in this book, sport and physical activity offer opportunities for people and communities to forge improved relations, providing the intended context is structured with care. *Case Studies in Sport Development* will illustrate how experiences from across our global community have served as the conduit to harmony within and among people.

The internationally regarded contributing authors to this edited book speak from the heart about sport and physical activity experiences they have lived. These cases are heartwarming, written in the first person, and intended to provide the reader with hope that sport and physical activity are indeed answers to many of today's and tomorrow's societal challenges within people and communities, and among countries, races, and religions. This book has been conceived to provide you, the reader, with some indication of how sport and physical activity, formally structured, can contribute to a better life and a better world.

The co-editors of this book have structured the compilation into three unique sections. In Section I, the reader is introduced to "Remedying Marginalization" through sport and physical activity contexts. In Section II, "Health and Well-Being," the reader learns how activity contexts can foster better lives for individuals and communities. Section III shifts the focus toward "Peace and Social Justice," perhaps the most widely recognizable theme in the overarching area of sport development.

Preface

Case Studies in Sport Development: Opening up the Discussion

Robert J. Schinke and Ronnie Lidor

We live in tumultuous times. Granted, there have been periods of uncertainty caused by civil unrest and economic hardship before now. Today, in this moment, we seem overwhelmed by fiscal and social challenges. Presently, the tendency is to look closely at our social ills through a critical lens, and to lament. Indeed, there is much to learn from our missteps—and what we learn is not easily integrated as better practices. Perhaps some feel a disconnect between present challenges and the hope for a better world. There is little question that we must, as individuals and also as members of social groups, strive to be (and to do) better. But how might we proceed and what context might we use as media?

The editors of this book choose to look at life and its opportunities through a positive lens. The contributing authors were asked to tell their personal stories or experiences within the sport-for-development area, employing an approach that might be regarded as idealistic. The task of looking for the positive in imperfect contexts is not easy. Sport development projects are sometimes criticized, especially when these programs colonize or silence the voices of the intended communities and their prospective participants. And yet, even within imperfect stories, there are "aha" moments when the reader can see what sport and physical activity can offer toward the realization of a better world.

Hence, following our introduction, positive cases are presented that embrace peace, remedy marginalization, and foster health and wellness. These cases are written as first-person narratives; they are highly personal. The language chosen to underpin the experiences is basic, intended to entice readers to think outside of academic boxes and silos. At the culmination of each story, the authors also provide takeaway messages that the reader might be able to consider and apply in similar circumstances. Before moving to these cases, we first provide the sole theoretical chapter in this book. Though our introduction is academic in comparison to what follows, this opening chapter serves as the platform for subsequent chapters.

WHAT IS SPORT FOR DEVELOPMENT?

As we look more closely at what sport development signifies, we might first consider the term by its components. The United Nations (UN) Inter-Agency Task Force on Sport for Development and Peace defines sport as "all forms of physical activity that contribute to physical fitness, mental well-being, and social interaction, such as play, recreation, organized or competitive sport, and indigenous sports and games" (United Nations, 2003). The parameters of this definition are broad, encompassing structured and unstructured play, as well as culturally diverse approaches to sport offerings (Hartmann, 2003). The focal point of sport within sport development is to engage people in meaningful physical activities, while fostering individual growth and social connections. Given all that sport offers, access to it is now regarded as a fundamental right for women, men, and children, regardless of race, religion, socioeconomic status, sexual orientation, gender, and health status (Sport for Peace International Working Group, 2005). Sport, loosely defined to also include physical activity, can contribute to the improvement of one's emotional and psychological health, as well as one's physical living conditions, regardless of geography and circumstance (Hanrahan, 2005, 2012). Finally, it is proposed that access to sport through sport development projects ought to be widespread, given that its financial cost is often nominal. Typically, all that is needed is physical space, little or no equipment, community engagement/mobilization, and a willingness to convene as a group to play and move (Sport for Development and Peace International Working Group, 2005).

The credence of *sport for development and peace* (SDP) as a movement is now affirmed through the International Olympic Committee and the United Nations. SDP has recently been tied to the UN's eight millennium development goals: (a) eradicating human hunger, (b) achieving primary universal education, (c) promoting gender equity, (d) reducing child mortality, (e) improving maternal health, (f) combating AIDS, (g) ensuring a sustainable environment, and (h) achieving global partnership (www.un.org/millenniumgoals/). These goals have recently been packaged for children and adolescent readers in the form of a comic book, published by the UN Office for Sport Development and Peace, titled "Score the Goals" (United Nations, 2010). Within the comic book story, the reader follows 10 international European football stars chosen to represent the UN, along with a few fans chosen to accompany the athletes to an out-of-country charity all-star game. The group travels by boat to a hypothetical destination, with the method of travel featured as environmentally friendly (i.e., no carbon footprint is created through the travel). The magazine exemplifies for the reader the importance of the aforementioned millennium goals within the context of the group's travels, as their ship becomes disabled and they are stranded on a secluded island. Questions of access to water, housing, leadership by women, and teamwork become integral to the group's unity.

The UN clearly recognizes that their educational mandate about global challenges must be directed in part to young readers, meaning the next generation of SDP advocates. Through sport and the integration of athletic superstars, the young reader finds SDP's focus areas of health and well-being, peace, and social justice more easily understood. The connection of elite sport to SDP is an inherent part of the larger movement. When high-profile athletes speak about social issues, they already have access to a high exposure forum through which SDP ideas can be created and promoted. Ronaldo, the Brazilian professional soccer icon, affirmed the potential role of elite athletes in sport development (SD) when he stated the following during an invited speech at the UN General Assembly in 2005:

> I have devoted my life to helping youth realize their dreams. Now working with the United Nations, I will be ready to help, through events, messages and any other means to help relieve the difficulties youth are confronted with, no matter which side they are on. (United Nations, 2006)

Consequently, elite athletes can serve as the media for bringing forward important societal messages pertaining to sport and development. In the city of Montreal, Canada, several of the first editor's professional boxers allocate significant portions of their spare time to youth sport programming in local impoverished neighborhoods. At Wikwemikong Unceded Indian Reserve, where one of the contributing authors resides, Indigenous high-profile elite athletes often visit and spend considerable time playing sports, coaching, and exchanging ideas with the community's youth and sport leaders. The program Right to Play (2008, 2010) exemplifies more globally how athletes might serve as catalysts for change within challenged communities and among targeted populations.

Though we propose that sport can serve as a catalyst to positive changes for individuals and communities, this is not to say that sport *always* contributes to human betterment. Within sport, there sometimes exists the unfair exploitation of athletic talent, a tolerance for violence and hooliganism among fans of opposing teams, and within competitive settings, a focus on winning at all cost over sport for human development (Sport for Development International Working Group, 2005). Embedded in a sport development project is the possibility that the program will fall short, with processes disempowering those engaged in the project. As Giles and Lynch (2012) recently proposed, projects in developing nations, conceived and quarterbacked from outside of the intended community, can serve to colonize sport participants through a perpetuation of power imbalances, such as when an SD project is created by an affluent outsider, where the focus of the project does not match the interests, challenges, or cultural standpoint(s) of the intended community. Right to Play (2008) has acknowledged that sport unto itself cannot be regarded as the silver bullet—a solution that eliminates problems and stands alone. When sport becomes *the* focus within projects or decisions are made on how to improve a social condition from afar, the correctly formed holistic approach that is required to better human conditions may be overlooked. SD projects require community engagement to meaningfully connect sport with the appropriate trajectory and vertical links with local, regional, national, and sometimes international resources, as needed.

Focus Areas in Sport Development

As the reader peruses the extensive number of SD websites, it becomes clear that there are several ways to classify projects. For example, Israel's Education and Social Project (Mifalot; www.mifalot.co.il/mifalot/Language/english/#) features various types of projects: (a) on the field, (b) knowing your neighbor, (c) civil service, (d) the game of life, and (e) sport leadership. Embedded within the above classifications, one can find a variety of foci, including physical activity, moral development, peace and reconciliation, and social justice. Right to Play differentiates among its programs in relation to the following: (a) promoting health and preventing disease; (b) stressing well-being for persons with disabilities; (c) enhancing social inclusion, preventing conflict, and building peace; (d) strengthening child youth development and education; and (e) promoting gender equity (www. righttoplay.com/International/our-impact/Pages/SportforDevelopmentcont%27d.aspx). Adding to the above, the Sport for Development and Peace International Working Group (2005) proposed that sport development can foster the following: (a) individual development, (b) social integration, (c) post-disaster trauma relief, (d) economic development, and (e) social mobilization. Pulling these classifications together, we have synthesized sport development into three focus areas that seem to reflect the topic matter featured in this compilation. These focus areas are *remedying marginalization, health and well-being,* and *peace and social justice.*

REMEDYING MARGINALIZATION

The trajectory of remedying marginalization encompasses how inequities in the treatment of people are presently being corrected through SDP. One might posit that his or her country is above social injustice, or in contrast, fertile ground for social injustice. Social injustices happen in large urban areas, in remote locations, and in developing and developed countries. Consider access to sport, for example, and how readily available it is to able-bodied youth versus youth with physical challenges or psychological conditions. When one speaks of social justice, the discussion, in keeping with the UN Millennium Goals (United Nations, 2010), might include the provision of *access* and *equity*. When reviewing the words of Giles and Lynch (2012), poorly conceived sport-for-development projects can integrate applications that misalign with a community's needs, cultural norms, and human resources (see also Hartmann, 2003). Sport practices are sometimes developed based upon education processes garnered in universities, formal coaching courses, main-stream readings, and the like. Within such initiatives, the best intentioned of sport-for-development projects can miss the mark, overlooking (and also silencing) readily available community resources or misidentifying their prospective participants. When incorrectly framed programming is proposed for (and on) the field, the programming creates a disconnect between provider and participant, and creates or perpetuates an uneven playing field by limiting access and contributing to social injustice.

The trajectory of remedying marginalization is exemplified by a case study written by Blodgett and Peltier. Duke Peltier has, for more than 10 years, served as the Wikwemikong Unceded Indian Reserve's community lead contact in a well-regarded series of decolonizing research projects, where SDP has been part of his work. Within Duke's story, as a former elite ice-hockey player, he shares how he overcame racism after relocating to a mainstream community in the pursuit of his athletic ambitions. Though his experience was not part of a formal SD project, what becomes apparent is how one person can, via sport, catalyze an educational process that teaches people in mainstream cultural contexts how to become more inclusive and sensitive to the standpoints of those at the margins.

HEALTH AND WELL-BEING

Within health and well-being, the focus in cases shifts to the promotion of physical health and psychological resilience. When one considers the parameters of this general grouping of SD experiences, the content spans programs that foster self-esteem, self-worth, and self-determination (Coakley, 2012). In addition, health and well-being projects can focus on the global rise in both noncommunicable and communicable diseases (Sport for Development and Peace International Working Group, 2005), and the growing epidemic of physical inactivity within some regions, among certain socioeconomic or cultural groups (The Next Step, 2008). The choice of how to focus a health or well-being SD project is a decision made within a *region* by a *specific group* and based upon *contextual necessity*. Within Tanzania (Maro, Roberts, & Sørensen, 2009), a central focus, initially proposed by the World Bank (1992), has been the HIV and AIDS crisis in that country. Consequently, a few Tanzanian SD providers, including Maro and colleagues, have promoted the awareness and prevention of the national HIV epidemic through holistically designed sport programming. Soccer, given its popularity as a Tanzanian national sport, was identified as the physical activity through which education about disease prevention would take place. Though a formal educational setting can serve as the context to bridge physical activity with the health topic of disease prevention, Maro and colleagues found that many of the Tanzanian youth at risk for the disease did not attend school. Consequently, the SD project they engage in is a community outreach program outside of the school system, open to a broader base of youth, including those without access to formal education. Hence, the best conceived SD projects take into account how to access the intended population, beyond the aforementioned criteria of geographic location and contextually and culturally relevant sport programs.

There are several cases that illustrate the power of existing health and wellness programs. Among these, consider the physical activity program that Tamar Semerjian provides, where she and a few academic colleagues have worked with physically challenged participants, seeking to develop their fitness and, in some cases, also their mobility. When one reads Tamar's case, it becomes clear that access to physical activity is often restricted to the able bodied. Within this section more generally, it becomes apparent that access to physical activity, when opened up to those often excluded from its offerings, can better lives. However, first, the potential SD provider must look beyond mainstream populations to subgroups who lack access to health and well-being opportunities.

PEACE AND SOCIAL JUSTICE

Peace is not characterized by the absence of violence (Keim, 2003, 2009), but by proactive strategies being developed to restore relationships among people in conflict. The following extract from the address of Secretary General of the UN to the World Conference on Education and Sport for a Culture of Peace underscores the objective of peace through the medium of sport:

> Be it team competition or individual athletics, sport has long displayed an inspiring ability to overcome national, political, ethnic, and cultural differences. Sport, in short, is an instrument of understanding among people. It is a vehicle for education about the world at large. It can be especially powerful in instilling in children and young people universal values such as respect and tolerance. (International Olympic Committee, 1999)

Sport-for-development projects can contribute to reconciliation processes, but we would caution that their potency is influenced by whether the structures and processes that underpin said projects are meaningfully conceived. Consequently, though generalities might be offered in terms of intervention guidelines across projects, effective SD projects can only be conceived when one is immersed, living within the context, and working with those touched by the conflict. Each conflict has a specific history and its own unique injustices, with both aspects viewed through the lens of context.

In this book, Ronnie Lidor considered how professional soccer in Israel has served as an informal opportunity to work through the hostilities among elite athletes from Israeli and Palestinian backgrounds (see also Liebmann & Rookwood, 2007). The physical and social context of the soccer field seems to pose many challenges for Israeli and Palestinian teammates. Depending on where a game is played, crowd/fan behavior tends to be more supportive of team members from one culture than the other culture. In the professional soccer context in Israel, Israeli and Palestinian fans sit in separate sections of the arena, spatially confirming a distinct cultural and ideological divide. Knowing that fans are divided by entrenched differences, the athletes working as teammates are left to seek a middle ground, all the while attempting to focus on elite sport performance. Given this, Lidor aspires to guide a process of sport psychology intervention, where shared objectives are identified among the athletes, even when the performance context sometimes crackles with hostility and tension. The athletes who succeed in becoming a unified group (i.e., team) within Israel's borders might serve as an example and perhaps a catalyst to reconciliation among soccer fans divided by religious and ideological strife. Clearly, one's intervention must be built to withstand the contextual challenges that those engaging in the intervention will encounter once they are reintroduced to the testing grounds of their social context.

Considering this Book

We offer each of the invited case studies as an example among a much wider breadth of possible topics and important experiences that bridge sport with holistic human development. Further, our classification of case types is highly simplistic and open to modification and definition. Turning now to the views we have shared: as a disclaimer, we are proposing sport development as a solution to some of today's most pressing challenges, proffering sport and physical activity as a solution. Watching the emergence of sport-for-development projects around the world, we propose that even the most promising of intentions can be stymied by misinformed leadership, inaccessible programs, and armchair leaders working from outside of the local context. The very best of what is to come in and through sport and physical activity happens when topics, structures, and processes encourage community engagement in the form of cultural and contextual knowledge, as well as a long-term commitment that ensures sustainability. Only then might resources align to support sport development in the comprehensive and insightful manner that will foster better circumstances for our civilization.

REFERENCES

Coakley, J. (2012). Youth sports: What counts as positive development. In R. J. Schinke & S. J. Hanrahan (Eds.), *Sport for Development, Peace, and Social Justice* (pp. 181-192). Morgantown, WV: Fitness Information Technology.

Giles, A., & Lynch, M. (2012). Post-colonial and feminist critiques of sport for development. In R. J. Schinke, & S. J. Hanrahan (Eds.), *Sport for Development, Peace, and Social Justice* (pp. 89-104). Morgantown, WV: Fitness Information Technology.

Hanrahan, S. J. (2005). Using psychological skills training from sport psychology to enhance the life satisfaction of Mexican orphans. *Athletic Insight, 7*(3). Retrieved from http://www.athleticinsight.com

Hanrahan, S. J. (2012). Developing adolescents' self-worth and life satisfaction through physically active games: Interventions with orphans and teenagers living in poverty. In R. J. Schinke & S. J. Hanrahan (Eds.), *Sport for Development, Peace, and Social Justice* (pp. 134-148). Morgantown, WV: Fitness Information Technology.

Hartmann, D. (2003). Theorizing sport as social intervention: A view from the grassroots. *Quest, 55*, 118-140.

International Olympic Committee. (1999). Peace cannot be built overnight. *Olympic Review, XXVI-28*, 34. Retrieved from http://la84foundation.org/OlympicInformationCenter/OlympicReview/1999/OREXXVI28/

Keim, M. (2003). *Nation-building at play—Sport as a tool for social integration in post-apartheid South Africa.* Oxford, UK: Meyer & Meyer Sport.

Keim, M. (2009) *Translating Olympic truce into community action in South Africa—Myth or possibility in Olympic truce-peace and sport.* Olympia, Greece: International Olympic Truce Centre.

Liebmann, S., & Rookwood, J. (2007). Football for peace? Bringing Jews and Arabs together in Northern Israel. *Journal of Qualitative Research in Sports Studies, 1*, 11-18.

Maro, C., Roberts, G. C., & Sørensen, M. (2009). Using sport to promote HIV/AIDS education for at-risk youths: An intervention using peer coaches in football. *Scandinavian Journal of Medicine & Science in Sports, 19*, 129-141.

The Next Step. (2008). *Toolkit sport for development.* Retrieved from http://www.toolkitsportdevelopment.org/

Right to Play. (2008). *Harnessing the power of sport for development and peace: Recommendations to governments.* Toronto, Canada: Right to Play.

Right to Play. (2010). Retrieved from http://www.righttoplay.com/International/Pages/Home.aspx

Sport for Development and Peace International Working Group. (2005). *Sport for development and peace: From practice to policy.* Toronto, Canada: Sport for Development and Peace International Working Group.

United Nations. (2003). *United Nations Task Force report: Sport for development and peace: Towards achieving the world millennium goals.* Geneva, Switzerland: United Nations. Retrieved from http://www.un.org/sport2005

United Nations. (2006). *Press conference by United Nations Office of Sport for Development and Peace.* Geneva, Switzerland: United Nations.

United Nations. (2010). *Scoring the goals: Teaming up to achieve the millennium goals.* Geneva, Switzerland: United Nations.

World Bank. (1992). *Tanzania: AIDS assessment and planning study.* Washington, DC: World Bank.

SECTION 1

REMEDYING MARGINALIZATION

Intending to Create a Landmark Will Change You

2

Carole A. Oglesby

All stories reside in a specific time and space. Spatial and temporal characteristics frame the narrative themes of the core elements of the story. In this chapter, the spatial elements include Temple University, a populist and urban institution in the heart of heavily African American-populated North Philadelphia. The city itself, iconic in America history, adds to the frame. Another focus is late 1970s to early 1980s USA. The country had barely moved past the antiwar and civil justice unrest of the 1960s. Various institutional contexts, such as education, politics, business, and sport, were enmeshed in the persistent turmoil of transformative change as the old gender and racial *percentages of participation* were no longer accepted or tolerated.

In the center of this frame is the story of a bond among four women, a relationship of purpose that through daunting obstacles generated a product that deepened and accelerated transformational change in sport, and propelled each woman forward in her own important career. This relationship remains more than 30 years later as a footprint of that long, arduous journey. I recently interviewed my three co-authors of our published product to complete this chapter.

I taught at Purdue University for three years after I completed my physical education PhD there. Then there were three quick and exciting years at University of Massachusetts, and in 1975, I made the third (and longest) stop on my academic journey at Temple University in Philadelphia, Pennsylvania.

Philadelphia (*philos* = loving; *adelphos* = brother) was anything but brotherly love in 1975. It was to me, then and now, a city with a fascinating trajectory. Founded in 1682 by Quaker William Penn, it was carefully and consciously built to be a seat of government and a port of great economic significance. It was the largest city in the colonies and the place where the United States of America was born. As the 19th century opened, Washington, DC, became the seat of US government, and as the 19th century rolled by, Philadelphia's neighbor to the north, New York City, became the leading financial center. Gradually, the vitality of the textile industries, the railroads, and the retail giants (e.g., Wanamakers) waned, and I felt that by the late 1970s Philadelphia was a city with a debilitating inferiority complex and an identity crisis.

From its beginnings, Philadelphia was a multiracial and multiethnic city as wave after wave of immigrant groups chose the city as home: Italian, Irish, German, and after WWII, many Russians and other Eastern Europeans. Consistently, however, the significant racial/ethnic community for Philadelphia was African American. In the 18th century, the region boasted the largest free Black population in the US. The area was a center for the Abolitionist Movement in the Civil War. Philadelphia was an important destination for the Underground Railroad and a frequent meeting place for leaders like Harriett Tubman and William Still. Philadelphia was also a major destination for what was called the Great Migration of African Americans from rural South to urban North. From 1880-1930, the population of African Americans in Philadelphia rose from 31,000 to 220,000.

Also important to a perception gap between Black and White cultures were the many iconic landmarks in the Philadelphia area virtually ignored by the mainstream. The city is the home of the *Philadelphia Tribune,* a newspaper founded in 1884 and the oldest, continually run, Black-owned newspaper in the US. Center City, which includes the central business district and central neighborhoods of Philadelphia, is the home of the Mother Bethel African Methodist Episcopal Church, founded in 1731 on the country's oldest parcel of land continually owned by African Americans. The childhood homes of operatic giants Marion Anderson and Paul Robeson can be found there (only if one looks hard).

By the mid-1950s, the so-called White flight from the city began in earnest. From 1950-1970, census numbers show Philadelphia losing 25% of its population, mostly to the suburbs. Nowhere did this flight become more visible than in North Philly, where Temple University is located. The Physical Education and Athletic Department building sits on beloved Broad Street (the champion Philadelphia Flyers ice hockey team were the Broad Street Bullies) and Montgomery Avenue, less than four miles north of City Hall (designed as ground zero center of the geometrically perfect William Penn design).

When founded by a Baptist minister in 1884, Temple College was located in middle-to-lower class, White ethnic neighborhoods. It was consciously offered as an affordable education in a city renowned for its affluent "privates": University of Pennsylvania, Haverford, Bryn Mawr, and Swarthmore out in the suburban "Main Line." In 1907, Temple College revised its institutional status; a hospital, a medical school, and a dental college were annexed and Temple University was born.

The fortunes of Temple University and North Philadelphia waxed and waned over the next 50 years, but the surrounding community became almost uniformly poor and Black. The community perception seemed to define Temple as an island (a White island, I would say) surrounded by an alienated community. A commissioned report on the occasion of the 125th anniversary of Temple's founding describes how the university attempted to grow during the 1960s, with 7,000 community residents being displaced by university acquisition of what officials saw as "unsightly property." To the surrounding community, these "properties" were homes. Protests began in earnest. At the height of the tensions, the Board of Trustees studied moving the entire campus about 20 miles out to a suburban location in Ambler, Pennsylvania. Even with all the anger and frustration felt toward Temple, this move would have the effect of abandoning all hope the community held for their children and generations to come.

Somehow, wisdom prevailed and an outside mediator was able to broker a *compact* between Temple and the community. A moratorium on building was declared, assenting to no further expansion or building without mutual agreement.

Even with Temple's image as a "White island," about 18% of the students were African American, a higher percentage than any American university except historically and predominantly Black colleges. In addition, there were many more African American professors and coaches than I had ever experienced before. The education of a lifetime in the area of diversity opened before me, and in the beginning I didn't even know it was happening.

There was so much to be done. Frank Rizzo was the mayor of Philadelphia, 1971-1979; he was a "law and order" former police commissioner with a reputation for brutal tactics and racism. It was said that his reply to a question about how to "improve the situation" in North Philadelphia was "burn it to the ground and start all over."

When I arrived in 1975, it was common for Temple students to lobby hard for student teaching assignments in suburban areas. Few wanted assignments in the Philadelphia School District inner city where it was perceived that racial difficulties, poor discipline and behavior, and chronic absenteeism (from all classes but especially physical education) were pandemic. Some Temple athletic teams had "subteams" of White and Black groups. Traveling to White, upper-class areas occasioned Temple players to cope with racial slurs and taunting, and many coaches and players voiced their frustrations that officials (mostly White but some Black as well) consistently used a different standard of physical contact for Temple players, seeming to prejudge that they would be rough.

During my three years at University of Massachusetts, I was introduced to an academic unit of psychology of education that would become a groundbreaking Department of Social Justice. One of their special approaches was to utilize the Piagetian "developmental levels of cognition" to create levels of developmental processes relating to the various -isms, especially anti-Semitism and racism. I learned about the early stages of Beverly Tatum's construct of a White racial identity, especially where the naive White person interacts with real Black people and is forced the confront the myriad ways real people act that are completely unlike the learned racial stereotypic "Black folk." I knew some theories, but during my first year or two at Temple I was at sea over the psychoemotional meanings of my experiences. The "U Mass way" had been White-on-White racial awareness training. This approach was premised on the notion that White people had created a dominant racial consciousness without Black participation and should heal themselves in the same way. I am sure this approach made great progress. My own education down the path towards an equitable personal racial identity was fostered and enhanced beyond measure by three African American women I encountered at Temple. We all worked together (with others, to be sure) to change students' orientations towards Philadelphia's inner city schools by creating materials and undergraduate and graduate classes to bring racial awareness into professional training, as well as by holding postgraduate professional training workshops for coaches, officials, and athletic administrators, initially in the Philadelphia area and then well beyond. The rest of this chapter attempts to capture the wondrous essence of these three great leaders, colleagues, and friends, and the primary material product we created to enable us to meet our goal: publishing a text titled *Black Women in Sport*. The first order of business is a brief, descriptive biography of each of the three co-authors of the book.

Dr. Nikki Franke

Nikki Franke was born in Harlem. She had an older brother who died at the age of 5. When she was 10, it was discovered that she had severe scoliosis, and she spent a good deal of time in a neck-to-waist cast. Eventually, the back issues receded and she was a very active child, involved in basketball, tennis, and the city specialty, stickball. When her medical issues were at their worst, Nikki had a home teacher, and as Nikki was recovering, the teacher wisely made sure Nikki got into a better school.

In her senior year in high school, a newly graduated teacher introduced her to the sport of fencing, and there was no turning back. The place for a would-be fencer to go to college in New York City was Brooklyn College, where former Olympic coach Denise O'Conner worked. Nikki graduated from Brooklyn College with honors, and she became the next in a line of Brooklyn College fencers to go to Temple University for graduate work, while also coaching there. She never left the coaching position.

Nikki represented the USA in the World University Games in Moscow in 1973 and was on the 1976 and 1980 Olympic teams. Nikki was the US Fencing Association foil champion in 1975 and 1980. She won a silver medal in the 1975 Pan American Games and a bronze medal in 1979.

Her coaching accomplishments have been even more phenomenal. She has coached at Temple University for 39 years, compiling a 601-158-1 career record. During that period, Temple's fencers have entered post-season competition 36 times. They were NCAA team champions in 1992, runners-up in 1987 and 1993, third in 1985 and 1991, and fourth in 1983, 1984, 1988, and 1990.

Nikki was the US Fencing Coaching Association Women's Coach of the Year in 1983, 1987, 1988, and 1991. She has been inducted into four different halls of fame: Brooklyn College, Temple University, US Fencing Association, and the International Hall of Fame of the Women's Sports Foundation. She was the first African American female fencing coach in the collegiate ranks and the only African American women to coach a Division I fencing team.

Nikki was one of the co-founders of the Black Women's Sport Foundation. Part of the motivation to start the Foundation, she says, was that "[w]e used to go to so many women's sports conferences and would see no women of color." Of the *Black Women in Sport* text, Nikki says that the most significant contribution was in consciousness-raising. She thought the release of the book was "neat" at the time, but over the years she has come to appreciate its significance much more than she had initially. Along this path, Nikki found time to earn a master's and a doctorate in community health, and is an associate professor at Temple along with her coaching duties. She is married to Norman (one of her role models, along with her two coaches, Tina, and myself), and has a daughter (also an athlete, but not a fencer).

Dr. Alpha Alexander

Alpha Alexander is the youngest of the trio of Black co-authors. Born in 1954, her mother and father lived in central Tennessee but moved to Dayton, Ohio, for her birth. Her father told her he did not want her "raised in the South" at that time. Alpha had twin brothers who were stillborn, so she was raised an only child, the apple of her parents' eyes. Her father was a postman and a schoolteacher, although he had earned a master's degree in mathematics at the University of Wisconsin, Madison. He could not find a way to utilize the degree except through public school teaching. Alpha's high school was 70% White when she was a freshman, but as affluent Black families began to move into the area, White families left. The school was 80% Black by the time she graduated, and all this was keenly noticed by Alpha.

College attendance was expected for Alpha. Her father wanted her to be a medical doctor, but she had a great love for sports. The College of Wooster in Ohio sponsored 13 varsity sports for women, so that was where she headed. She played volleyball, basketball, and tennis, and in 1991 was inducted into the Wooster Athletic Hall of Fame.

Although an excellent athlete, it was Alpha's contributions as a researcher, educator, mentor, and advocate that prompted the NCAA in 2006 to name her one of the 100 Most Influential Student Athletes of the century. Her own mentors, Drs. Ginny Hunt, Nan Nichols, and Maria Sexton (all legendary Midwestern figures in women's sport), encouraged Alpha to go to Temple University for her master's and doctoral degrees. Alpha's master's thesis catalogued the participation (or lack thereof) of women of color in the Association of Intercollegiate Athletics for Women (AIAW) collegiate program at that time. The AIAW named Alpha and Tina to a Task Force to study and enhance minority involvement through the 1980s and early 1990s.

Alpha's role in the AIAW and the NCAA, along with her years as Education Director for the YWCA International, led to her extensive involvement with the US Olympic Committee, the IOC Youth Camps, the IOC Olympic Academy, and Citizen Ambassadors, for whom she led several international tours. Alpha also served as President of the Arthur Ashe Foundation and Executive Board Member of both the Peter Westbrook Foundation (African American Olympic fencer) and the Wendy Hilliard Rhythmic Gymnastics Foundation. To all this must be added, of course, her role as cofounder of the Black Women's Sport Foundation.

Alpha's interview with me for this chapter produced several poignant moments. She described how racism, sexism, and economic barriers had challenged her. "I was so poor in graduate school that I could only eat a Philly cheese-steak once a day. It was lucky I received a graduate assistantship to cover my tuition." She described the tensions involved in the continual experience of being the only person of color in a room (she had been very surprised to find that Temple was not the Black school she had assumed it was). Alpha's mother had died within two months of her graduation as an EdD and her father two years after that, so Alpha knew the toll of the chronic and stressful lifestyle-related diseases still rampant among African Americans, but that did not deter her. Of Black Women in Sport's publication, Alpha said "I was very young when the book was published, but I knew it was badly needed. There were so few documentations of African American women in sport. The book spearheaded many other recognitions to follow."

Professor Tina Sloan-Green

Tina Sloan-Green is the most senior of these three African American leaders. She was born to a family of five biological siblings and three foster siblings in the community of Eastwich, a suburb of Philadelphia. Her father was an electrician and carpenter, while her mother was an entrepreneur operating from home. She attended an elementary school with only 13 students, 12 of whom were Black. Because of her grades and standardized test scores, she was admitted to the Philadelphia High School for Girls, the second most elite secondary school in Philadelphia. Girls High had an excellent physical education program; almost all its teachers were Temple graduates. They took note of Tina immediately. She stood out in the predominately White student body, but as she puts it, her talent was respected. Many of the girls were Jewish and had attended private preparatory schools, all of which emphasized sports development. Tina says today that had it not been for her sports involvement, she would not have survived.

Tina played field hockey in high school and went on to West Chester University of Pennsylvania, which had a famously successful hockey program. Vonnie Gros, a legendary coach of both field hockey and lacrosse, immediately saw Tina's potential and persuaded her to take up lacrosse for the first time in college. Lacrosse was not in the Olympic or traditional collegiate program, but Tina received many All America credentials for lacrosse in the United States Women's Lacrosse Association collegiate programs.

Upon graduation, Tina became the first African American teacher at Unionville High School, an affluent Philadelphia suburb, and also quickly became a coach at Lincoln University, a public, Black university in Pennsylvania. In 1973-74, for reasons already described in the history of Temple, the university officials perceived an urgent need for more African American teachers and coaches, and Tina was recruited and hired. She was the first African American head coach of collegiate lacrosse. She coached at Temple from 1973 to 1992, compiling a record of 207-62-4, three national championships, and 11 consecutive Final Four appearances. During her coaching career, the program produced 23 All Americans, and literally, scores of collegiate coaches today came from the Temple program.

Tina Sloan-Green has been inducted into the Halls of Fame of Temple University, West Chester University, the Lacrosse Hall of Fame, and the Women's Sports Foundation. Additionally, she has been awarded Lifetime Achievement Awards from the National Association of Collegiate Women's Athletic Administrators, the National Women's Lacrosse Association, and the National Association of Girls and Women in Sport.

All of these sports awards are only a small part of Tina's legacy. She was very influential in the creation of the "Studies in Race" general education requirement unique to Temple University, and co-created two very popular courses to meet the requirement. Along with our text, she published chapters in all editions of the Brooks and Althouse text, *Racism in Collegiate Athletics.*

During the course of her illustrious career, Tina has been told by White administrators that she cannot represent the athletic department in corporate circles because her skin is too dark; she doesn't smile enough; she talks funny; and she makes White people feel uncomfortable. She has shared that being aware that the stellar results of her teams and players were diminished because she didn't fit the mold. Through her creation of the Black Women's Sport Foundation and our text, she had the deep contentment that the concerns, needs, and accomplishments of Black women were addressed at last. In her interview with me to prepare this section of our chapter, Tina described these landmarks in very personal terms: "The publication was important for my promotion and tenure. It was symbolic of change in that era. Traci Green [Tina's daughter] was a baby at the time the book was published, and now she is the first African American female coach in the history of Harvard University."

It seems appropriate now to provide an overview of the 75-page monograph the four of us created. The creation process was one of compiling and organizing the various segments we were preparing to meet various ordinary demands of our lives. Alpha Alexander was a doctoral student, and she was preparing papers along the way. I was working alongside Tina and Nikki to prepare class materials and workshops for presentation around the state and nation in our roles as professors, coaches, and officers in women's sport organizations. Because of my close and long-held ties to the National Association of Girls and Women's Sport (NAGWS) of the American Alliance for Health, Physical Education, Recreation and Dance, we knew we had a publisher for a quality product, and that was what we were committed to creating.

Black Women in Sport

Forward: NAGWS President Doris Corbett. Dr. Corbett was already an associate professor at Howard University and would go on to become the first Black woman to be elected President of the America Alliance of Health, Physical Education, Recreation and Dance. She had also completed two terms as President of the International Congress of Health, Physical Education, Recreation, Sport, and Dance.

Chapter One was a literature review on the topic of Black women and sport. In the mainstream, there has been practically no attention to the topic. The review was a summary of 16 bibliography citations including four unpublished graduate works, classics by W.E.B. Dubois and Eldridge Cleaver, and several pieces from feminist psychology publications such as the renowned journal, *Signs*.

Chapter Two featured biographical sketches of 17 outstanding Black sportswomen. The sportswomen were Olympians, collegiate champions, officials, coaches, administrators, and sport federation leaders. There were women in basketball, track and field, lacrosse, fencing, field hockey, tennis, crew, golf, team handball, and volleyball. This incredible diversity of sport and performance role was crucial to belying the myth that Black women's involvement in sport is limited to basketball and track and field.

Chapter Three was created to provide on-the-ground suggestions for solving real and practical problems. Four scenarios were discussed and evidence-based or empirically tested solutions were presented:

a. low participation rates, not only of Black women, but of other women of color as well (Asian, Latina, Native American);

b. focus groups exploring the experiences and reactions of Black female youths in confronting and coping with racial abuse and discrimination;

c. a full description of a case study of a consciousness-raising workshop actually staged in three different university settings;

d. a full description of a White-on-White racial awareness training session.

Chapter Four was a database research report on perceptions of Nigerian women concerning their own participation, or lack of it, in sport. The introduction made clear that this one selection was not designed to tell the story of African women, or even Nigerian women, in sport. The article gave a taste of some similarities and differences between African American women and one set of African women.

In Chapter Five, the book's conclusion, the two of us who were most senior allowed ourselves to run free and say what was really on our mind. Tina Sloan-Green devoted her conclusion to the future of Black women in sport.

Tina described many predictions and now, 30 years later, at least three have, importantly, proven accurate. In 1978, she said that the future would hold more opportunities for Black girls in sport nongovernmental agencies (NGOs) and schools would expand sport development. As predicted, organizations such as Girl Scouts, Girls Inc., and Boys and Girls Club of America have embraced sport as an important element of their programming. Research, especially that made public by the Women's Sport Foundation, has shown that although growth in opportunities for African American girls has not been proportional to that of Caucasians, it has still been astounding in absolute numbers.

Additionally, Tina predicted that more athletic scholarships would go to Black female athletes, enabling college attendance. Similar to opportunity numbers, the growth in awarding of athletic scholarships has not been proportional for Black women but has still dramatically increased. As was suggested in 1978, this increase in college athletic scholarships for Black women has contributed to the great increase in numbers of Black women in the traditionally upper class sports of golf and tennis.

Tina also predicted that more Black women would migrate from their sport experience into sport careers. In fact, organizations like the NCAA and National Association of Collegiate Women's Athletic have developed institutionalized programs of several types to both encourage entry into and progression through athletic administration. Report Cards, like that from Northeastern's Center for Study of Sport and Society, the Women's Sport Foundation, and the landmark Acosta/Carpenter study of women's coaching consistently remind us of what has been accomplished and how much there is yet to do. Tina, Nikki, and Alpha founded the Black Women's Sports Foundation (BWSF), and its leaders have tirelessly worked to produce programs and materials to bring about the growth of Black women's leadership in sport.

Lastly, Tina predicted that more recognition would rightly come to the pioneers in Black women's sport. Just in case not enough was happening to make this prediction come true, the BWSF developed and promoted a beautiful documentary on this topic, *Amazing Grace,* and has also instituted an annual awards program to honor the accomplishments of significant figures in Black women's sport history.

No one is 100% accurate with predictions, and there are two important "misses" to report. Media coverage of Black women in sport has not increased. Research, both from the Tucker Center at the University of Minnesota and the LA84 Foundation (created as a legacy of the 1984 LA Olympic Games), shows that the coverage of all women's sport amounts to roughly 5% of sports coverage. Also, it was believed (or hoped) that increases in sport participation among all Black women would result in better health. Unfortunately, the incidence of chronic, sedentary, lifestyle-related diseases are epidemic among Black men and women, and have resisted efforts to reverse this situation.

My own concluding comments in the book deal with the traditional "women's way of sport" as it touches Black women and, indeed, all women. I described how, for me, the most important learned insight about racism was about the nature of its dysfunction, to master and slave. The truly great African American rights activists did not preach hatred and retribution, just the opposite. They exhorted African Americans and all Americans to transcend the evil of oppression and the outrage the people had sustained, and to practice a disciplined approach in order to hold accountable and to forgive. In this way, life would be filled with love and peace. From my own studies in counseling, I came to know that this transcendence the activists were seeking was what humanistic psychologists deem *second-order change,* instead of just more-of-the-same behavior.

There is a parallel for me in the observation that second-order change transcends racism, and that second-order change transforms elitist, business-driven, violent sport into a sport-for-development framework very like that emanating from "women's way of sport." This one concept could be spun into a book all in itself. Let me just close with three tenets that characterize the sport-for-development movement:

a. Sport is a human right for ALL;

b. Sport roles must be open and accessible to all, and men/women of all diversities are welcomed as federation leaders, coaches, officials of play, sport medicine doctors, trainers, and researchers; and

c. Sports' purpose is always and only for the good (development) of those who play.

The bond of purpose had worked its near-magical effect on us all. Organizations were formed, students were produced, records were set, and new recognitions for African American women were attained. Sometimes it becomes hard to remember that things were as difficult as they had been. We helped to make things change, for the better. It's a great feeling to know that.

CONCLUSIONS

1. There remains a great need for specific sport and physical activity programming and policy designed to serve Black girls and women, across all age categories. Research has shown that chronic diseases of sedentary lifestyle afflict Black women. Affirmative political efforts, such as Title IX in the US, tend to benefit Black women less than other women. Planned efforts are necessary to change the face of what is; specially designed programs and policies are needed if Black women are to be reached.

2. Research also has shown that Black women are not found in the ranks of coaches, athletic administrators, or sport scientists in proportion to their numbers as athletes. Educational institutions must implement and increase their recruitment and training efforts aimed at increasing the numbers of Black women in athletic leadership. Sport leadership in national governing bodies must also take on this mission as an important organization goal.

3. Research on both the qualitative and quantitative methodologies is needed to better document and describe the effects of athletic and physical activity involvement for Black women in both organized sport and healthy lifestyle activities. The positive, as well as any potential negative, effects must be better understood so that the clearest benefits (in relation to health, social, and economic factors) are obtained.

The Bridge Goes Both Ways: Lessons Learned from Athletes Searching for Direction and Meaning

3

William D. Parham

The following narrative portrays the journey, still unfolding, of two athletes. Their quest for a life of meaning and purpose found them sharing a road on which this author was also traveling, as it turns out, in a parallel quest. The athletes, one female and one male, both African American, sought this author's counsel and guidance, believing that our shared ethnicity and their perception of me as a successful professional would provide safety and solace to talk about the challenges that made each feel alone and isolated at many times during their respective journeys. Our respective and shared travels, though each of us was at different points along life's path, fueled discoveries that continue to benefit all of us.

The journey of the female athlete was seemingly marked by a mixture of family dysfunction, fueled in part by the mental health issues of two family members and athletic successes from her days of participating in youth sports. As a youngster she showed athletic talent in two sports, and in time she found herself blossoming in one of the sports, to which she subsequently devoted a lot of time and attention throughout her collegiate career. Her involvement in athletics stemmed initially from the strong desire to escape the "craziness" of the environment and circumstances within which she was reared and that continued to influence her life up to the time when our paths first crossed. Surface relationships between and among family and extended family and the peers with whom she associated masked the depression, domestic violence, and sexual assault scars she felt as permanent as tattoos. The considerable success she enjoyed in athletics came as an unexpected but nonetheless satisfying byproduct of her desire to retreat into an environment that provided a reprieve, albeit brief, from the enormous burden of the challenges of her home and community life.

The journey of the male athlete was a similar confluence of family dysfunction and the harsh realities of a crime-ridden, poorly educated inner-city community with abundant churches, liquor stores, and virtually no safe zones for childhood play and recreation. Success, outside of athletics, was defined by daily survival of an inner-city-blues reality that had defined the lives of this athlete's family for at least three generations. Two family members had served jail time, and during the time I visited with this athlete, his younger sibling was tempting fate with the legal system. Athletics provided an alternative arena from which this athlete could derive the emotional rewards that came with distinguished athletic performances. Of equal fortune, bonding with teammates as "family" represented opportunities to reconcile the lack of true family bonds unfulfilled by brothers, sisters, stepsiblings, parents, and grandparents, all of whom fell captive to the venomous hostility of urban blight.

A single-parent, middle-to-low socioeconomic status household shared with three siblings during the period of the 1960s was the environment within which I was raised. I did not fully understand the true significance of the 1960s zeitgeist, with its civil rights movement; cultural-, ethnic-, and gender identity-based personal and community reclamations; political assassinations (The Reverend Martin Luther King, Jr.; President John F. Kennedy; and presidential hopeful and brother Robert Kennedy); race riots; and the Vietnam War, to name a few. However, I came to know and realize the significant influence these and related events had on my development as a professional. One of many of these childhood events remains fresh in my memory.

The turbulence of the 1960s civil rights movement provided fodder for daily television news in cities across the United States. One particular evening I happened upon a news story of a peaceful civil rights march in Birmingham, Alabama, that was viciously interrupted by police using high-powered water hoses and German Shepherds to attack law-abiding African American (*Negro* during the 1960s) citizens. An image was emblazoned in my mind of the eyes of a White (Caucasian) police officer daring an African American male, who was exercising his right to protest, to make a false move and give the policeman justification for releasing the angry attack dog to kill the peaceful protester.

Fast forward: As a developing young man the lure of "the movement" caught my attention, so I devoted some time to studying these events I couldn't yet fully appreciate. All the while I carried in my mind the image of the police officer releasing the attack dog on an innocent African American man (now memorialized in a bronze statue that stands in Kelly Ingram Civil Rights Memorial Park in Birmingham, Alabama); I desperately grasped for the reasons that fueled the venomous expressions of hatred that spewed from one man to another. One day, the answer came to me!

While walking one morning to the corner where I caught the bus to school, I experienced an exhilarating light-bulb moment. The revelation resulted from the following musing on the one-half mile walk:

If some White folks really believe that Black people are dumb, stupid, and imbecilic, as we are portrayed, then the normal and expected reaction to imbeciles and heathens would be to leave us alone knowing that our dumb, stupid, and imbecilic dispositions would lead us to self-destruct. However, White folks spend all of their political, social, economic, legislative, educational, and even spiritual might trying to wipe us off the face of the earth. This reaction from White folks is more consistent with seeing us as a threat. Thus, in a strikingly distasteful and offensive way, White folks are, unbeknownst even to them, affirming our worth as individuals and as a culturally rich community. At the same time, they are expressing their fear and compromised self-assurance regarding the "real" control they believe they have over African Americans.

I took solace in this revelation, one of many that have sustained me through the years, especially when matters of race and ethnicity framed the experiences I was having at any given point in time. Frequently, I call upon the aforementioned story, as well as others, and use them as invitations for athletes to ponder as they seek to reconcile the challenges that bring them to my office. For me, the repository of experiences and lessons I have learned allows me to withdraw pay-it-forward tokens that I can now invest in persons needing assistance finding their way. The two athletes just introduced represent cases in point.

Each of the athletes came to me via referrals from their respective coaches, presenting concerns centered on recently emerged needs to learn how to respond more effectively to performance pressures. Both athletes were standouts on their teams and within the athletic conference in which their teams held standing. Both envisioned their collegiate careers as bridges to their careers as elite professional athletes; also, across the bridges each athlete dreamed of crossing were opportunities to go for the gold. Perhaps more importantly, each athlete saw crossing the bridge as their way out of the seemingly circumscribed inevitability of their back-home neighborhoods, in which many in their respective families and entourage of peers seemed perpetually trapped.

Their records of athletic accomplishments were quite impressive, so much so that their stellar performances over time sharpened the focus on their decreases in performance, which seemed to come from out of nowhere, and the corresponding increases in excuses about why they were not doing as well athletically as everyone had come to expect.

Of the two, the female athlete proved to be the most challenging, especially for a male colleague of mine, who had agreed to see the athlete because my schedule was booked four weeks ahead at the time she initially presented to the clinic. I trusted and had confidence in my colleague, knowing he was well trained and experienced. He was a talented clinician with a cognitive-behavioral orientation that primed him to intervene with cognitive reframing and relaxation techniques that, on the surface, seemed to be exactly what was called for given the athlete's presenting problem. Several weeks into their work my colleague referred the athlete back to me, claiming she was too anxious and couldn't relax. He shared with me that he considered referring her to a psychiatrist for consultation regarding use of antianxiety medication, but wasn't sure how national athletic conference guidelines about athletes taking medication would affect her receptivity to the suggested intervention.

Our first session provided an important breakthrough. Approximately 20 minutes into it, following a fairly detailed synopsis of the athlete's recent athletic performance struggles, I initiated an assessment procedure using a standard clinical interview. One set of questions had to do with assessing past and current experiences with abuse: physical, sexual, and emotional. During this portion of the interview the athlete reacted initially as if she were stunned. Her halting expression then quickly turned into agitation. Her right leg, which crossed her left, shook and her hands fumbled, as if wiping off the perspiration that had suddenly begun to accumulate.

Gentle and respectful probing of her sudden reaction triggered a denial that she had become uncomfortable. Moments of silence, however, seemed to chisel away her defenses and resulted in her very tearful disclosure of childhood physical and sexual assaults. Exploration of her abusive past, about which she felt embarrassed and ashamed, segued cautiously and nervously into her disclosure of another sexual assault several months just prior to our interview. The sexual assault resulted in a pregnancy that she subsequently terminated. The athlete's secrets had never been told. The fear, trepidation, dread, and foreboding associated with having an unwanted pregnancy provided an extra layer of emotional complexity to her sense of feeling alone, isolated, terrified, and horror-stricken during the pregnancy termination. As difficult as it was for the athlete to disclose her past and current experiences, and as unsettling (I was angry at the violation of innocence) as it was for me to learn about the private horror this very public athlete had to mask, the constant ruminations about these two traumatic experiences were not, as it turned out, the salient triggers of the athlete's decrease in athletic performance. As the interview progressed it became clear that an upcoming athletic event in which she would be competing was scheduled to be held in the location where she was sexually assaulted. Further, she knew with reasonable certainty that her assailant, also a prized athlete, would attend the athletic event in which she was competing and would likely want to make contact with her.

This athlete's on-the-surface athletic performance problems were, in reality, not the problem at all. Her performance decrements represented self-protective responses to past, fairly recent, and soon-upcoming events, all of which contributed to the athlete feeling she was not in control of the forces around her. I recall sharing with her the analogy of a smoke detector. I invited her to consider that when a smoke detector goes off it is not then removed because it is broken. The fact that the smoke detector went off suggested that it was indeed working and alerting all those in ear shot that possible danger lurks. The markers of her recently decreased athletic performances, in actuality, represented her smoke detectors that were alerting her and others around her that she felt threatened and unprotected.

This athlete resonated to this observation and cried as if to express relief that someone other than herself knew about the emotional journey she heretofore had felt forced to keep hidden. Gradually, she began to open up and share her fears and worries about seeing her assailant, whom she had met at a social gathering. The assault took place following attendance at a second well-attended social gathering during which both athletes had been drinking.

Ways of responding to her assailant, to the environment where the transgression took place, and to the competition were explored with short- and longer-term interventions being suggested. We met for several sessions up to and following what turned out to be a successful resolution to the situation regarding her assailant and a heralded athletic performance that resulted in post-competition honors. Our work, for now, had ended with the athlete expressing appreciation and gratitude for my support and counsel. She went on to complete her collegiate career achieving all but one accomplishment on her to-do list. Importantly, she graduated having done well academically. She subsequently crossed the bridge over into the ranks as a professional athlete where she enjoyed a distinguished career, albeit a short one.

I felt honored to serve this athlete. Admittedly, I wrestled internally with the work of my colleague, feeling a bit stymied by his lack of success with her. Post hoc consultation with him revealed that he selectively omitted some of the questions in a standard clinical interview, key of which were the questions regarding sexual assault. His omission resulted from thinking that she was gifted, obviously successful, and appeared to be well adjusted, simply needing only to learn how to relax. His star-struck response got in the way of him doing his best work.

As we continued to explore what happened between him and this athlete it became clear that suspicion of her inability to relax surfaced when he introduced a relaxation exercise as an intervention he thought would be useful. Unsurprisingly, the athlete hiding secrets of past and relatively recent sexual assaults responded self-protectively to instructions to close her eyes, recline, and relax in a room with subdued lighting. The apprehension and tension she experienced in response to being asked to surrender herself under those circumstances, and with a male only several feet from her, made sense and represented a normal response to real threats. I will provide more details on this athlete later in this chapter, including another trip across the bridge.

The male athlete's performance, like his female athlete peer, presented as him feeling highly anxious, especially when he needed to perform in competitions he deemed important. What was surprising was that this high-profile athlete had performed well, even exceeding his and others' expectations, in competitions that were believed by the greater athletic community to be hallmark and significant.

During our initial session a synopsis of his athletics journey was followed by an assessment using a standard clinical interview. Among the key findings, this athlete denied a history of seeking mental health services of any kind, psychological or psychiatric. This declaration proved interesting given this athlete's later-in-the-session admission, with little provocation, to a history of depression including past suicide ideation and one past failed suicide attempt. As the athlete's story unfolded it became clear he had spent a lifetime working hard to manage his depression. His mental health management task was made measurably more difficult given the execrable family, social, and community dysfunction within which his life and training as an athlete evolved. A long-term and tremendous fear of his mental health condition being exposed exacerbated his panic and regularly challenged his belief about the amount of real personal control he possessed to protect his secret.

Pressures associated with the highly publicized upcoming competitions coupled with the sudden emergence of two other challenges, one related to his health, precipitated the athlete's sense of desperation, the feeling that ultimately brought him to my office. We spent several sessions sorting through the situations that had recently summoned his attention, and we co-constructed a multitiered intervention plan aimed at addressing his varied concerns, including the matter of his health. We strategized about his approach to the upcoming competitions, and his subsequent embrace of his success plan was as apparent as his relief in having tasks that would serve as emotional management anchors if he began to again feel encumbered with thoughts of vulnerability.

Fast forward: This athlete's multiple successes through the time he graduated from college allowed him to cross over the bridge to become the professional athlete he had dreamed about being since childhood. A richly exciting lifestyle combined with the rigors of training required the athlete to work even harder and more deliberately to manage his depression, which felt unshakable, as he admitted during an unexpected encounter two years following graduation. Further probing about his post-college professional and emotional journey brought to light his awareness that the professional life to which he had aspired turned out to be a good-news/bad-news situation. On the one side he enjoyed the fortunes of success. On the flip side of the coin the internal pressures triggered by publicity and the need to satisfy sponsors pulled constantly at the seams of his internal sense of emotional control. I will provide more details on this athlete later in this chapter, including another trip across the bridge.

Illustrated, hopefully, in these two stories are two examples of persistence in spite of overwhelming odds, hope for brighter days when life seems full of doom and gloom, and discovery of heretofore unknown reservoirs of esteem, confidence, motivation, and courage to create a way when a way out is not immediately apparent. A second lesson I learned and not infrequently share with athletes who seek my counsel comes in the form of questions I ask regarding their recollections of sunrises and sunsets. Invariably, they respond that, yes, they have seen sunrises and sunsets, and they further indicate the approximate times the sun rises in the east and sets in the west. Their answers to a third question, however, baits a pause and an anticipation about a punch line.

Those to whom the sunrise/sunset questions are posed are then invited to recall lessons learned about the solar system that were first presented to them in the fourth grade. Most athletes recall several basic facts. The sun's position at the center of the universe, the earth's simultaneous rotation on its axis and around the sun, the earth's surface being mostly water and its uniqueness as the only planet on which human's live constitute the collection of early memories of lessons learned about the solar system. Listeners are then asked which of their beliefs (e.g., sunrise/sunset vs. solar system) constitutes truth. Without fail, most responders are surprised to learn that they have never, ever seen a sun actually rise or set. Instead, they reconnect with their fourth grade lessons wherein they first learned that sunrises and sunsets represent illusions of movement. The sun does not move! Further, the sun is ever-present even when it is not visible. Lastly, it does not abate or diminish in intensity as time passes. In the pitch black of midnight or during the deepest, darkest, most horrendous storm when inclement conditions (wet, cold, dark and dreary) seem to indicate the absence of the sun, the sun in all of its glory is still there at the center of the solar system.

The bridge from this story to the lives of the athletes with whom I work is suspended with two invitations serving as structural foundations. The first invitation to every athlete kindly requests that they consider that they have an internal sun: their confidence, motivation, self-esteem, and will power. Like the sun, their confidence, motivation, self-esteem, and will power never move, are ever-present even when they are not visible or felt, and do not diminish in intensity as time passes. The second invitation encourages athletes to believe that they can access their sun at any time they wish. The journeys of the two athletes serving as the focus of this narrative affirm my beliefs in the boundless energy athletes possess and have access to if they know and believe that such an emotional reservoir exists, and that they can tap into their personal reserves without fear of depleting any of their emotional energy stores.

The athletes about whom I have written and with whom I feel blessed to have worked acknowledge that entertaining the notion that they possess endless supplies of emotional energy (confidence, motivation, self-esteem, and will power) is easy; accessing the alleged-to-be-available emotional energy on a consistent and sustained basis is not. The reality of these assertions is seen in the rest of their respective stories.

Vicissitudes of fate and her own psychological storms eventually caused the female athlete to cross back over the bridge to a life far more arduous and less glamorous. The acclaim she received from her hard work and discipline faded, and she returned to circumstances similar to the compromised and dysfunctional environment of her developmental and early college years when we first met. She had been lured by life's good promises only to fall prey to formidable challenges she now faced and would likely continue to face for years to come. The emotionally inclement weather against which she felt mostly defenseless followed harsh conditions that included underemployment, a spouse on permanent disability, and two of her three children with special needs, one with a chronic medical condition. The third child's problems with aggression, bullying, and truancy seemed manageable by comparison. Her unexpected call to me provided a forum for us to catch up on all that had transpired since we formally ended our work many years earlier. The notion that the bridge goes both ways was as resonate to both of us as the hope that at some time in the future this athlete could go back across the bridge. She continues to fight through the obstacles she now confronts and is determined to overcome her challenges; I wonder if I could do the same under similar circumstances. Our conversation brought home a reality about which we talked in the past and currently remain aware: life can change immediately and our only control is how we respond to the new realities with which we are now faced.

This reality played out in the life of the male athlete. His persistent and two-fisted struggle to combat his depression on top of facing the challenges inherent in the fortunes of a successful life was a battle he ultimately lost. His collapse spawned a depression that resulted in two hospitalizations, one of which was involuntary, and a medication and therapy regimen that continues to this day. I don't know the details of his journey back across the bridge to a life that was less dazzling and exhilarating. The truth be told, I have not had direct contact with him since our formal work ended. I hear about him very sporadically through colleagues and others who know him personally. Interestingly, this athlete's name first resurfaced several years ago while I was attending a sporting event. In a conversation I overheard while eating lunch, two athletes referred to him and spoke of his athletic accomplishments as if they were urban lore. The two athletes whose conversation I overheard did not personally know him, yet his athletic records represented goals they unabashedly believed they would surpass. I wondered if they knew that the bridge goes both ways. Time will tell.

There are many benefits to the work I do. One benefit is to experience the privilege of serving others who feel adrift from the life course they charted. A second and related benefit comes with the opportunity to spread light, either as the candle illuminating the sea on which they are now sailing or as the mirror reflecting a yet-to-be-discovered light that shines inside them. As an added bonus, I have had opportunities in abundance to bear witness to the tremendous fortitude, stamina, toughness, determination, and tenacity that fuels the human spirit especially in times of hardship and misfortune. Witnessing others' responses to significant trials and tribulations also helps me keep perspective on the way I confront and manage my own professional and personal challenges. I feel blessed with ever-present reminders about the fragility of life and about the importance of being thankful.

Reminders about responses to life's challenges surface frequently in my work with athletes from privileged backgrounds, a population actually seen by me more frequently than athletes from harsher backgrounds and upbringings. Two lessons stand out! The first lesson reminds me that money, privilege, and prestige can't buy drive, heart, hunger, passion, or unbridled and sustained dedication to excellence. There are no shortcuts to being your best, irrespective of one's social or economic standing! Money, privilege, and prestige, on the other hand, do afford a level of comfort, convenience, and cushion for athletes interested in being good but not the best at which they are capable. The invitation hidden behind a life grounded in economic fortune, often inherited, comes in the form of asking privileged athletes that if they had no economic backing and no immediate prospect of securing needed financial support, would they be as or more dedicated to their pursuit of athletic excellence? Real struggles with answering this question represent normative responses from both male and female privileged athletes with whom I have worked. For many, the reality of having little to no financial stability is not one with which they easily resonate, and thus seem forced to safely declare, "I'm not sure!" Privilege, however, does bait the following questions: To what degree does surrender to the comfort, convenience, and cushion of current and likely future financial stability rob or impede an athlete's deep discovery and subsequent achievement of athletic excellence? And to what degree does surrender to the comfort, convenience, and cushion of current and likely future financial stability rob or impede an athlete's dig-deep discovery and subsequent achievement of excellence in other life areas such as academic, career, relational, and social pursuits?

A second lesson reminds me that financial stability does not render privileged athletes immune from harsh and painful awareness brought on by unexpected changes in personal circumstances and life trajectories. The unanticipated life circumstances faced by the athletes discussed in this chapter, before and after their athletic careers, could befall even those with the most stable resources. Dysfunctional family experiences—including all forms of abuse, mental health issues, learning disabilities, chronic health challenges, and a profusion of life's problems and complications—cross economic, racial, ethnic, and gender-related boundaries, and include individual, family, and community identity. Athletics gives rise to opportunities, both fortunate and unfortunate, for authentic and truly meaningful intrapersonal discoveries. In the final analysis, direction and meaning can be found in every one of life's twists and turns if the unanticipated obstacles are used to ignite the drive, passion, and curiosity required for the search.

CONCLUSIONS

The observations and reflections in this narrative stimulate recollections of other consultations in which I have been engaged. The following final thoughts represent a partial synthesis of collected takeaway insights I discovered while serving others as I journeyed and searched for direction and meaning.

1. When we listen to our clients long enough, they will tell us what is wrong with them. When we listen to our clients just a little longer, they will tell us what we can do to help them feel better. In essence, the true therapist in the room is actually the client. The therapist's role is to facilitate the client's discovery and embrace of the wisdom they already possess.

2. Hidden in the verbal, emotional, and behavioral expressions of persons seeking counsel are clues to the truer and often longer-term challenges they are facing.

3. We are creatures of habit and pattern. That said, know that deviations from a person's normative (relative to the individual's observed and expressed custom) cognitive, emotional, and behavioral responses to life's challenges represent activations of their smoke detectors that should alert both the client and the therapist that something feels threatening.

4. On-the-surface presentations of circumstances and situations are sometimes merely portals to the more salient challenges clients confront.

5. Therapists, both seasoned and novice, need to be ever mindful of their responses to images of stardom and celebrity. Ignoring said awareness clouds the lens through which a therapist sees the person seeking counsel. Failure to monitor responses to a celebrity image can block a therapist's access to the tools that might better help the person and result in more precise problem resolution.

6. Life's twists and turns, irrespective of the gravity of their imposed challenges, represent opportunities for growth and forward movement.

7. Recorded life events can't be altered or erased. However, when we change the way we think about things, then the things we think about change.

And I say to myself, what a wonderful world!

Run Your Dream

Hussain Haleem

Growing up in a low-income family in the Maldives during the 1970s was to me harder than trying to complete an Ironman race. We were continuously challenged with physical and psychological obstacles as we strove for acceptance in a society infested with hypocrisy and social prejudice.

March 5, 1969, born premature, I stepped into the world as a burden to my family. The complications were many. Even the doctors had no hope I'd make it to my first birthday. Being tiny with an underdeveloped immune system, I was constantly ill. There was never an epidemic outbreak that did not affect me. I remember a time when I had to sleep crouched on the bed with only my knees and elbows touching the sheets because my whole body was covered in boils. My parents did their best to give me as normal a life as possible.

My world was within the boundaries of our house. Our modest home had a relatively big backyard, well equipped with primitive swings and slides and lots of trees to keep us entertained and occupied. I was one of 12 kids from three marriages. Life was anything but easy; it was either a continuous party or a constant scuffle. I, being the weakest, usually wound up at the tapered end.

However, I had many fond memories of being with my father. Usually, it was my father who woke me up in the morning. He would gently tickle me awake and ask, "Are you ready to get up?" and carry me to the bathroom in a big bear hug. I would cling to him, revelling in the closeness as he carried me. I wished he would hold me forever. If I woke up before he arrived, I would lie in bed and wait for him, pretending to be asleep. If he were late, which was rare, I would call out to him and stay in bed until he showed up. I loved being tickled out of bed. It was one of our special moments.

I loved my father very much, and I was very attached to him. He was big, strong, and handsome, and I loved the way he smelled. I loved everything he liked and always tried to tag along with him. He allowed me to pick fruits from the trees. He even took me to the market on weekends. Fishing was one of his many hobbies and sometimes he let me tag along. I learned to hook a fish when I was very young. He was my superhero.

I remember my first experience outside the walls of my home. It was the day I started kindergarten. I was three years old, and so excited about going to school. I kept rambling on about all the fun I would have. My father took me on his pushbike. I stood on the pedals while he pushed along. He made me read all the sign boards all the way to the school. I was ecstatic until we reached the school, and it was time for me to say goodbye to my father. I said, "I don't want to go to school, Daddy," and my eyes welled up. I was clinging to my father and bawling until a teacher came and took my hand and coerced me to class. I kept looking over my shoulder to make sure my father was there. He was.

School was a scary place for me. It was big and intimidating, and there were so many strangers. I felt very uncomfortable. But after the initial drama, the first day went pretty well. We were all strangers trying to fit in. Week two, the nightmare began. I was the shortest and the skinniest kid in the classroom. This perhaps made me an easy target for all the bullying and pranks. One experience stands out: As I was in the playground, four students chased me for no apparent reason. When they caught me they pulled down my pants around my ankles and dragged me across the field. All the kids who saw applauded and laughed at me. No one came to my rescue. I retreated into my shell in embarrassment. There were no teachers around so they did not see my humiliation, and I did not tell anyone. I have no explanation as to why I was being bullied. It was frightening. Such experiences shattered my confidence.

After three years of kindergarten I was enrolled in Majeediyya School, where I hoped things would be different. I expected the students to be nicer. I wanted the teachers to be role models, and I expected them to nurture and protect me and help me rebuild my confidence. Most of all, I expected them to help me excel academically and was very excited at the prospect. However, I was in for a rude awakening. I was still small for my age and was bullied and the level of abuse increased. No one came to my rescue, not even the teachers I had held in such high esteem. In fact, they contributed to my humiliation. They preferred students from well-to-do families.

On one occasion I was actually used as a guinea pig to demonstrate a lesson. The teacher pulled me up to the front of the class and, despite my protests, made me take off my shirt. I was forced to stand helplessly in front of my giggling classmates, stripped to the waist while he used a stick to point at different parts of my quivering frame to demonstrate the lesson. I felt violated, abused. I was too embarrassed to share the debilitating experience with my family and became even more withdrawn and shy. Confused and afraid, I started to hate school and teachers and lost faith in the system. After that, despite my best efforts to study hard and make my parents proud, I fell inadequately short.

At the age of 12 I faced the biggest blow of my young life. My parents decided to separate. Since neither of them was capable of looking after all the children, they decided to separate us as well. My older brothers stayed with our father and the younger children, including myself, went to live with our mother. I was devastated. Given the choice, I would have preferred to stay with my father.

My mother's house was a tiny one-room place at the opposite end of the island. There was not enough space to sleep comfortably. Having idolized my father all my life, I missed him the most. He was kind and generous and had a wonderful sense of humor. I was miserable without him. Between the abuse at school and the tension at home, I became more confused, frustrated, and lonely. I became a rebel in the making. Attending school became a chore and my grades fell drastically. I started to rebel, and misbehaved and annoyed the teachers. I started to spend an increasing amount of time in detention, standing or kneeling outside the classroom. I spent more time outside the classroom than inside.

Soon I hooked up with a bunch of other boys like me. I felt a sense of camaraderie with them and wanted to do everything they did. I tried my hand at smoking but did not enjoy the bitter taste it left in my mouth. I felt nauseous and had to brush my teeth and eat something sweet to get the taste out. It became too much of an inconvenience. After five cigarettes, I decided I could not do it and quit. This was one of the best decisions I ever made.

By then I was a ticking time bomb. I was frustrated, depressed, lonely, sad, and angry, all at the same time. At one point I even contemplated suicide, but fortunately was smart enough not to see it through. Apart from the fear of committing the act, I was too scared at the prospect of going to hell. In Islam, suicide is considered the greatest sin and is strictly forbidden. Anyone who commits suicide is destined to go to hell. I was mad at myself for weeks for not going through with it.

I scraped through school up to seventh grade, where we were required to sit the newly introduced National Exams. The results determined who continued on to secondary school. I, of course, failed and had to repeat the class and suffer the embarrassment of failing it twice in a row. In one subject I received 18 out of 100! I was kicked out of school at the age of 15. My mother pleaded with the principal to let me stay. He rudely dismissed her with, "He has no future." I vowed to prove him wrong and make something out of myself—one day.

Joining a lowly private school immediately after being dismissed from a supposedly better government school was not in my agenda at the time. But I had to swallow my pride and join English Preparatory and Secondary School. Starting secondary education at a private school was a turning point in my life. In the new school, as in most other private schools, academics took a back seat to sports. This was a welcome change for me. My life became easier. I usually managed to top the class without having to put too much effort into my studies. Cheating was so much easier. I was able to complete my secondary education and sit the London O level exams without further drama. My results, of course, were a whole different story.

My experience in sports was poor to say the least. I participated in most sports played at school—badminton, table tennis, football (soccer), and so on. Needless to say, I wasn't much good at any of them. When I was about 11 and in primary school, I tried out for a few events to be held at the sports meet. Even though I qualified for the long jump, finishing third, I was not allowed to participate. One of the officials walked up to me and said, "We have decided that Ahmed, who finished fourth, will participate as he is taller than you. We are sure he can perform better on the competition day." He smiled at me and added, "You can still come to cheer if you want." I could not believe my ears! Earlier I had tried out and failed to qualify for either running or the high jump. And now they were taking away my only opportunity to participate because I was short! I was angry and distraught and cried all the way home. That was the end of my sports participation in school.

My sporting life really began after we moved to a new neighborhood. Before long I had several "bad boy" friends. Most of them were from poor and broken families just like me. We shared a common bond. They were good at the things they did, including sports. Even though some of the things they did were bad and illegal, I wanted to be just like them. My mother hated them and did not like me hanging around with them, but I hardly ever listened to her.

My new friends and I loved to play soccer. The road was our field. Unlike me, they were quite good. I found out I was good at one thing—goal keeping. I quickly found myself fantasizing about being the best goalkeeper in the country. But alas, this turned out to be just a fantasy. You see, I never seemed to grow. I was always the shortest. This meant I had more to prove. I couldn't allow anything, even a painful injury, hold me back.

Our gang of friends was playing a match with another neighborhood team. They were bigger, better, and far more aggressive than we were. I was the goalkeeper. I fought valiantly to defend our goal. In a freak accident while trying to save a goal from being scored, I fractured my arm. Although the pain was almost unbearable, I didn't stop until I almost passed out on the field. As luck would have it, my mother was out of the country at the time, so I was forced to endure the pain for two more days before I asked a neighbor for assistance.

While recovering, I saw the most beautiful girl I had ever seen. I fell for her like a ton of bricks. To make a long story short, after showering her with gifts I approached her, only to be dismissed bluntly with, "How can a beautiful girl like me date an ugly guy like you?" I nearly fainted. That was my love story in a nutshell.

After this short romantic detour, I tried to focus on sports. But despite my enthusiasm and perseverance, my dreams of sporting greatness seemed to become even more distant. I tried every sport I knew and failed. I had been rejected by love and was a social outcast. I just wasn't good enough for anything!

In August 1986, one of my soccer friends started to talk about an announcement he had heard on the radio. "Guys, the Olympic Committee is recruiting potential runners to go overseas for a competition. I just heard it on the radio." "Really?" I was curious. He turned to me and teased, "Hussain, maybe you should try out. . ." to giggles from everyone around. I was very embarrassed at the sarcasm, but then I had been the butt of their jokes for a long time. "Maybe I will," I responded, even though I had serious doubts about my ability.

As it turned out, one of my other friends wanted to try out and asked me to accompany him. I decided to tag along to see what it was all about, and maybe even try out. A considerable crowd was already present when we arrived. I was mortified to see I was the only one wearing studded soccer shoes. Sensing that I did not belong there, I hid behind the taller runners hoping no one would spot me. Soon, the president of the Olympic Committee arrived and everyone was asked to gather around as he addressed us.

"I am pleased to see we have a good turnout," he began, and continued to talk about the endeavors of becoming a good athlete. After a few minutes I was bored and restless until he said, "We want to get some runners who would be interested in training for the Olympic Games to be held in two years." "What the hell are Olympic Games?" I thought. This was the first time I had ever heard of them and did not have a clue. Now my interest was piqued. As he continued to speak, I gathered that the competition would not be held in the Maldives. Then he introduced the foreigner standing next to him, "This is Sato from Japan. He will be the coach for those of you who make the squad today." I was excited. Now what?

He turned to the coach and asked him to conduct the trials. The coach spoke very little English and used gestures to demonstrate the message. We were asked to form two groups—potential sprinters and distance runners. I didn't know what either meant. Not knowing what to do, I got into the same group as my friend. It turned out to be the distance runners. We were asked to run two kilometers around the park. It seemed simple enough, and I thought I could do it in a fairly short time. I wanted to show coach how good I was. "Let's do it" I said to myself as I psyched myself for the race.

I darted off at the coach's starting signal and ran as fast as I could. After only a hundred meters or so, my lungs burning and my head spinning, I almost collapsed. I was breathless and my body felt like jelly. I struggled to stay on my feet but by the second lap, my legs felt like lead and I dropped out from the race, nearly passing out. "Crap! What am I doing here? I don't belong here!" I thought. I have failed once again. My dream was over before it even began.

When all the runners had finished, the coach asked us to gather around. I walked back and hid behind everyone. I stood there, shoulders drooped and head hanging in defeat. Certain it was the end of the road for me, I stood there trying to focus on a spot on my shoe.

"Good, good, no problem," he started and rambled on with several hand and body gestures to explain what he was trying to say. We were able to make out most of what he said. He said that although we had not run well—which I was sure was a comment meant for me—with commitment and regular training, we could all become good runners. We had to commit ourselves, be punctual and do whatever he asked and he would make us good runners. That was the most powerful message I had ever received. Despite my dismal performance, I went home content and hopeful. I thought as I got into bed, "I can do it. I, too, have a chance." I was so excited I hardly slept all night. But the next morning I woke up doubting myself again. "Who am I fooling? There is no way I can do this."

Meeting the coach was a turning point in my life. I bought into his words and believed in him. He gave me hope, which up until that moment, no one other than my father had done. He encouraged me and the squad to train hard to achieve our full potential. I willingly did everything I was asked, and then some. I improved immensely. As my self-confidence grew, my way of thinking changed. I started to believe in myself. When I first started training with Coach Sato, I was a shy and timid young boy. I was hesitant to run around the island as he asked. I was worried about what people might say. It was not normal to run around the island. Up until then, no one had done it. Sports participation was something frowned upon by the majority, and for most, running around the island was not even a sport. Nonetheless, I persisted and continued to do my laps around the island.

Soon people started to make comments as I ran past. Some offered welcome words of encouragement, but most were sarcastic and insulting. I ignored the urge to confront them. I became more determined and developed an intense desire to prove them wrong. "There is no room for failure this time. My feet will do the talking."

My life began to revolve around running. All my time apart from my working hours was invested in running. It gave my life routine, structure, and direction. Coach Sato provided me with some English and Japanese running magazines. I couldn't understand the text in either, so I scanned the faces of the athletes and learned their statistics. I memorized every detail. In no time I was able to recall names, faces, and the personal best times of the world's top 20 runners. Running became my obsession. I even had a stack of magazine cut-outs of great runners beside my bed.

Coach Sato was very impressed with the progress I made and suggested that I watch "Running Brave," a movie based on the true story of a Native American named Billy Mills. The movie depicts the many challenges he faced, including racism, and how he overcame them and persisted to achieve his Olympic dream. His triumphant story ended with the biggest upset in Olympic history, with Mills winning the 10,000-meter race at the 1964 Tokyo Olympics. I loved the movie so much, watching it became a routine. I identified with and embodied Billy Mills. I became the Billy Mills of the Maldives.

After four months of rigorous training, I was ready to face my first real test—the first Maldives Marathon. January 1, 1987, the morning of the race day, was wet with traces of rain. We had had heavy rainfall the night before and the race route had several knee-deep potholes full of muddy water. I was as prepared as I could be, except that since I did not have a pair of running shoes yet I was wearing a borrowed pair one size too big. I did not let that deter me. I was ready and excited. "This is it. Let's do it." I told myself. The gun went off and we all started running. For the early stages of the race, I ran alongside the best runners in the country. We had to run eight-and-a-half laps around the island to cover the distance. By the third lap, many of the leading runners had started to drop back. "This is easier than I thought." By the fifth lap, I was in the lead with the best runner at the time. I could not believe it!

Despite my own fatigue, I picked up speed. My legs got heavier with every step. "I can do it. I can do it." I tried psyching myself not to give up. Finally, I was able to drop him right around the 25-kilometer point and I was leading the race. I was relieved. Then, at around the 32 km mark, I hit the "wall." Although I tried valiantly, I simply could not lift my feet off the ground. I had to drag them. I could not allow myself to give up, so I started walking. The more I walked, the more I felt like walking instead of running.

I walked for about 20 minutes. Then I jogged and walked alternately for a while up until around the 37 km mark. I kept a slow pace until the final kilometer. I wanted to look good for the people waiting at the finish line. When I saw the finish line looming in front of me, I picked up the pace and ran as fast as I could. A feeling of euphoria engulfed me as I broke the finish line. "I did it. I did it." I was screaming in my mind. I was exhausted. Being unable to even walk properly from exhaustion, I was dragged aside. That was the moment I realized that anything is possible. I was overwhelmed and cried for several minutes.

The next day the newspapers carried my photo. I was very flattered. "I have come a long way," I thought. The exertion had left me weak and severely dehydrated. It was several days before everything got back to normal and I was able to even relieve myself. My feet had blisters and were sore. I limped badly for weeks. I welcomed this discomfort and pain, as it gave me a gratifying sense of triumph.

Six months after I began the journey, I kept my promise and did not miss a single training session. I was hooked on running. I had finally found something I was good at. Running gave me an avenue to prove my worth. As a child, I never dreamt of going overseas. A lot has changed since then. After intense melancholy and many sacrifices, I had found my calling—running—and it was now going to take me on a journey beyond my wildest imagination.

In 1987 I was about to embark on my first trip out of the country. I had been chosen to represent Maldives at the 7th Asian Track and Field Championships, to be held in Singapore. I was both nervous and excited. I could not sleep properly and when I did sleep, I had vivid dreams of the impending trip. I bragged to all my friends and anyone who would listen that I was going to Singapore. It was a huge deal for anyone at that time. I could hardly contain my excitement in the plane. Beaming from ear to ear, I was a typical tourist and took photos of everything, as I was seeing most of these things for the first time. I even took a picture of myself sitting on the side of the bathtub wearing my new sunglasses! I was amazed at all the new things I saw and got to experience.

I participated in the 5,000 and 10,000 meter events. My performance in both events was below par. Despite having set national records in both distances, I finished well down the line. Although badly defeated, my determination was not marred. It was an eye-opening experience. I realized I had a long way to go and knew exactly what needed to be done in order to succeed at top-level competitions. I was confident that with commitment to training I would continue to progress and close the gap over time. The trip to Singapore was the first time I had run on or even seen a purpose-built track. In sharp contrast to the road surfaces I trained on at home, the track was bouncy and difficult to run. It took a toll on my legs, and they were extremely sore for days. I returned home with a greater enthusiasm and motivation to improve my performance as a distance runner.

Fuelled by my desire to become a better runner, I started training twice a day. I woke up early and ran two laps around the island before work. Training sessions with the coach began at 4 p.m. I always showed up 20 to 30 minutes early. The training session usually ended around 6:30 p.m. I went straight home to shower and sleep. I did not socialize and even gave up my regular clothes and switched to athletic gear. They were hand-me-downs from the coach and were my trophies. They symbolically confirmed my status as an athlete. Soon my wardrobe consisted of only a few hand-me-down tracksuits and a pair of cheap running shoes that I had purchased with my first paycheck. They were my prized possessions, and I loved and treasured them.

My love for my chosen sport grew steadily. I began to revel in the sheer joy of it. Running gave me the much-needed outlet to free my mind of the painful memories associated with my broken family, the bitterness of my failed academic experiences, and the constant bullying. I chose to run to escape the real world. Soon running became an obsession. I started sleeping with my running shoes on so that I could go running as soon as I woke up. One night, I just could not wait until dawn. I had to go out. I had to run. In my desperation, I went out on a run at 2 a.m. Halfway into the lap, a policeman caught up to me and, assuming I was a thief making a getaway, took me to the station. I was let off with a warning to run at more acceptable hours.

Addicted to running, I began to idolize the great Kenyan and Ethiopian runners. I wanted to dress and look like them, with their bright-colored tracksuits and crew cuts. I, of course, went one step further and shaved my head. Ironically, my shaved head made me popular among my peers. I took pride in this newfound attention and admiration. I began to like myself!

Training was tough. Trying to keep the pace set for the session was tougher. I put in a valiant effort even when I was exhausted. There were no athletics tracks. Instead we had to run on the roads around the island or around the park. The sandy, unpaved roads were bumpy and uneven. If it rained we had to face the hazard of potholes, which we had to zigzag around, in addition to the traffic and pedestrians. By now, I was used to these obstacles. My determination to succeed overruled them, and I welcomed the considerable pain and discomfort associated with the training. I loved sporting a limp when I walked. It reinforced my willingness to sacrifice in order to achieve success. Eventually, I adapted and became insensitive to the pain from ignoring it for so long. I was no longer sure if the pain was real or imagined!

Life, on the other hand, was extremely hard. A low-income family, we could not afford a decent standard of living, let alone to sustain me during my demanding training routines. Occasionally, a neighbor would offer me a hearty meal, but I went to bed hungry several nights a week. As a result of poor nutrition, I was constantly fatigued. Then Coach Salto came to my rescue. He started to cook and serve me food at his expense. This soon became a routine, and I started helping him with the cooking and cleaning.

Most people did not understand my passion for running. My family, friends, neighbors, and even my boss began to question my intentions. My obsession for running to the point of neglecting everything else in life was scorned. "Hussain, why are you running all the time? Do you have nothing better to do?" Usually, I tried to ignore them or vaguely mumbled something in response. I did not expect them to understand the sense of fulfilment I got from running. It was pointless to try and explain my vision. A void developed between my old and new life. Any relationship I had with my family and friends started to deteriorate rapidly. "Why do I run?" I asked myself. I run because I want to, because I need to expend my energy productively. I run to give hope to other kids like me that they can rise above what people expect.

But I did not expect people to understand. As everything else in life, my dreams had to be achieved at a price. Unbeknown to most, my coach and I had several ideological issues that somewhat tarnished our coach-athlete relationship. As Muslims, we fast during the month of Ramadan. Although we practice it from a young age and our bodies adapt to the fasting, the extremely rigorous training would leave me drained. So I tried to schedule my training around the fasting time, and unfortunately Coach Sato, being non-Muslim, failed to understand my reasoning. Training during Ramadan was usually extremely strained for both of us.

Also as Muslims, we are forbidden to consume alcohol. Coach Sato was, of course, aware of this, and yet one day he tried to forcefully make me drink. It was normal for me and some other athletes to crash at the coach's place. When I walked in that day, he was having a drink.

"Hussain, come and join me for a drink," he said.

"I'm not allowed to drink," I replied meekly.

"Why not? Just take a little bit," he insisted.

"I'm not even allowed to take a sip, coach."

"Drink, damn it. I want you to drink this. Here. . ." Refusing to be denied, he pushed the glass towards me, spilling some of the contents on my shirt. Now that he was getting physical, I was petrified.

"No coach, NO!" I screamed, and ran out of his house, wondering if he would throw me off the squad for that. That was the first and only time I refused to do something he asked.

The next day was like any other day. He did not mention the incident of the night before. Perhaps he couldn't remember. Even though I had gotten away with it that time, there came several occasions when I was forced to obey him and compromise my religious obligations. Given the choice to train with him and go the Olympic Games or report him and lose an Olympic spot, I chose the first option (silence).

January 1, 1988, was the day of the Second Maldives Marathon. It was also going to be the trial race for the Olympic Games. I was 18. My plan was simple—win the race in under three hours, to break the national record. I looked around at my competition. There were a few good runners and some not so good ones. We set off with the gun and for the first three laps I ran with the best. I was pacing myself as planned; I took the lead in the fourth lap and never looked back. I was strong throughout the race and crossed the finish line in 2:57:03, setting a new national record. I would be in Seoul in eight months. It was the best day of my young life. Twenty minutes later, the second runner crossed the finish line. Maldives was going to be represented at the Olympics for the first time, and I was chosen to captain the team. I had the honor to carry the Maldivian flag at the opening ceremony. Words fail to describe the pride I felt as I walked into the stadium carrying the national flag of my beloved country. The patriot in me couldn't have been happier as I shed tears of joy.

At the end of 1988, however, tragedy struck. My father was suddenly taken seriously ill and hospitalized. I was devastated to learn that he had been paralyzed on one side of his body. He was unable to talk. Although we were not able to spend much time together, he was my security blanket, my pillar of strength. To see him in a hospital bed on life-support was unbearable. His health deteriorated rapidly. In the last few months of his life, I spent every night at his bedside in the hospital. I slept on a chair at his bedside and woke up early to go running before I went to work. My life was in chaos and my schedule hectic. He passed away on April, 29, 1990.

I received the news while I was coaching a school team, and I immediately ran to the hospital. I walked in to see my father covered with a white sheet. I broke down. The reality of it hit me with a jolt. My idol, my role model was no more. As I clung to his lifeless body, memories of all the good times we had flashed through my mind. How could he leave me so early? I had so much to tell him. I needed to tell him how much I loved him. But he was gone, leaving a huge void in my life never to be filled again. As I mourned the death of my father, I took refuge in running. I ran until I could run no more. I ran to drown my sorrow and ran myself to exhaustion every time the memories surfaced. It kept me sane.

In 1991 I was presented the opportunity to go to Japan to train for the 1992 Olympic Games. While training in Japan I suffered many injuries, mostly due to the sudden drastic increase in training load—from 70 km per week to 150 km within a week of reaching Japan. Yet I made the team and went to the Olympic Games. I was given the honor of carrying the flag at the opening ceremony for the second time. Words cannot describe how I felt. Also, I had unfinished business from 1988. I could not finish the race then; I was determined to finish this time—at any cost. Although I was injured weeks before the race, I decided to compete. I barely managed to complete the race.

After the Olympics, I had to reflect on my running career. Injuries come as part of the package for all athletes in any sport. I had my share as well, but would not exchange them for anything. I suffered several cuts and bruises, a busted eye, a broken finger, a fractured arm, and a cracked head. I even had to be treated for a torn meniscus. Running on uneven surfaces, in cheap running shoes, with average coaches had broken my body. I realized that with the minimal support I was getting from the local association, I had no chance for success at the international level. In my frustration I wrote a bold comment in my diary, "If I cannot break 2:35:00 in a marathon by 1992, I will give up running and allow either my coach or the Maldivian Government to cut off one of my legs" (diary entry, December 24, 1991). Given the opportunity, I knew I could achieve that goal, but I came to a dead end with the Athletic Association of Maldives and the other relevant organizations. Since I had only a few chances to break that barrier, I never managed to achieve it and thus reluctantly ended my competitive running career at the age of 24.

I had no choice but to keep running at a mediocre level, so I forced myself to look for other options. Taking from the example of Billy Mills, who succeeded against all odds, I decided to get an education and applied to universities for a scholarship. Being a high school dropout posed several obstacles. I knew it would be unlikely for me to get a standard placement at a university. Neither did I have the financial capacity to support my education. But I was not willing to give up without trying. Since I could not write a decent letter in English, I turned to a co-worker for assistance. Over 30 universities rejected my application before I received a comparatively long letter from an Australian college. I was awarded a scholarship as a result of my running prowess. However, I needed to secure living expenses. Fortunately, my popularity as a runner had brought me in contact with several powerful people in the Maldives. I approached the Minister in charge of funding scholarships, and within two weeks I was granted the required funds. So began my academic race.

In 1994 I left for Australia in pursuit of academic excellence. I was ready to apply the same commitment and determination to this new venture. Failure was not an option. At first, my progress was slow as studying in English had major setbacks, but I persevered. I took English classes with a tutor, four hours a night for two years, to enable me to tackle the course, and every minute was worth it. The funding I received from the Ministry was not sufficient, as the cost of living was higher than expected. In order to earn the extra money I needed, I started working for the college. I cleaned the lecture rooms after classes. It was a difficult time for me.

As soon as I arrived in Sydney, I became acquainted with a new reality—racism. It was a new word for me but I instantly learned its meaning. I had never imagined that people would be treated differently because of their skin color! Being a colored Muslim presented even more issues. I was subjected to a near strip search every time I entered Australia because of my name. Hussain is a very common Muslim name. On the other hand, everything changed as soon as people found out that I was an Olympian. I became everyone's best friend! As you can understand, I had to flaunt the Olympian bit often in order to survive my five years in Australia. I barely managed it. But, as the Aussies say, "I gutted it out."

I returned home and worked for a year before I secured funds to pursue my postgraduate studies, this time in New Zealand. During that time I got a recommendation letter from the national Olympic committee President (from 1978-2009), Mr. Zahir Naseer, and following is what he had to say about me.

> I have known Hussain Haleem since 1985 when he was only a little boy. His frame is small, but I don't know of anyone with a bigger heart than this young man. . . . I have been holding the position of Olympic Committee President since 1978, and I have not come across anyone like Hussain, who has such determination to succeed in whatever field of work or study that he undertakes.

Anyway, New Zealand was a welcome change compared to Australia. I always felt welcomed there and was never treated like a terrorist. I love New Zealand and consider the country as my home away from home.

Within 10 years I completed two bachelor's degrees, two master's degrees, and a PhD. I became the first Maldivian to earn a PhD in a sport-related field. I guess I am also the only high school dropout with one. My life has taken many twists and turns. I have achieved success at a level beyond my wildest dreams. Running opened the doors!

In 2005 I returned home to several changes within the Maldives. The most significant was that the one-party autocracy changed to a chaotic multiparty system. Hesitant to take sides, I decided to join the armed forces and took the rank of Captain at the Maldives National Defence Force (MNDF). I became the first person to join at such a high rank in the organization's 100-year history. One year later, the Maldives national Olympic committee held the first elections. I am honored now to be the vice president and look forward to helping my country improve its sport performances.

As for my running records, I still hold multiple national records, including the marathon. My marathon best of 2:45:03 is slow by today's world standards. But in the context of sport, the Maldives are at least more than half a century behind in most sports if compared to the current Olympic Games standards.

Before I found running, my life was on a downward spiral, sure to take a wrong turn and leave me on the opposite side of the law. I was able to change my life and make it a decent one with the help of sports. I am thankful to have found and pursued it. I have not been beaten in a distance race locally and still hold the national records for 10,000 m, 20 km, 30 km, and the marathon. Running has enabled me to visit many countries so far, and provided me with the opportunity to meet many of my heroes, like Billy Mills, Muhammad Ali, Kip Keino, and Haile Gebrselassie, among others.

I still dream. My most ardent dream at the moment is to raise my kids well and give them the opportunities I missed out on as a child. I also would like to complete one more PhD and write at least 20 books. Sportswise, I am currently training to complete an Ironman. I want to become the first Maldivian to complete an Ironman and do so in 12 hours or under. Visiting all the stadiums that have hosted the Olympic Games is also on my wish list. In the not-so-distant future, I would also like to work at the International Olympic Committee to pass on the message of Olympianism to the less fortunate people of the world.

In 2011 another dream came true for me. After 18 years since running a marathon, I just completed the most historical marathon of all. I ran the Athens classical marathon from Marathon to Athens that finishes at the 1896 Olympic Stadium. I cried for the first km and in the last from happiness of achieving a life-long dream. We all need to have dreams. We also need to strive to achieve those dreams. Run towards the light at the end of the tunnel. I did and came out at a place beyond my wildest dreams.

CONCLUSIONS

Below are a few thoughts and reflections that I wish to leave you with:

1. Life is a very arduous journey, with many twists and turns. Surely each of us will face a hardship that is almost impossible to overcome, but then somehow we manage to overcome it. In order to beat the challenges, we need guidance from other people, be it family or others.

2. We are faced with making crucial decisions. We are the ones who have to process the information and decide in order to map our life. One thing is for sure: each of us has to develop a willingness to persist in the face of hardship and uncertainty.

3. I never thought my life would turn out the way it has. I am very glad that I ventured into the unknown against the advice of those closest to me, and dared to be different despite the consequences. I must thank the sports context, particularly the marathon. I can honestly say that if not for my running, my life would not have become such a demanding, yet rewarding, experience.

Queering Sport One Team at a Time

Barbara Ravel

INTRODUCTION

As far as I can remember, I have always loved sports and was a real tomboy. The first organized sport that I played was soccer. I played on a boys' team because there were no girls' teams in my village at the time. I also played volleyball on the schoolboys' team—because I was too good for the girls' team. I also played tennis, first in my village, then in the nearest big city when I moved there. I eventually quit these sports to focus on another one when I discovered the wonderful sport of ice hockey. Ice hockey was, for me, love at first sight. It became a passion of mine and for many years it was central to my life.

Over the years, hockey has provided me with opportunities to have fun, to excel at something, to compete at a high level, to travel across Europe and Canada, to meet new people, and to develop long-lasting friendships. But hockey has also greatly influenced my life in two other areas. First, sport became the focus of my studies, which eventually led me to my current position as an assistant professor in the School of Human Kinetics at Laurentian University (Ontario, Canada). My job involves teaching sports-related courses as well as conducting research on different aspects of sport. I can credit hockey for this career path. Second, I discovered that I might be gay while playing hockey when I met two former players who, according to my teammates, were lesbians. As odd as it may sound, just seeing them in person and knowing that they were lesbians made me realize that I might be gay, too. This encounter was a moment in my life that defined who I am today.

Moreover, it is amusing to witness how these two aspects of sport and academics became interconnected, since my research deals with issues of gender and sexuality in sport.

WHILE IN FRANCE

When I was growing up in France, homosexuality was a taboo subject. What I heard was how "masculine" certain women were—and how "bad" it was to be "masculine" when you were a woman. I eventually learned that it was a way to condemn homosexuality, since being "masculine" was associated with lesbianism. Even though I probably fit the "masculine" description, I mostly escaped it because I was playing sports. I was not "masculine," I was an athlete! But when I joined an elite ice hockey team at 18 years old I soon discovered how homophobia worked and how subtle (or not) it could be. Ice hockey is a contact sport and as a result tends to have a reputation of being "masculine." However, women's ice hockey teams in France, and my team in particular, tended to pride themselves on their "feminine" looks. As a team, we were not "masculine" (contrary to female soccer players), and we were not lesbians (like some hockey players in Canada).

Compared to my (mostly) "feminine"-looking teammates, I felt I did not fit in, even though it was not usually acknowledged that I did not exactly meet the standard of femininity. However, a celebration of various athletic achievements in our city provided me with a brutal reminder of the importance of conforming to gender norms. Our team was honored for winning the national championship the year before and for having several international players on its roster. Other teams' successes were acknowledged as well as the accomplishments of individual athletes. On this occasion, homophobia, in the form of the obligation to conform to gender norms, was displayed in two separate ways. First, our team leader ordered us to dress appropriately for the ceremony, which meant wearing a skirt or dress and makeup. In other words, we had to look "feminine." To me, this proved difficult since I did not possess a skirt or a dress—and did not intend to either buy one or borrow one for the occasion; I also refused to wear make-up. As a result, I was one of the two players on my team who did not conform to the team leader's orders and I was explicitly reminded of this. "You could have made an effort, Barbara!" Of course, I could have. I could also have explained my point, which was that I was free to dress according to what I felt was appropriate, not to what others thought was appropriate, no matter how "masculine" this might be. Instead, I opted for an act of passive resistance by saying nothing and smiling as if embarrassed. Second, among the celebrated athletes were female soccer players who had similar achievements: national champions and many players selected on Team France. To this day, I still clearly remember seeing them on stage and wishing I were part of their team! I so looked like them that I could have easily passed as a soccer player during the event. I immediately felt a connection with them—they were "my people." Looking at them made me realize there was another way to be a woman. I felt relief, happiness, and hope, all together. I was relieved that I was not the only one and happy because I was able to witness other women who seemed unapologetic about not conforming to gender norms and who, with their approach, had tremendous success in sport. Finally, it gave me hope that, one day, I could be in a team where I would completely fit in. For my teammates, catching a glimpse of the soccer team was enough to incite them to make derogatory comments. It was difficult for me to witness how my wonderful teammates could suddenly change into homophobic individuals and apparently not see the evidence—that I was what they mocked. I decided to remain silent about my feelings of discomfort about their comments and realized that it would be difficult to tell them that I was gay.

It was never clear to me how somebody on my team knew that some Canadian hockey players were lesbians, but somebody did and thought it was information worth sharing. The information was not circulated in a neutral tone, though. On the contrary, I could sense the aversion in their voices. These offensive comments towards suspected lesbian hockey players were intended to warn us in case we were to go play in Canada. According to what they were saying, playing hockey in Canada would be dangerous for us. The relation between lesbians and sexual predators was alluded to. I thought that it was contradictory to insist on distancing ourselves from lesbianism when the two former players who were lesbians were warmly welcomed every time that they came back to see us. I also wondered if they realized that they did not perceive their former teammates as sexual predators. How could they reconcile these two different images of lesbians? Again, I understood that being gay in this context would not be easy. Switching back to soccer for a more welcoming environment was not an option, but moving to Canada, at first a crazy idea, soon became a much-planned project. Fortunately and conveniently, the realization of this project was facilitated by a concomitant purpose—participating in an exchange student program with a Canadian university. As a result, I officially moved to Canada in order to study as a graduate student and to play hockey. But I also had a secret objective: finally being able to live as an openly gay woman!

IN CANADA!

I arrived in Montreal on August 19, 1998. I was ready for a fresh start, and it really felt like the first day of my new life. Living in Montreal was great and exceeded even my highest expectations. First, there was hockey. Ice hockey in France is a very marginal sport, but in Canada it is the equivalent of soccer in France: It is everywhere! I had so many opportunities to play that I was on the ice almost every day of the week! Then, there were my studies. Studying at the University of Montreal was stimulating at the academic level and at the interpersonal level. I met engaged professors and was registered for great courses. Moreover, whereas I had few friends at my university in France, in Montreal I found myself meeting many new people and building several friendships. How different my experience was as a student all of a sudden! Finally, I discovered a city that embraced diversity like no other I had been in before. I would wander around town and be amazed by the different neighborhoods. Of course, I particularly enjoyed the "gay village!" My secret goal was about to become a reality. Again, hockey played a central part in my coming out as a gay woman.

Coming from France, I faced a lot of skepticism towards my hockey skills. I had to prove my abilities even more than the Canadians did, because it was assumed that French people were not good hockey players. I also experienced something that I had not expected when planning my departure: having to learn a new language to be able to communicate with my new teammates. French in France and French in Québec are not exactly the same. There are different expressions and a different accent. But being in a locker room with French Canadian hockey players was the worst! Many technical or tactical terms related to hockey and pieces of equipment were called by different words than I was accustomed to or by English words in French conversations. I was linguistically lost! Nonetheless, I felt a sense of peace and unity in the midst of this culture shock. I had finally found "my" people. I was not alone anymore. In a way, it was like coming home. Maybe I had to adapt my vocabulary and to prove that I belonged on the ice, but I was able to be an openly (i.e., out) gay hockey player. To an outsider, it looked as if I was indeed "perverted" by the many lesbians surrounding me on the ice and in the locker room. My former teammates would have thought they were right to warn me against the risks of playing in such an environment. I knew better—I was just waiting for the right context to express who I really was. During my 10 years in Montreal, I played on many teams, most of them embracing diversity: from teams with a minority of nonheterosexual players to teams with a minority of "straight" (i.e., heterosexual) players. Remembering what my French teammates had said about Canadian hockey players, I had to smile because, in a sense, they were right. What they could probably not have predicted is the fact that it was not bad at all. It is difficult to describe how liberating and fun it was to play hockey in a context where my nonconformity to gender norms was not an issue and where my sexuality could be revealed without fear. It was so much simpler to just have to focus on playing hockey!

After a year in an exchange program with my university in France, I chose to apply to a Canadian graduate program. With my previous degree being in psychology and my personal interest leading me to sport, I opted for a master's in sports psychology. Having witnessed how an athletic context could be so different from one country to the next and how sport could have such an influence on the expression or repression of nonconventional sexualities, I eventually decided to investigate the issue in women's ice hockey for my master's project. Several years later, I was finishing my PhD and was a published author, with my first article titled "The Lightness of Being 'Gay': Discursive Constructions of Gender and Sexuality in Quebec's Women's Sport." For my dissertation, I interviewed women with a nonconventional sexuality playing different team sports. With this project, I wanted to find elements of answers to my initial questions. For example, how open could sport be towards sexual diversity and how sport could influence the expression of nonconventional sexualities. The methodology adopted for the study favored the establishment of a conversation with the participants and the sharing of experiences as nonheterosexual women playing sports between the researcher and the interviewees. As difficult as it was at first for a novice qualitative researcher using such an emotionally charged method of data collection, it was fascinating to conduct the interviews and to learn about other athletes' experiences, so much so that it was certainly one of the highlights of my PhD. Another highlight of my doctoral journey was when I wrote a fictional story in order to present the main results to the participants towards the end of the study. This fictional story was designed to illustrate how women with a nonconventional sexuality are present and visible in sport; how open conversations can be between "straight" and "nonstraight" players when it comes to nonconventional sexualities; and how sport is more open towards sexual diversity than other contexts. The story is called "Locker Room Conversations" and it is staged in a fictional hockey locker room while the various players of a team, each also with a social role, get ready for a game. What follows is the dialogue.

LOCKER ROOM CONVERSATIONS

Alex, a 24-year-old gay forward: Have you seen the other team?

Sandra, a 28-year-old heterosexual defense player: Why? What's wrong with them?

Alex: Oh, they're really charming!

Natalie, a 30-year-old gay defense player: They're all so butch!

Sandra: They're what???

Natalie: Gosh, good thing we're here to educate you! For your information, a butch is a woman like the ones we saw earlier, before coming into the locker room. … Let's just say not very feminine.

Alex: A truck driver or a mechanic!

Sandra: Oh, I see.

Natalie: To say the least, they're not very attractive.

Alex: Well, just because you're gay it doesn't mean that you shouldn't pay attention to how you look.

Natalie: Sorry to sound mean, but I don't want to be associated with them. It's not very flattering.

Alex: No wonder people don't like lesbians!

Isabelle, a 24-year-old heterosexual forward: Why do you care what they look like anyways? I don't find you very supportive of the people in your community. Don't you think you should stand by each other instead of discriminating against one another? There's enough discrimination in our society as it is. Live and let live.

Alex: All right, all right, I admit it's not nice. Let's just say that their style is different from mine, that they're older and so I don't want to be associated with them.

Isabelle: It seems to me that they fought for the rights you have today. So you should be grateful, no?

Jen, a 22-year-old queer-identified goalie: Yeah, respect!

Alex: You may be right, but I refuse to associate myself with the "pretty" ladies working at the hardware store, for instance.

Lana, a 26-year-old heterosexual defense player: Oh, there she goes again! What do you have against Home Depot? My grandmother always told me there are no stupid jobs. Just because you go to university it doesn't mean that you should only hang out with university people.

Natalie: By the way, Alex, what's going on with you and that girl in your department?

Alex: Oh, I don't know. … She might be gay but she might not be. … It's hard to tell and it's driving me crazy!

Natalie: On a scale from one to ten, how gay does she look?

Alex: I don't know. … A five maybe? She's quite sporty looking but at the same time she's pretty feminine. She could be straight but just not be a bimbo. Or she could be gay but not look like a truck driver! It's really hard to tell. If I were 100% sure that she was gay, I could say something or do something. But if she's straight …

Jen: She might be straight today but who knows about tomorrow? Maybe she'll be gay … or bisexual!

Alex: Oh no, not bi!

Jen: Why not?

Alex: Well, I don't understand why they can't just choose. I mean, it's not very complicated. Who are you attracted to? Men or women?

Jen: What does it matter to you? Even if she's gay it doesn't mean she's going to be interested in you anyways! Straight, gay, that can change. They're only categories! I really feel that you fall in love with a person, not with a gender.

Alex: I know she's had a boyfriend.

Jen: Well, that doesn't mean anything, does it, Natalie?

Natalie: Very funny!

Alex: It's annoying. I see her almost every day at university, and I can't seem to figure it out. … On top of it, it's a tricky situation because she might not even know I am gay. I don't hide it, but I don't really talk about it either. Some of my friends know, but that's it. And I'll never tell certain people—they're way too straight!

Isabelle: Hey, Sandra and I might be straight but we play hockey with you so … not all straight people are narrow-minded.

Alex: Okay, you and Sandra are open-minded but with people outside of hockey, like at university, I'm not sure it would go over that well.

Natalie: It's true that it's probably better to keep certain things private when it comes to your professional future. I've told several people at work that I'm gay but not really those that could have a direct influence on my career. I haven't told my boss, and I don't think that he knows. I don't really think it would change anything, but I don't want to take the chance. He seems cool, but he's still my boss. But I have other colleagues that I've told and others have probably found out. I think it helps that people are pretty young at my work.

Jen: Yeah, it's clearly a matter of generations. Just look, now teenagers think it's cool to be gay or to know people who are gay.

Natalie: And don't forget, we live in Montreal! I'm not sure it's as cool to be gay in a small town. I don't think people in a small town would be pleased to know that their neighbors are flamers or a butchy lesbian couple with their dog!

Alex: I know I shouldn't generalize but I think that in the suburbs or in small towns people are less open. It's like they're not as exposed to gays. In Montreal, people are used to diversity, cultural and otherwise, and everybody knows someone who's gay!

Jen: My parents have always lived in the suburbs, and it wasn't a problem when I came out, but look at Kim and her new girlfriend's parents.

Kim, a 27-year-old gay forward: They probably just need a little time.

Natalie: It's incredible though, isn't it? We have the right to get married, but we can't bring our girlfriend home for dinner! It just sucks. I can't complain because my parents are super cool, they're really open, but if I were with a girl whose parents were against being gay, I don't know what I'd do. I'm not sure it would be very good for our relationship.

Alex: What about you, Julie? Do your parents still not know?

Julie, a 31-year-old gay forward: No.

Alex: What? You haven't told them yet? You don't think they're going to wonder why you want to buy a condo with your "roommate?!"

Julie: I don't know, but my mom won't stop talking to me about her neighbor's son and how nice and good looking he is!

Michelle, a 29 year old gay defense player: I still have aunts and uncles who ask me every time I see them—which isn't very often thank goodness!—if I have a boyfriend. … My sister and I just look at each other. … It's not my problem if they don't want to see or understand anything. I bet that even if I brought my girlfriend to a family party, some of them would ask her where I was hiding my boyfriend! Yeah, we're not all as lucky as you, Jen, to have such cool parents!

Jen: Well, guys, I don't want to interrupt you but we have a game to play.

Alex: Yeah, against our charming opponents!

POST-STORY REFLECTIONS

In this story, the presence of traditionally masculine-looking players on the opposing team sparks a conversation about nonconventional sexualities among teammates with different sexualities (e.g., heterosexual, gay, queer). Although certain passages are clearly butch-phobic, the majority of the interactions demonstrate an openness to sexual diversity. Moreover, the story depicts the ease with which heterosexual and nonheterosexual players can discuss sexuality, both conventional and nonconventional. As a result, this locker room offers a unique environment of exchange and acceptance towards sexual diversity, which is in stark contrast to other milieus such as work or family. As Alex, Natalie, and Michelle suggested, it is not always as easy to be out to your family or your coworkers.

THE CURRENT SITUATION FOR NONHETEROSEXUAL ATHLETES

The fictional story presents the situation for sportswomen with a nonconventional sexuality as enviable. Nonheterosexual women could be out about their sexuality in sport and thrive in this environment. This very encouraging result, however, needs to be nuanced and put in perspective. The study was conducted in Montreal in 2004-2005 and certainly reflected the city's climate of tolerance and inclusion. Nevertheless, anecdotal evidence suggests that homophobia in sport is also decreasing in other cities and countries. Many initiatives have been created to challenge homophobia in sport and many sports organizations actively fight discrimination based on sexual orientation. To name a few: Step Up! Speak Out!; Gay, Lesbian and Straight Education Network (GLSEN); Canadian Association for the Advancement of Women and Sport (CAAWS); Pride Houses during the Vancouver 2010 Olympic and Paralympic Games; and Hockey Against Hate. For example, according to its website, Hockey Against Hate

> aims to spread understanding, tolerance and compassion through the game of hockey. It promotes a message of diversity, equality and acceptance on and off the ice in the hope that no one who loves the game should ever feel threatened, demeaned or persecuted for the person they love, the color of their skin or the team they cheer for. (hockeyagainsthate.com/pledge/)

To me, this is encouraging!

Moreover, several high-profile athletes have recently come out as gay in the media. These brave athletes come from all over the world: Canada (soccer player David Testo), England (cricket player Steven Davies), Australia (field hockey player Gus Johnson), New Zealand (speed skater Blake Skjellerup), Sweden (soccer player Anton Hysen), and the United States of America (figure skater Johnny Weir and basketball player Jason Collins). This list is desperately lacking names of female athletes, which seems paradoxical since so many women are out to their teammates and coaches, yet when they are part of elite teams, they are reluctant to publicly come out. Canadian hockey player Sarah Vaillancourt is probably the exception, but she stated in an article that while she came out as a student in an Ivy League university, when she plays for Team Canada she is quieter about her sexuality. The situation for high-profile athletes who recently came out leaves me with mixed emotions. On the one hand, I am delighted when I read about another coming out story. On the other hand, if we rely on their reports, it appears that the sport context is not always welcoming to athletes who are not heterosexual. In general, progress still needs to be made in the fight against different forms of homophobia (heterocentrism, reinforcement of gender norms, silence or invisibility of sexual diversity in locker rooms as well as in the media).

WHERE I AM NOW

I never regretted my decision to move to Canada, and I became a Canadian citizen once I finished my PhD. To this day, I appreciate how fortunate I am to live in a country where I am free to express my sexuality, where I am free to marry my female partner and to be recognized as one of the parents of my nonbiological children on their birth certificate. Among Western countries, Canada is at the forefront of the battle against discrimination based on sexual orientation either with legislation (the legalization of same-sex marriage, for instance) or with social acceptance in general. A new Research Chair on homophobia has been created in a Quebec university, apparently the first of its kind in North America. Research in sport is also vibrant in Canada, with researchers from various provinces leading the way in terms of studies on LGBT athletes. As for me, I have been hired as an assistant professor based on my nonconventional research interests, and I have discovered another part of Canada, Northern Ontario, where it is not so bad to be gay after all. It seems that there is hope outside Montreal, too! Always curious, I intend to investigate how it is to be nonheterosexual in sport here. My athletic career may be behind me, but my professional career is in its early stages and, according to one of my former students, I am now considered a model—a model of, I guess, a woman who is a successful professional and married with kids, which seems to still be rare when it applies to a nonheterosexual woman. I must say that I was proud to hear this comment from my former student because I feel a sense of responsibility towards my students to use my position in order to challenge heterocentrism, the traditional assumption that everyone is heterosexual. At the same time, I fear that I present a very normative version of what it is to be a woman with a nonconventional sexuality: I decided to formalize my (same-sex) union with marriage; I chose to have kids and, as a result, almost feel more connected to my straight colleagues who have kids than my queer peers who do not; I am a White educated woman with a somewhat enviable social status, which grants me a certain freedom and independence, as well as privileges.

I used to be involved in sports as an athlete. Now I am involved in sport mostly because sport is central to my teaching and research and because, as a professor in human kinetics, I notably teach future actors of the sports world (e.g., physical education teachers, sports administrators, coaches). I often tell my students that I have the best job in the world because I am paid to study sport. I am a sports enthusiast, so therefore it really is a dream job. But I also know, first hand and through my expertise in the field of sport sociology, that sport may not always be welcoming when you are "different" (e.g., LGBTQ, Black, overweight). Being able to challenge my students by using sport to reflect upon sexism and homophobia, for example, is one of the highlights of my job. Most of them just love sports, in the same way that I do, but hopefully, after my sport sociology classes, they can see sport through a more critical lens and will make sure that sport is indeed a good place to be for all.

CONCLUSIONS

The fictional story based on the participants' narratives showed how sexuality could be fluid but also how gender norms were more difficult to transgress. In other words, it was okay to be gay, bisexual, or even to refuse to label your sexuality as long as you did not look too "masculine." I was okay because I was not a "butch," but as a researcher I had to highlight this form of discrimination. If I were asked what still needs to be done, based on my research and personal experience, I would answer the following: challenge gender norms and fight butchphobia. More broadly, additional education and research need to be done to increase social acceptance towards individuals with a nonconventional sexuality, whether in sport or in other contexts. In particular, more physical education teachers, coaches, and sports administrators have to become aware of the different forms of homophobia and how to put an end to discrimination based on sexual orientation. We also need more diversity in the public sphere. While an increasing number of elite male athletes have been less reluctant to come out in the recent past, out lesbians in sport are still scarce and tend to be discreet. Furthermore, we can ask ourselves: Where are gays of color? Who is going to challenge the gay normativity? How can we make more gains to better protect sexual minorities around the world?

This chapter was intended to provide inspiration from an athletic and a professional journey. I can attest that there is hope: Hope that it is possible to enjoy life as an out lesbian woman. Hope that sport may be the answer to homophobia and to discrimination against sexual minorities. Hope that sport allows nonheterosexual individuals to thrive and excel in sport without their sexuality being an issue. Hope that sport can offer a mutually enriching environment for straight and nonstraight players alike, an environment within which people from diverse sexualities compete together, learn to respect each other, and embrace their differences. To borrow from the Hockey Against Hate organization: "At the end of the day, we all love hockey." I could not agree more. Below are a few final conclusions:

1. Make sure that sport is a welcoming environment for all, regardless of gender or sexuality, and within which differences are respected and valued.

2. Challenge heteronormativity in sport and other sports-related contexts, for example, by using inclusive language and by positively talking about people with a nonconventional sexuality or gender.

3. Become a "straight" ally if you are heterosexual and help fight homophobia and heterosexism.

4. Be "out and proud" if you are a person with a nonconventional sexuality—it is a good way to tackle heteronormativity!

From the Reserve to the Rink: Pursuing a Hockey Dream as an Aboriginal Athlete

Amy T. Blodgett and Duke Peltier

FOUNDATIONS OF A HOCKEY DREAM

My name is Duke Peltier, and I can always recall being in love with hockey. It is a sport that has always been a part of my life. My community, Wikwemikong Unceded Indian Reserve, is an ice hockey community, with many fans and a lot of support for our local teams. My family is also a hockey family. From a very young age, I was immersed in the hockey culture of Wikwemikong, spending much of my time at the arena. Some of my earliest memories are of being in the dressing room with our local senior men's hockey team, the Wikwemikong T-Birds, who were provincial and regional champions for many years. They were a powerhouse team, often referred to around town as the "T-Bird Dynasty." My father was on the team as one of its captains and a lead organizer, so I was always around all the players—I was very attached to the team from a young age. It was from there that I got my start in sport and built up the confidence to pursue my own dreams. Because I spent so much time watching and admiring the T-Birds, I tried to emulate the players. They were role models and leaders in the community, and really, they were nothing short of hometown heroes. They exemplified positive community values and instilled a sense of local pride that continues to this day. A passion was instilled in me being around these successful athletes, and I realized that I wanted to do what they were doing. The T-Birds were one of the building blocks in establishing my identity as an aspiring athlete and creating my passion for hockey.

As soon as I was old enough I began playing hockey in our community youth leagues. In one of my first years, I remember getting a penalty for roughing up an opposing player. For whatever reason—most likely reflecting what I had seen in the older league games and the hockey I watched on television—I felt proud for getting the penalty. I thought it showed that I was a dominant player on the ice and that I wasn't afraid to play an aggressive game. But after the game I was quickly scolded by my father and informed that this was not how to play hockey. He explained to me that sport was supposed to be fun for everyone, and so my opponents, my teammates, and the rules of the game had to be respected. He said that hockey was not to be spent in the penalty box, but rather, played on the ice. My father passed away shortly after that, when I was about 4 years old, and this is one of my only recollections of him—introducing me to the spirit of the game of hockey.

Unfortunately, my father's passing left a big gap in my life where a positive male role model was needed, especially as I got older and moved into competitive hockey, where I had to make more decisions about my future and my hockey development. My natural instinct was to look to sport for that guiding figure, for someone who understood my passion for the game and would support my hockey development. I did end up finding much of the support that I needed in various people linked to my hockey involvement. These people included my uncles and my grandmother, the parents and grandparents of some of my teammates, and several of my coaches. These people rallied behind me and helped ensure that I was able to play the game I loved by providing me with transportation to the games (which were often three or four hours away from home at the competitive level) and giving guidance when I needed it. But in terms of a real role model I could look up to, I was drawn to the young men who were playing hockey at the Junior level and had established a degree of success for themselves as Canadian Aboriginal athletes.

One of these established players was Gerard Peltier. He was one of the youngest players of the final Wikwemikong T-Birds teams, and he went on to play in the Ontario Hockey League (OHL); he also played professional hockey in Europe and the United States. Gerard came from my community, our little reserve, and was able to make it into the elite levels of hockey in spite of the odds and the racism that were against him at the time. He was a huge inspiration and source of pride in Wikwemikong, and I can remember our community taking busloads of people to go watch his games when he was playing in our home region. Fortunately for me, a few years after Gerard completed his hockey career he returned to the Wikwemikong community and became a coach for the team I was playing on. It was such an exciting day when I found that out because he was one of my idols, and he was returning to teach my teammates and me how to play better hockey. That was one of the turning points that really kickstarted my hockey dreams. Gerard brought a new level of structure, discipline, and knowledge to my hockey game, and he motivated me to want to work harder and become a better player. He gave me specific feedback and constructive criticism on what I needed to work on, and he also showed me how to utilize the strengths that I had. I remember him saying once, "To make it in hockey you're going to have to be twice as good as everyone else before you're going to be given an opportunity." Those were really motivating words to me, despite the harsh truth underlying them, because they let me know that I could succeed as an Aboriginal hockey player—as long as I was prepared to give it everything I had in order to overcome the disadvantage many people would hold over me.

Gerard was one positive role model that I found through sport, and he helped to fill the absence that was left by my father's passing and propelled my hockey dreams into the realm of possibility. He laid the foundation for me to develop my talents to the fullest as I prepared mentally for what was to come. He set me up to succeed in pursuing my hockey dreams. There were others along the way who also nurtured my hockey dreams and development, but Gerard stands out as the key figure.

PURSUING OPPORTUNITIES AWAY FROM HOME

As I got a bit older I ended up moving off reserve to play Midget hockey in a nearby city. I wanted to compete at a higher level, which meant integrating into the mainstream hockey leagues in the region. Unfortunately, it didn't take long for me to realize that I wasn't being given a fair opportunity to play at the highest caliber of hockey in the city. When you come from a different race and try to make it into the mainstream teams, it's easy to be overlooked or not be given a real opportunity. In my case I think it had to do with the negative stereotypes that existed about Native people not being able to pay the costs of playing and not being disciplined or motivated enough to stick with the team through the whole season. It is a constant battle to fight against these stereotypes, and that's why Gerard told me that I would have to work twice as hard to get any of my hockey opportunities.

As I watched more of my peers move up to higher levels of hockey while I remained stagnant, I began to doubt my abilities. I was repeatedly being told that I wasn't big enough, I wasn't strong enough, I wasn't whatever enough; I was given many reasons why I couldn't make it up to the higher levels of hockey. Over time, those comments began to take a mental toll on me and the seeds of self-doubt took root. Then, one night I was at a team fundraising function when a local fan approached me and questioned me about what my dreams were. He asked me, "When are you going to play in the OHL?" Without much thought I said, "I'm not big enough to play at that level." He replied, "Yes, you are." And this simple conversation became so significant for me, because at that point I realized that I had lost some of my focus and I had let a few people break my sense of self-confidence and destroy my belief that I was capable of playing in the OHL. I hadn't questioned whether those other people might have been wrong and might have underestimated me. This gentleman told me that I was big enough to play and that I did have the ability to do so, and his words changed my outlook. I think the reason I believed him and felt the impact of his words was because he was an external person, outside of my family and community, who saw the ability within me and believed that I could go further with my talents if I was willing to put in the work. He didn't have to offer those words of support to me, because he didn't know me personally. He reminded me that I had been given everything I needed to succeed on my life's journey. From a traditional Aboriginal perspective that is one of our teachings—that we are provided with everything we need to survive and succeed in life. We all have our own skills, our own abilities, and our own ways of doing things that help us survive and reach our full potential. It was a real wake-up call, which reinvigorated me and motivated me to work harder than ever.

Not long after, when I was 17 years old, I ended up getting the opportunity that I had been waiting for: I was invited to attend a prospects hockey camp in Alberta with my cousin, who also played hockey. It was for Native individuals from all across Canada, and it was a chance to get scouted for a Junior level team. Our families raised money for my cousin and myself to travel there, then they placed us on a plane (our first flight ever) and sent us on our way. I didn't know who was going to meet us in Alberta or where we were going to be staying; all I knew was that we were flying three provinces away from our home (more than 1500 km) to play hockey and try to make something of ourselves. I gave everything I had at the camp and, luckily, got noticed by one of the scouts who asked me to move to Saskatchewan into a residential school setting, where I would play hockey and have all my expenses paid for. It was a Midget team rather than a Junior team, but I knew this was an opportunity that I wasn't going to get back home, and I knew it would relieve my family of the financial burden of having to pay for my hockey. So I took it. I moved to St. Michael's Indian Residential School in Saskatchewan all alone.

Going to this residential school put me in a very different setting, because I was coming in as a recruit. I was put on a bit of a pedestal because I was coming from Ontario and brought in from such a distance, so there were high expectations placed onto me by the rest of the team and the coaching staff. This was quite a new experience because back in Ontario there were few expectations that I would make it among the non-Native (i.e., non-Aboriginal) players. Back home I almost felt like people were waiting for me to fall on my face just because I'm a Native person. I got the sense that people were wondering "When are you going to quit?" or "When are you going to become another Native stereotype?" But when I was in Saskatchewan it felt more like people were wondering: "What other great things can you do for the team?" This helped reaffirm many of the positive comments I had received from my home community, and it instilled greater confidence in me since there were now people outside of my community saying the same things. As the expectations shifted from low to high, I realized that for the first time I was in a position where I would be showcased as a talented athlete.

My experience wasn't entirely positive, because I found life in the residential school to be very lonesome. Even though we were all Native people, I was from a completely different tribe than everyone else, and I didn't know the local language because it was different from my own. I spoke the Odawa language and everyone else was speaking Cree. A lot of my peers were still able to communicate in their own language among each other, but I wasn't able to so I kind of felt like an outsider. Even though I was meant to fit in I wasn't really one of them, so I wasn't able to build any relationships. In addition, people seemed to think that I was being favored because I was brought in from Ontario to play on the hockey team. So there was a bit of jealousy and even a sense of hostility at times. One of the guys actually made a point of saying to me, "You think you're the king because you have a hard slap shot." That was a big statement to me, and there were a number of other instances like that.

But in spite of being lonely and dealing with the jealousy of others, I went through a great Midget hockey season at the residential school, and I was receiving interest in being picked up for different Junior teams, which is what I was focusing on. One Native team in Saskatchewan was considering putting me on their protected players list, which meant that they would have the rights to sign me to their team, but they hesitated because of some questions circulating about why I wasn't playing hockey in my home province if I had the talent for that level, and why I had come all the way out to Alberta. They were unsure of me, and while they wavered back and forth on a decision, another (non-Native) Saskatchewan team saw me play and immediately put me on their protected players list. That team was the Weyburn Redwings Junior team. The Weyburn coaching staff watched me play in the Western Canadians Championship, where my team became the first Native team to win, with my assist on the winning goal. The coaches were pretty impressed with what they saw so they offered me a spot on their team for the following year.

The management and coaching staff on my Midget team asked why I wanted to take the opportunity to go to Weyburn, because they told me it was "redneck" country. They said it wasn't a good place for me to be going because I was a Native person, and they weren't sure how I was going to be treated. They said I most likely wouldn't be accepted because there was a lot of racism present in that region. But ultimately I made my decision to go to Weyburn because I thought it would be a better opportunity for me. It was an organization that had a long history of providing players with opportunities to move on to higher levels of hockey, and the coaching and management structure was well established. It was a stable and credible organization. So I was willing to put aside the fact that I would be called names based on my race—I had heard it all before and it didn't bother me much anymore. Luckily, my family supported my decision to move to Weyburn, which helped me feel more confident in my decision.

So I moved to Weyburn Saskatchewan and began another chapter in my hockey journey. It turned out to be a really eye-opening experience, because we had many different nationalities on the team. I hadn't expected such diversity given what I was told about it being in redneck country. But there were Finnish players, Ukrainian players, French players, African Americans, African-Canadians, Aboriginals, and Anglo-Canadians. Everyone had completely different backgrounds, different languages, and different ways of doing things, and it was really interesting to experience such diversity. During our pregame practices and stretching, each teammate took turns leading the group in their own language, so we got to learn bits of each other's language. It was really cool. Little things like that helped create an open team environment where everyone was comfortable sharing some of their culture and learning from one another, and it brought us closer together.

I lived with one of the Ukrainian guys, and we could only communicate through our own attempts at sign language, since he didn't speak English and I didn't speak Ukrainian. I had been thinking I was very poor coming from a Native reserve, but here was a guy who came to the team with just one suitcase containing one pair of pants, a couple of shirts and some socks, and a hockey bag. That's all he had. And one day I saw him trying to clean his clothes in the sink with just a bar of soap. I tried to tell him that there were machines he could use to do that. I knew I had to help him learn his way around and get accustomed to a different lifestyle, especially since communication was a challenge for him. On another occasion, after he went to the store with his translator, he came home to the room that I shared with him carrying a bag from the pharmacy. He started pulling out the stuff he bought, like a toothbrush and toothpaste, and then he looked at me, smiling away, and pulled out a stick of deodorant. I couldn't help laughing to myself because it was women's deodorant. But I didn't say anything to him; I just let him enjoy it. Later on the other guys on the team noticed the deodorant, too, and they just let him use it. To us in Canada there is an expectation that people will maintain hygiene and smell nice, but this Ukrainian guy came from a different place where the things that we take for granted every day weren't readily available to him (like running water and laundry facilities). So the reason he didn't have deodorant and didn't know anything about it was because it was such a trivial, nonessential item in the larger scheme of his life. He had a very poor upbringing and was used to just getting by with the minimum necessities of life; deodorant was a luxury item to him. Even when he received a $50 honorarium, which was given to each player on the team every couple of weeks to make sure we had the things we needed, this guy would send almost all that money home to his family in the Ukraine. It was a lot of money to him and his family, whereas to us that amount was really nothing—we could spend it in an instant without thinking twice about it.

These experiences really helped me to appreciate the different life experiences and cultural backgrounds of others, bringing a whole new light to my thinking about the struggles humans encounter in their lives, even in attempting to pursue sport. For myself, coming from a Native reserve and going across the country to play hockey, there really wasn't any comparison to what my Ukrainian teammate felt moving across continents and settling in a new country where he didn't speak the language and was all alone. It really put things into perspective for me, as well as for others on the team. Ultimately, I think these experiences helped our team develop a deep respect for one another in that we recognized we each came from different backgrounds and different life paths, but we each had to struggle through our own circumstances in order to get to where we were. Some people had to overcome greater challenges than others, but no one had made it onto that team without blood, sweat, and tears. There was something comforting in knowing that you weren't the only one who had struggled on your journey and that people around you could understand and sympathize with your experiences.

Being on this team was probably one of the first times I had the opportunity to meet people from a variety of different cultures and was able to listen to their stories and get a sense of what life was like for them in their communities back home. Our team was naturally able to appreciate the life stories, life experiences, and cultural practices of others, which went a long way in our developing a sense of trust in and support for one another. I think this environment largely reflected the quality leadership that was present in both players and coaches. The effects of this leadership translated onto the ice, too, because we were the provincial champions that year.

I stayed with the Weyburn Redwings for two years and enjoyed my experience there. During the second year, college teams heavily recruited me, but I ended up sustaining a significant shoulder injury, which led several of the college teams to back out because they didn't want to take a chance on me. I'd had my heart set on going to one of the big schools, like an Ivy League school, or to one of the big hockey schools like Michigan State or Notre Dame. But because of my injury I was relegated to the lower-tier schools with lower caliber hockey teams, and I ended up accepting a scholarship from Ferris State University in Michigan. Unfortunately, I didn't fully research what I was getting into. Upon arriving at the university I was immediately told by the hockey coach that I wasn't going to play that year—I was going to be sitting on the bench. This caught me off guard because I had assumed that since they were giving me a full scholarship I would be playing. I had always been on teams where I played, and here I was coming into a situation where, as it turned out, I was only brought in to replace one of the veteran players when he graduated the following year. They brought me onto the team a year before they needed me because they wanted me to be integrated into the system when the time came to step up. This wasn't a role I wanted or had expected to play, and it took away from the enjoyment I got out of the game and changed my outlook. It was part of a very structured system of hockey where everything was choreographed and planned out, and this wasn't how I had grown up playing the game. Everything became so technical; it was like playing hockey out of a manual rather than just playing. There were some philosophical differences between the coach and myself in terms of our hockey expectations, and after one semester I ended up quitting the team. I finished my semester and then I returned to Weyburn so I could finish out my last year of Junior hockey there. Weyburn essentially had the same make-up of the team as we'd had for the last two years, and we went all the way to the National Championships that year. So I was happy to end my Junior career on that note.

TAKING ACTION AGAINST RACISM

Throughout the course of my hockey journey I achieved a certain level of tolerance for being called names and hearing racial slurs on the ice, because it had just seemed to come with the territory of being a Native athlete. It occurred frequently enough, so I had no choice but to learn to ignore it and keep focused on my game. When I played on the all-Native team at the residential school and we would play against non-Native teams, I repeatedly saw fist fights going on outside the arena between the players' parents. It always started with one parent yelling insults at the other team's players for something on the ice, and then parents from both teams would start yelling back and forth and begin insulting one another, and then it escalated from there. In one situation it got to a point where there was so much hostility our team had to get the police to escort us out of town after the game was over. I think this was a reflection of the political climate at the time, because it was during the 1990s when there was real anger between the mainstream people and Native people. Here we were an all-Native team, which was virtually unheard of at that time, playing against non-Native teams in a period when cultural tensions were running high. Another time I remember being on the ice in the middle of a game and all I could hear was this one guy yelling from way back in the stands, telling me to go back to the reserve to my tepee. These comments were the norm more than the exception, so I accepted them as part of my hockey experience and just tried not to focus on the situation or let it bother me.

Over the years I built up such a tolerance for the racist comments that I didn't even pay attention to a particular instance while playing at the university level. During a game against a Manitoba team I was being called some degrading names from the opposing team's bench. It was obvious that their coach wasn't bothered by what was going on because he was sitting right there with the players, allowing it to continue, and likewise, I didn't react or say anything about it. I didn't give a second thought to the situation after the game was over until I received a phone call from the president of the hockey league. He told me that somebody from my team—he never told me specifically who it was—had advised my coach that there were racial slurs being thrown around in the game and he thought it was totally inappropriate. The coach agreed with this person and ended up complaining to the league. The president of the league confirmed with me what had been said and then asked me what I wanted done to this other team. I had never been asked this question before, but I thought about it and asked for an apology, in writing, to me and to my team. I also requested that the team volunteer their time at an inner city school in their community. My hope was that by insisting that they volunteer at an inner city school, maybe they would see some of the struggles that the Native people encounter. There would be a large population of Native youth at an inner city school in that particular community, and I'm sure it would have been quite shocking for many of the players on that hockey team to see what these kids' lives were like. I hoped that this volunteer experience would be eye-opening for the hockey team and would really bring a new understanding of how racist comments undermine the hard work and struggles that Native people have to overcome to make it to where they are today.

Within a day of my talking to the league's president, there was a letter sent to me, signed by the other team, stating their commitment to volunteering at an inner city school. It was a big moment for me, one that I'll never forget. I still have the letter to this day, and it's still quite significant to me. I think this letter and the whole situation around it really showed that a shift was slowly starting to take place, at least in the hockey world, where racism wasn't being tolerated anymore. Up until that point nothing had ever been done about racism—at least not in my own experience—which is why I had developed a thick skin and didn't find it unusual to be called racist names. I gained a sense of satisfaction from knowing that I might have played a small part in changing the views of a few people, hopefully opening up their minds to becoming more accepting and respectful of other cultures.

Looking back, my experiences of racism were tied to feelings of fear more than anger, because I didn't want to see anybody get hurt needlessly, through physical acts of violence or verbal attacks. I never felt anger because I recognized that a lot of non-Native people were not educated about our people and our history, and I realized that they didn't know anything about me as a person. I think one of the reasons why I was able to move past all those experiences of racism and name-calling without letting it get to me was because growing up I always had a really good understanding of who I was. A lot of that had to do with having an upbringing in my home community with my own language, which helped me feel rooted in who I was and where I came from. I wasn't searching around trying to find myself, trying to piece together my identity; I was in a position of strength in that regard. I had no reason to question my qualities or character, or even my ability on the ice. And I wasn't going to let anyone else pass judgment on me based on their own lack of knowledge about me. This is an important foundation that every person requires. You need to know who you are and what your talents and abilities are so that you can set out on your life journey with the strength to succeed, and not be pulled down by the negativity of others.

CULTURAL EDUCATION THROUGH SPORT

From my journey, I have realized that sport provides an opportunity for people from different cultures and backgrounds to come together as part of a team and really learn from one another, first-hand. When you're on a team, you spend large amounts of time together—playing and practicing, traveling, even living together—and you're going to want to build connections with those people around you and share pieces of your background and your life. You share your history, your values, your beliefs, your struggles, and your triumphs. And in that sharing process people will find commonalities as well as differences, both of which provide learning opportunities at the personal and social level. But in order for that sharing and learning to occur, there has to be an atmosphere of openness to and appreciation of diversity, which I believe needs to be facilitated by the team's leadership (coaches and players). It requires a certain skill, and I'm not sure exactly how to nurture that skill, but if it's recognized early enough by a coach or team leader it is something that can be incorporated into the team's practices (for example, the way my team conducted warm ups in the different languages of the players, or through other team-building exercises that recognize and play on the strengths of people's diverse backgrounds). In these situations opportunities are created to bridge cultural gaps or tensions that might exist, and to build deeper connections based on understanding and respect for one another.

People can gain cultural education through the sport experience, maybe even more than they can get out of a book or school course, because in sport the education can be lived and experienced, and it is personalized. As a Native, when I get questions like "Do you still live in tepees?" it tells me that there is a real lack of knowledge about our culture that is not being addressed in the Canadian school system. But as for my teammates with whom I played hockey, if they were interested in learning more about my culture I was willing to teach them about it and show them where I come from. It's an opportunity to break down stereotypes and open people's minds. When I started playing Junior hockey, it was a real rarity for a Native person to be playing at that level. There were only a handful of Native players up there. But now there are so many that you can't even count them. Something happened along the way that opened the door for Native people to have these opportunities to pursue elite levels of hockey, and this is truly opening up a space within sport to share our culture with others.

CONCLUSIONS

1. Every athlete needs to develop an understanding of who they are as a person in order to ground themselves throughout their sport journey and help them overcome the challenges that they will inevitably face. In knowing where you come from, including the culture you are rooted in, there is an inner strength that others cannot take away. There is an understanding that you are a part of

something bigger than yourself, and you can't let the negativity of people who don't know you keep you from succeeding. Athletes should be encouraged to constantly develop their identity and reflect on their cultural roots as a way of developing personal resiliency.

2. Leaders should help foster an atmosphere of openness and respect for cultural diversity among sports teams, so that opportunities are created to bridge cultural gaps or tensions that might exist and ultimately to build deeper team connections. Through such efforts, stereotypes can be broken down and people can gain a first-hand education that is probably more meaningful than anything that could be gleaned through books or school courses. As such, team leaders should make an effort to encourage athletes to share their backgrounds with one another and even integrate cultural aspects into the team's practices.

3. There should be no tolerance for racism within sports leagues and individual teams, and action should be taken against any such instances. When people stand up against racism, they are sending the message that sport is a space in which all people should be able to safely and respectfully participate. No athlete should have to worry about being confronted with racial slurs or being denied opportunities to succeed simply because of his or her race. It is both a personal and social responsibility that each of us—players, coaches, referees, and administrators—stand up against racism and refuse to accept it as part of the sport experience.

HEALTH AND WELL-BEING

Exercising Fat Control, Resistance, and Self-Compassion: Two Ethnographic Stories from the Field

Kerry R. McGannon and Kathi A. Cameron

INTRODUCTION: SETTING THE SOCIOCULTURAL CONTEXT

I was in a group discussion recently, and when one woman said, "I actually feel okay about the way I look," another woman scrunched up her face and said, "I have never in my whole life heard anyone say that—and I'm not sure I even believe you." That's how pervasive this negative body-talk is. It's actually more acceptable to insult your body than to praise it.

"Shocking Body Image News: 97% of Women Will Be Cruel to Their Bodies Today" (*Glamour,* February, 2011)

Within contemporary discussions of overweight and obesity, the so-called war on fat and the advocacy of using physical activity to fight the war, a "truism" exists: many women—regardless of their shape and size and regardless of whether they are fit and healthy—are at war with their bodies and themselves. The above headline comes from a recent issue of *Glamour* magazine, whose poll of 300 women found that some women have over 100 negative or anxious thoughts about their body shape. The average number of negative thoughts was 13—almost one for every waking hour. Why is this happening? With the help of a psychologist specializing in the treatment of adolescents and adults with eating disorders and body image distortion, *Glamour* identified a key influence: the media's narrow and unrealistic beauty standards. The irony of such revelations are not lost upon further inspection of *Glamour's* magazine cover, which featured an image of a thin woman and extolled the virtues of weight loss and "getting one's best body," all to be more attractive to the opposite sex. While men are not immune to body ideals generated by the media concerning fitness and masculinity, media messages and the effects of a negative body image disproportionately impact women across the lifespan.

How does the above relate to social justice and peace? For the purposes of our stories, the term *social justice* refers to creating a society based on the principles of *equality* and *solidarity* that strives to understand and value *human rights* and recognizes the dignity of human beings. The notion of *peace* refers to inner self-acceptance and self-compassion (e.g., kindness toward one's self rather than being harshly self-critical) regardless of flaws and imperfections. Viewed within the context of social justice, the angst and turmoil (i.e., lack of inner peace) women experience concerning their bodies becomes a social justice issue, not only because women are disproportionately impacted but because the uniformity of the fitness and beauty images stand in sharp contrast to the actual range of shapes and sizes of women's bodies. In turn, negative body-talk compromises dignity and inner peace, and, ultimately, women's health and well-being.

Self-loathing and feelings of turmoil in relation to one's body may be further verbalized *between* women as a way to create social bonds, further normalizing "negative body-talk" at individual and social levels. Research exploring the impact of media and social narratives surrounding obesity and fatness has shown that the normalization of negative body-talk is also turned outward toward others (i.e., overweight individuals), creating prejudice and stigma toward bodies that do not conform to, or approach, the (unattainable) ideal. These negative body-talk norms contribute to a society and a health and fitness culture that are less tolerant of a range of bodies and identities within the physical activity context and exercise space, creating a divide between people, and compromising their dignity and value as human beings.

The revelations from the *Glamour* survey are not news to feminists who demonstrated as early as the 1970s that the media and beauty industry create impossible ideals for women to attain by promoting a narrow version of beauty and femininity. Exercise and fitness are a vital part of the media industry and the portrayal and promotion of unrealistic and narrow body standards for women. By equating exercise and the female body with appearance and weight loss to sell products and services, the media has created and perpetuated an ideal, yet unattainable, narrow version of the fit female body (e.g., slim, toned, sculpted muscles, White, heterosexual). Such representations of women's exercise and bodies further encourage and normalize negative feelings surrounding the physical self (e.g., feeling guilty about not exercising, feeling ashamed for not exercising correctly, or feeling anxious or afraid that our bodies do not measure up within and/or outside the exercise context), and further promote the stigma and lack of compassion and acceptance toward bodies that deviate (e.g., muscular women, overweight women, older women).

Women who experience such feelings have greater difficulty finding inner peace and self-compassion when it comes to their bodies and exercise and/or accepting others. Feeling dissatisfied with one's body is further linked to avoidance of public places to be active, avoidance of particular forms of exercise (e.g., weight training, skill-based activities, and group exercise), overexercising and withdrawal from exercise when appearance-related motives are not attained, and eating disorders and disordered eating.

What is it like for women to incorporate these ideas (e.g., body dissatisfaction, antifat attitudes) into their psyches and everyday lives? Do women ever resist and/or transcend the dominant and narrow body ideals communicated to them, and if so, how? Many women do not experience self-loathing and/or the consumption of dominant media narratives concerning women's fitness in the black-and-white manner that *Glamour* proposed. In fact, some women resist the dominant messages and meanings perpetuated by the media and fitness industry, and some experience both liberating and disempowering effects simultaneously or in varying degrees. Researchers in exercise psychology have begun to explore the potential of self-compassion as a tool for women to resist negative body-talk and associated negative emotions within the exercise context. The aim of this chapter is to illustrate this complexity through the creation of two different stories of female exercisers who experience their bodies as deviating from the narrow version of the fit female body, as each enters an exercise context (i.e., gym). We conclude what may be learned from such stories in terms of social justice and self-compassion with respect to women's exercise and body (dis)satisfaction.

CONTEXTUALIZING THE STORIES: OUR "SELVES" AND ETHNOGRAPHIC STORIES

While the gym context creates power imbalances and inequalities in society by privileging White middle class individuals who can afford to purchase gym memberships, our stories are set in fitness gyms, as they are cultural spaces that exemplify an antifat ethic through the promotion of physical activity as a way of attaining appearance and weight loss goals. Our interest in fitness cultures and women's physical activity stems from our long-term involvement as fitness participants (e.g., aerobics, running), practitioners (i.e., fitness instructors, trainers), and academics (i.e., Kerry as a professor in sport and exercise psychology, Kathi as a health educator), with both authors as health promotion researchers.

As physically active woman whose journeys have spanned over 24 years, we are each a conglomeration of these multiple voices and perspectives. Having met in the gym, our 22-year friendship has been founded upon, and remains solidified by, our love and promotion of exercise and fitness. During each of our respective exercise journeys, we have experienced paradoxical feelings in relation to our bodies, such as fear and apprehension, guilt, anxiety, happiness, elation, a sense of freedom and control, and a loss of control. Though we would each characterize ourselves as having been thin and fit, fat and unfit, fit and fat, and even thin and unfit throughout our fitness journeys, neither of us has ever been fat in the clinical or empirical sense of the word. We have also been beginners/new in the exercise context, fearing the space and gaze of others due to not having bodies that measured up in terms of appearance ideals and not being able to perform correct movements in the gym space. Admittedly, we are not immune to the social and cultural messages that construct the ideal fit body, and as such, have not always been self-compassionate throughout the exercise and fitness experience. Regardless of our feelings toward our bodies, we acknowledge that we are privileged in terms of the exercise opportunities we have been afforded in light of being able-bodied, healthy, educated, White, middle-class females.

The result of these voices and experiences is that we each have a sense of self that is shifting and contradictory rather than fixed and straightforward. On the one hand, we have experienced our physical selves as flawed and in need of fixing, via various exercise practices during our 24 plus-year journeys. On the other hand, we have experienced ourselves as empowered and have been self-accepting due to the liberating features of our exercise and/or by liberating others (e.g., fitness participants, students), through challenging the "truth games" of women's fitness and the narrowly constructed fit female body. We thus position the two stories that follow with our broader work—as practitioners, educators, and researchers—as feminists, as we have an ethical commitment to producing knowledge that contributes toward social justice issues concerning gender, femininity, and fitness in order to promote more healthful physical activity practices and experiences for women.

Drawing upon our voices and experiences (i.e., exercise participant, practitioner, academic researcher) two ethnographic stories of two different women's (i.e., Carole's story, Jane's story) experiences within the exercise context (i.e., gym) were constructed and will be presented next. Writing ethnographic stories is a reflexive writing practice (i.e., being aware of one's identities during the write-up process and incorporating such identities into the process) whereby techniques such as emotional tone, character development, and plot (e.g., dramatic tension is built through flashbacks) are used in conjunction with data (e.g., participant-observation, interviews, focus groups, field notes) to construct a fictionalized story. An ethnographic story is fiction, but it is not merely a story; it is the result of having been there in a multitude of ways. It is also a way of presenting themes grounded in research data and real-life social and cultural contexts in an accessible story format that evokes emotion, empathy, and understanding from readers. Given this latter point, we view ethnographic stories as an excellent storytelling device to help raise awareness of social justice issues concerning the distress women may experience in relation to their bodies and exercise.

UNDERSTANDING EXERCISE EXPERIENCES AND (LACK OF) SELF-COMPASSION: TWO STORIES

The character of Carole is a conglomeration of Kathi's experiences and work as a personal trainer with obese clients, her observations and discussions with overweight clients during 20 years as a practitioner, and a study of aerobics participants' experiences of fitness leadership. Carole's story is told through the eyes of an overweight woman navigating the gym for the first time. The story of Jane represents Kerry's experiences with aerobics participants as a practitioner and participant observer over 15 years, the results of in-depth case studies collected from women who are sporadic exercisers, and her embodied experiences in the gym over 24 years. The character of Jane may or may not be read as overweight—this is for readers to decide. Jane's body-talk reflects the taken-for-granted body-talk women often engage in regardless of shape and size. As noted, such body-talk is an inherent and persistent theme in academic research and in both Kathi's and Kerry's experiences within the health and fitness industry and health education.

Carole's Story

Hi, I'm Carole. I am a 35-year-old government employee with a graduate degree and have done pretty well for myself if you don't count the fact that I'm still single and living alone. I'm also fat and have struggled with my weight since elementary school. My mother started me on my first diet at the age of 7, and to date I haven't lost any weight. I have no motivation to cook dinner as I'm by myself and can't seem to stop my cravings for fast food. I feel ashamed of my size and want to apologize for it all the time. . . sometimes I do. When I go shopping, I feel the stares of people in the grocery store as I walk the aisles. I'm especially aware of the shaking heads and looks of disgust when I go down the junk food aisle. Just the other day, a stranger came up to me, reached into my basket, picked out my tub of ice cream and told me I won't be losing any weight if I eat that. I was horrified, ashamed, and left the store (and my ice cream) as fast as I could. I haven't gone back there since. I don't have the self-control others have; I never have.

Moving is hard, my knees hurt, my back hurts, and my doctor tells me that I'm at risk for diabetes and an early death. She has suggested I get bariatric surgery but I'm still hanging on for a miracle. As I make my way to work in the morning, I see people staring at me as I carefully walk by. I have to watch my step on the sidewalk or else if I trip or stumble people either chuckle to themselves or think it's my fault 'cause I'm so fat. It is normal for me to get yelled at by a driver or passenger in a car. They call me names like pig and cow, or worse. It used to bug me, but today I just keep walking. It's just a part of my routine now; it's normal and it really doesn't matter. Runners jog by me in their little spandex outfits with their legs all strong and athletic. I know they judge me; I see it in their eyes as they peer at me with disgusted looks on their skinny little faces. I hate them.

Today, I have finally decided to go to the fitness center down the street and start an exercise program. I work with somebody who goes there, and she suggested I check it out. Although she is one of the fitness people, she says there are other people "like me" who work out there and the trainers are nice. The only problem is I don't have anything to wear to exercise in. Buying clothes in my size is hard, let alone exercise clothes that fit properly. I found an old, extra large t-shirt that barely fits; breathing in it is a little hard and everyone can see my fat rolls, but it's all I have. I bought a cheap pair of sweat pants from a second-hand store, but they certainly don't look like what everyone else wears. I haven't worn running shoes since PE class in school. Just slipping them on reminds me of how the other kids made fun of me. I was always picked last and no one ever passed me the ball. The PE teacher said it was a waste of his time and mine that I was even there. I will never forget that. I have never been athletic, why would I start now? I must be crazy.

As I drive towards the fitness center I feel my heart pounding in my chest, and my hands are cold and wet as I tightly grip the wheel. Maybe I should try again next week. I'm feeling sick; I must be coming down with a cold. I drive on. Pulling up to the facility, I see large groups of men and women leaving to run. They are thin, fit, and beautiful, wearing almost nothing to show the world their 8-packs and biceps. I park the car and wait a few minutes until they leave. When I think it's safe, I begin the process of getting out of the car. Once I'm out, I take a long, hard look at the fitness club. Windows expand the entire length of the lower floor and through them you can see sweaty people exercising on different machines; the treadmill people are most noticeable as they run with fierce looks and perfect bodies. As I plan my route I realize there is no way I can hide from their stares to get to the front desk; I must walk through the sea of black vinyl and chrome.

As I make my way through the sliding glass doors my stomach twists in knots, my face feels hot and red, my hands are clammy cold, and my legs start to feel weak. Oh my God, there's a crowd in the foyer, and to get to the counter I have to move straight through a near-naked, sweaty crowd of muscle and skin, and the hot steamy smell of perfume and body odor. I stand for what seems like forever as the desk staff laugh and flirt with all the fitness people. I feel invisible as I fight the urge to turn around and go home. In front of me is a wall of exercise clothes for sale that I couldn't get one of my meaty arms through. There is nothing for me on that wall, just a reminder of how fat and pathetic I am. I have never felt so out of place than I do now. Fitness centers are for the fit, not the fat.

Finally, a fitness person walks up to me and introduces himself as Jake. After asking me a few questions, Jake introduces me to Stephanie. She is going to be my trainer today and will set up a program for me suited to my needs. Stephanie is my worst nightmare. Next to her I look like a large beast from the scariest monster movie. She is wearing tight fitted yoga pants showing off her peach-like butt and one of those tight tank tops that highlight her toned, perfect arms. She is tanned, tight, young, energetic, pretty, thin, and everything I have come to hate about fitness. This time, however, Stephanie is promising me an exercise program that I will like. She promises that my body will be transformed into one that's long, lean, and rock hard—if only I stick to what she tells me to do.

For the first time in years, I feel a sense of hope and excitement. So what if I'm the fattest person in the room right now? I won't be for long. I hope Stephanie shows me exactly what she does to look like that. While I wait for my personal trainer to come back with the measuring tape (for what purpose, I have no idea), I imagine myself wearing normal-person clothes, yoga pants and tank tops. Stephanie invites me into a little room with a scale and a bike. My stomach flips and I feel like I'm going to throw up. She wants to measure my waistline but that tape measure looks really short. Thank God she doesn't ask me to take my top off. How is she going to get that tape around me? She's so little, and I'm so huge. Stephanie fumbles around me at first, but cannot reach the tape so she asks me to hold one end while she wraps around the other. I start feeling hot again, stomach flipping, heart racing. … The tape measure isn't long enough. I fight back the tears; I don't want this fitness person to see me cry. My heart is breaking as I apologize for my fat body. After explaining there isn't a measuring tape long enough, Stephanie leads me into the cardio room.

As I follow her through the maze of machines, Stephanie doesn't look at me or talk to me. It feels awkward and cold as I follow her like a child following a parent. I hear her chirping the odd greeting to an exerciser and laughing with others as we move closer to her machine of choice. The room is filled with the hum of treadmills, Stairmasters, rowing machines, and stationary bikes. The air is warm, wet, and smells like a combination of mold, rubber, and workout gear that has been worn too many times without washing. I can hear the consistent thump of the spin music coming from the studio next door as the instructor belts out orders in the same manner as a drill sergeant yelling at her troops. The thought of being in that room makes chills run down my body as I come to a stop next to my trainer. Because of my size, she explains, the rowing machine is the only option for me. Again, I feel the urge to run, as there is *no way* I can get down on that tiny seat without looking like an idiot. Everyone is watching me as they exercise on their own sweaty machines; the rowing machines are placed at the front of the room while the other machines surround them. I feel like the evening's entertainment as I struggle to get my butt onto the extra small, unstable, plastic seat. What if it collapses under my weight? What if this machine isn't built for someone like me? What if? All eyes are watching my every clumsy move. People in spandex are watching the fat lady with a mix of disgust and pity. How did she let herself get like this? How can someone let themselves go like that? Perhaps I'm serving as a warning to others to keep exercising lest they turn into the fat pig on the itty bitty rowing machine.

I finally sit down on the seat but can't reach the bar nor keep my balance as I fall to one side, barely catching myself with one arm. It's uncontrollable now; I start welling up with tears wondering how the hell I am going to pull myself off this floor without the entire fitness center watching from their mechanized perches. Stephanie has been talking with another member this whole time and doesn't even notice I need help. I finally right myself and, through some small miracle, grasp the bar in front of me. Stephanie finally looks down to see that I have accomplished what she set out for me and begins to instruct me on proper technique. I can hardly keep my body steady on the microscopic seat let alone attempt good technique. After a few short minutes, I'm done. I'm ready to pull myself off this machine, slug Stephanie in her perfect face, and go for a drink. Instead, I follow my trainer into the weight room feeling like a prisoner walking to her death. We pass the free weight area where the grunts and groans of bodybuilders fill the room like a woman giving birth to twins would fill the hallway of a hospital. The sound of dropping and clanging metal is so loud I feel like my eardrums will burst. It's official. . . I'm scared.

Stephanie continues to lead me like a child as we come to another small area, filled with metal and pink vinyl upholstery and a lot of women. Most say nothing and keep their eyes down as they slip into their machines and work their muscles with more determination than a mountaineer ascending Everest. They all look like they know what they are doing, like they've been doing it all their lives. I have no idea what these machines do, but they look painful and unnecessary. Stephanie tells me this is a great way to tone my upper arms and get rid of my trouble areas, so I listen as best I can over the din of metal slamming on metal and the constant mist of chemical cleaner in the air that makes my lungs burn. Her words sound almost medical; she's talking a language that I can't understand no matter how hard I try. Reps, sets, concentric, eccentric contractions, biceps what? I start tuning her out and just do what I have to do to get my own set of beautifully toned arms.

The next machine promises to firm and shape my legs and butt, but as I try to fit my legs onto the plate in front of me it's everything I can do just to breathe. My knees start to hurt, I start losing the feeling in my toes and then panic sets in: My heart rate goes up, I'm feeling hot, and my stomach is flipping. Stephanie finally notices my anxiety and with a deep sigh suggests another machine. I can just tell from her body language she's just not that into me; she can't seem to find anything that works for me. And why should she? I'm too fat for any of this equipment. A familiar feeling of hopelessness washes over me again as she settles on an abdominal machine that looks wide enough to slip my fat ass into. This is the machine that will give me tight abdominals and maybe, if I do it enough, flat abs. I turn around and try and sit down on the small seat, but I can't slip my hips past the metal frame (let alone slip in between the chest pad and back of the seat). The tears start coming. For the first time, Stephanie looks right at me as she reassures me that this happens to a lot of her clients and that just coming into the fitness center for a stretch will help me get fit. So we move to the stretch room. I choke back the tears, put on a fake smile, and provide her with a less than enthusiastic, "Okay. . ." and follow her into the stretch room.

She makes space for me by placing a mat on the floor and instructs me to lie down. Although I'm able to do it, the fear of not being able to get myself up without a struggle or request for assistance has me preoccupied. Stephanie, lying next to me, starts showing me a stretch for my butt and lower back. She pulls her muscular leg close to her chest and holds it there as she continues to instruct me to do the same. There is no way I can pull my leg even halfway up let alone all the way; the fat on my leg and my stomach won't allow for it. God, I can't even reach; I'm so pathetic. It's obvious Stephanie is running out of patience, as she appears to struggle to think of another way for me to stretch. She can't; there's nothing for me. She quickly jumps up and waits, hands on hips, as I slowly rise from my mat, not unlike a hot air balloon as it slowly, yet clumsily, rises off the ground. This workout is over. She ends our time together right in the middle of the stretch room. I watch Stephanie's ass stay perfectly firm as she walks briskly across the stretching room floor and out the door. I'm left standing alone in the middle of the fitness center, among the perfect bodies, spandex, and laughter. An all-too-familiar wave of hopelessness washes over me as I gather my things and make it through my own personal house of horrors. I know I won't be back. I'll never be back. I was right all along: fitness centers are for the fit, not the fat.

Jane's Story

I feel sick. There is a sinking feeling in my stomach; it is rumbling and churning. There is a rising loaf of bread in my stomach. A surge of energy trickles through my body, slowly at first, like water dripping from a leaky faucet, but then quickly the surge becomes faster, as if the water has been turned on to rush out all at once. It spikes up one side of me and down another. . . and then, a wave of nausea. I just ate a muffin . . . *sigh*. . . and I have not exercised in four days. I rarely eat muffins, so I don't know why I feel guilty. Butterflies are floating freely in my stomach. I feel like I cheated on a test but nobody knows. I need to atone for this sin—exercise is the best way.

I stand in front of the mirror in freshly washed jeans that need stretching out. The irony hits me like a ton of bricks: I have a muffin top.* I can see how pronounced it is. Like the doughiest, most abundant part of the muffin that spills out over the stump, my fat runneth over the top of my jeans. I can feel it. It is like a little rubber tire tube I remember seeing when my brother changed the tire on his bike. I poke the sides. Flesh bounces back. *Boing!* Like the loud sound of a spring one hears in cartoons on television. It also jiggles like jelly. It is official; I am having a fat day, maybe even a fat month. Okay—maybe a fat decade. It is there! I can't even look at it anymore.

---

* A derogatory term used to describe overhanging flesh [fat] when it spills over the waistline of pants or skirts in a manner resembling the top of a muffin spilling over its paper casing.

I need to get to the gym. I had joined a month ago, but I kept to myself, going at less busy times—usually after 8 p.m. I didn't have to worry about people then. I don't like crowds all that much. I like to work hard though, get my heart rate up—hopefully to get some results in terms of this damn muffin top. I'm not as thin and fit as I once was. . . . Was I ever thin and fit enough? I don't remember now. Now that I am older, my body won't move as quickly as I would like, or as quickly as I need to in order to get the results that should happen from exercise. The lack of results makes me not want to move at all but exercise is a punishment for the food crimes I just committed. So I will drag my ass there, get it over with, and feel better once I get home and have forced myself to do something. I hate it, it's so boring.

I did step aerobics eight years ago and I enjoyed those classes. Everyone smiled. I smiled. We would laugh. The room was bright and airy. There was unspoken camaraderie. When a new face would appear I would sometimes stare, wondering if she was as scared as I was the first time I came to a class, or if she was already fit enough to be there and would outshine us all. Our instructor was always welcoming, regardless. She taught us the moves and the choreography so we could do it. Eventually, it got to be where we would be able to anticipate those moves, sometimes before she even queued them. She motivated with encouragement, "You can do it!" and with hoots and hollers—"yip!" and "woo-hoo!" Some days I wanted to zone out and not speak, and I could do that, too, if I wanted. No pressure. The instructor could anticipate our moods and responded accordingly. I hadn't been to one of those classes in over eight years.

I hadn't tried a class at my new gym but I peered into one last week, a "cardio combat class" (yes, we are apparently at war!) that was described on the schedule as a mixed martial arts class that would allow us to "lose our butts while we kicked butt." It sounded painful and didn't look inviting. The music was at ear-bleeding levels and the tiny instructor was on a raised podium so everyone could see her. She belted out commands in a military-like manner: "Now people, PEOPLE! Don't try to kick as high as me. You WON'T. GO! GO! GO!" People's faces were serious—like stone walls. Sometimes she would come off her podium to mingle. She went over to a woman doing kicks and shouted, "Is that it? Is that as high as you can go?" I wondered if the woman would magically kick higher just because she was told to do so. She did not. As the instructor moved toward the back of the room, during her off-podium journey the back-row women shrank like wilted flowers that had missed their watering. The front-row women were transfixed on themselves. They all glowed and worked to keep up. Part of me felt envious but nervous. I didn't want to take the risk. It didn't look like how I remembered it. For now, I will stick to the treadmill that goes nowhere but at least makes me feel like I have gone somewhere when I am done.

The shiny reflection in my own mirror breaks my gym-thoughts. Damn. Who is that? I'm old. And fat. It will feel good to come off the cardio equipment, stop being a hamster that goes nowhere if I go to the gym, and try one of those classes. But I think I will go with what I know—the step class. I stare at the mirror. My reflection brings me back to "reality." Muffin top. Alright, that's it—I'm going to the gym. I will work this off and feel better after. I won't feel all this guilt. It's going to suck, though. It's going to hurt. As the instructor reminds us, "This will be the hardest 60 minutes of your life. But feeling good takes hard work. No pain. No gain." That's it … I'm going … in 10 minutes, I'm going … 10 more minutes.

I have made it and I am here. It is 5 p.m.—prime time in the gym. Yet I am back in high school. All the beautiful and coolest people are here on display and are having a great time! They know what to wear, how to talk, and what to do to fit in. The desk girl, Deb, who in high school would have been the social director of "the crew"—breaks my high school thoughts with a squeaky voice: "Unfortunately, the step class is full." Perky Deb beamed at me. "But you're in luck! The cycle-spin class has a few spots open. It's really awesome! You'll love it!" She already had her pen out, poised to write my name down on a list. I felt panicked; my heart sank. My face went ashen. I looked at Deb, then toward the exit door, then toward the back of the gym, past the gauntlet of weight equipment that looked like a torture chamber filled with torture devices to "work" the body. Men were pacing the floor and gesticulating like executioners. Which was closer, the exit door or the cycling room?

Warmth crept up the back of my neck at the thought of going into unchartered territory. I didn't want people looking at me. I was having a fat day. What if I didn't know what I was doing or couldn't keep up? I didn't have much concept of what this class would be like, other than it looked hard based on the saturated bodies and t-shirts that emerged from the room where the class was. Deb said, "It's really fun, and you can go at your own pace. Plus, it's *the best* calorie burner." Well, there it was. Deb was saying I needed to burn off calories. Deep in my muffin-top shame spiral, I thought, "Deb is right." The class would be a chance to atone for food sins and exercise the demon food baby growing within. "Alright," I said. "Sign me up."

The cycling room was a small box-like room with about 40 mini-bikes. The bikes were very small. It smelled of rubber, sweat, and a light whiff of Windex cleaning solution. It didn't seem well ventilated. Dimly lit, a yellow glow was cast in the room. People were setting up their bikes, moving seats up and down, adjusting handlebars. Then they placed towels on the handlebars, as well as water bottles. There appeared to be no cliques. There were a range of ages, shapes, and sizes. There were men and women, about an equal number of each. I was confused. But then something familiar— mirrors lined the walls. I quickly looked down and walked over to a bike. I slid my feet into the pedals and sat down. The tiny seat instantly made me think of how big my butt was, as it barely fit. My heart rate quickened when I noticed the instructor setting up. She welcomed everyone and asked, "Anyone new?" Did I have to answer that question? No one raised their hand. I peddled a bit faster to match my heart rate, which was now racing due to fear of being singled out. I did not raise my hand. I would rather remain ignorant and just watch the others to find out what to do.

The instructor wore special shoes that clipped into the bike pedals. She started the music, but it was at a comfortable volume, and I could actually hear what she was saying. "We are going to go through a series of races. Some will be on a flat surface—you will need to add tension on your bikes so you can simulate what that feels like." I added tension. There were multiple explanations and cues for what to do and why we were doing it. We went through a series of drills, simulated races, and hill climbs. When we climbed a hill, we added tension on the bike. My thighs would tighten and my pace would slow. "Try to keep the pace up with the music," the instructor directed. "We are raising those heart rates and holding this for 45 seconds." Boom, boom, boom, the music was loud and the bass in the song was pounding through my chest. I felt afraid of not being able to keep up.

To my surprise, I kept up. The instructor provided breaks and an opportunity for rest. Some of my fear dissipated. And I shifted focus. I imagined myself on a road excelling on the ride. I closed my eyes and added tension on the bike as the instructor told us sternly, "We are going up the side of a mountain, so THREE turns on that tension as we climb." My upper thighs tightened. My legs burned as I pedaled more quickly to keep up with the music. Tom Cochrane sang, "Life is a highway. I want to ride it all night long!" I was breathing deeply in and out, my shoulders creeping up toward my ears when the instructor shouted, "Remember to relax the shoulders. Keep the energy going into the legs." My hands had tiny circular beads of sweat on them, translucent. Everyone strained to get up the last hill. Four fans hummed beneath the music, blowing hot air. T-shirts were changing colors, going from light grey to black, and from light blue to dark blue, as they became saturated with sweat. The instructor yelled, "Forty-five seconds and then we are at the top! Push, push. We are going to get to the top of that hill and then we will go down the other side for the reward!" We were huffing and puffing, like little engines that could. My legs were like lead, heavy, worn out, drained. Finally, we were there. I released the tension on the bike and flushed out the fatigue from the climb. Whoosh! I was saturated in sweat; my t-shirt had changed color like everyone else's. I felt tired but energized. I couldn't believe I made it through the entire class.

CONCLUSIONS

We are reluctant to tell readers how to interpret the above stories. The value and impact of them lies in what they evoke for readers, in light of each reader's background and the degree to which each reader engages in self-reflexive awareness. There are several take-away messages we wish to highlight in terms of self-compassion and the sociocultural context of women's exercise. When looking at Carole's and Jane's body-talk, it is striking how lacking in self-compassion it is. While Jane's body-talk shifts toward self-compassion as she gains competence in the exercise context and because she has had successful past and present social experiences in the gym, Carole is never afforded this opportunity in light of her past experiences, shaped by her mother and having been teased by peers, which were further reinforced through her present experiences in the gym and the social and cultural stigma of fatness.

Ultimately, each woman's experiences were based on her body not measuring up—in Carole's case, literally, when she did not conform to a weight and a measuring tape—to an ideal, fit body in terms of appearance and ability to conform to fitness and movement ideals. The gym environment exposed and reinforced each woman's perceived flaws and negative emotions in a multitude of ways, through the meanings ascribed to fit bodies (known through ideal body and beauty standards), through reflections of self and others in mirrors, through what fitness instructors do and say in terms of body shaping and/or inadequate bodies, and through the exposure gym equipment and tight gym clothing create for female bodies that do not "fit." At first glance, it is easy to say that the women have something wrong with them, that each has distorted thinking and motivational issues. Viewed in this simplistic manner, it is tempting to revert to forms of advice women are often given as solutions to these dilemmas: change the thoughts and/or change the self-talk so that it is more positive in order to increase motivation, suck it up, and then get one's ass to the gym! Or even "Just get in shape—it's easy, just do it!"

While this is not the intended meaning we wish for people to take away from the stories, we recognize that self-responsibility notions are pervasive when it comes to exercise behavior and motivation, particularly in light of the stigma and prejudice associated with fatness, and the (incorrect) messages that everyone can have an ideal body if they work hard. However, placing responsibility entirely on the individual, regardless of shape or size, ignores the sociocultural influences that contribute to the foregoing, making change and lasting change difficult. Moreover, such ideas silence the fact that weight loss regimes and diets are ineffectual, that the ideal body is unattainable, and that dietary and weight loss practices do damage to the psychological and physical self. People are not islands; they are greatly affected by the social world. With these points raised, it is tempting to blame the fitness industry and the social context entirely for women's negative body-talk and associated emotions. Blame in either direction oversimplifies the issue and will not lead to creative and effective solutions facilitating social justice and peace in terms of women's health and well-being, as social justice involves creating a society based on equality and solidarity, and striving to understand and value human rights and recognize the dignity of human beings. Solutions that deal with social acceptance and self-acceptance will be useful toward realizing social justice goals.

To keep dialogue flowing, we advocate increasing self-compassion (i.e., a nonjudgmental attitude toward one's perceived imperfections, limitations, and failures) by looking at how the fitness culture may be structured to facilitate a common sense of humanity (i.e., we are in this together, let's be supportive and value one another as human beings rather than tear ourselves down). Emerging research in exercise psychology has shown great promise in this regard by identifying ways to facilitate the appreciation of unique bodies by acknowledging and respecting body limitations and flaws. This may be accomplished by providing a range of role models (e.g., instructors, trainers, fitness participants) who represent a range of body shapes and sizes as well as exemplify body appreciation of body variation by using positive body-talk. An important part of facilitating this process is creating exercise environments that place less emphasis on social comparisons of bodies and greater emphasis on tolerance, acceptance, and a theme of common humanity. Additional factors contributing toward these goals are having fewer mirrors in the gym space, by instructors placing emphasis on what is positive about exercise and bodies outside of appearance and weight loss (e.g., enjoyment, accomplishment, gaining strength and competence), not emphasizing obligatory exercise goals (e.g., using exercise as a punishment for food eaten or calories consumed, using exercise as a form of punishment because of how one looks or because one took a day off), and a regendering of the weight room (i.e., women lifting weights in a nonthreatening and more egalitarian atmosphere).

While we are only beginning to understand how self-compassion may be developed and be useful in the exercise context to impact the psychological well-being of women and decrease negative body-talk, we hope that such work will continue. We envision self-compassion work in multiple ways, such as in one's own fitness practices and self-talk, in one's interactions with others, in one's behaviors as a practitioner, and in the educational and academic realms. Finally, we hope that by providing space for stories such as ours, additional stories may be told in order to raise further awareness and give voice to other avenues of resistance for women to enhance their well-being.

To summarize, we leave the reader with several final points that our chapter sought to raise and draw attention to:

1. Ubiquitous media and social messages position women's bodies as flawed and in need of fixing via exercise and normalizing negative body-talk toward one's self and others. Negative body-talk is a social justice issue because women's dignity, inner peace, health, and well-being are compromised.

2. Listening to women's embodied exercise stories increases awareness and creates understanding and empathy as to what women go through in relation to their bodies and exercise, and how their well-being is compromised.

3. Awareness, understanding, and empathy are important steps toward creating a society that values unique individual, social, and cultural differences, rather than stigmatizing and marginalizing individuals for such differences.

4. Creating health and fitness cultures that strive toward less social comparison and negative body-talk, via the promotion of solidarity, tolerance, and a common sense of humanity, will increase self-compassion and self-acceptance.

5. Being more compassionate and accepting toward one's self and others may ultimately lead to less inner turmoil and increased inner peace for women, further contributing toward social justice goals.

Using Games to Enhance Life Satisfaction and Self Worth of Orphans, Teenagers Living in Poverty, and Ex-Gang Members in Latin America

Stephanie J. Hanrahan

I was born in the United States and have been living in Australia for over 25 years. My primary job is teaching and doing research at a university, but I do not consider myself to be a typical academic. I struggle with the concept of professors engaging in research with the main goals being to obtain large grants and to publish in top journals. There is nothing inherently wrong with those outcomes (and a lot of public good has been achieved as a result of big grant money and academics publishing to get promoted), but if the focus remains on publishing in scientific journals that are generally read only by other academics and researchers, I question how keeping the knowledge in the ivory towers of academia promotes social justice. I've held multiple grants, but must admit that the large grants that bring professional kudos have not tended to result in any meaningful, real-life changes. On the other hand, I believe my work done with small grants (and even unfunded intervention programs) has made a difference in people's lives. One could probably argue that I just haven't figured out how to play the game to get large funding for social justice projects, but I guess my point is that one does not need a lot of money to attempt to enhance the quality of life of people who have been marginalized.

In addition to being an academic, I am a registered sport and exercise psychologist. I've worked with athletes and coaches from many sports and at all levels from social and recreational to professional. For many years my applied work tended to focus on elite level competitors and coaches (after all, they tended to be the ones who could pay). I believe two situations combined to change my applied focus. First, I was invited to teach personal development in an Indigenous performing arts school. Being performing artists, the students tended to be much more engaged in activities that involved movement than in typical handouts, lectures, or discussions. Although I had frequently used games as ice-breaking activities in groups, my work with the performing artists was the first time I made a point of including physically active games as part of the educational process in every session I ran.

The second situation that provoked my change in focus was a serendipitous mixture of three incidents on the same day: (a) I gave a lecture in an introductory psychology class and pointed out that mental skills training not only increases performance and enjoyment of participation, but also enhances general psychological well-being; (b) I had a frustrating afternoon working with a professional sporting team where many of the athletes appeared to have entitlement issues—they seemed to have no appreciation for the opportunities being provided to them; and (c) I received a newsletter in the mail from an orphanage in Mexico. Grumbling to myself about the elite athletes, I read the orphanage newsletter. My earlier lecture on the role of mental skills in enhancing well-being then flashed in my head. It suddenly seemed obvious to me that the orphans could definitely do with a dose of well-being and at the same time I seriously doubted they would have any entitlement issues. The next day I wrote a proposal about a mental skills training program that incorporated games and sent it off to the orphanage. Three months later I received an email that said, "Please come." I immediately arranged to spend a month of my summer (North American winter) living at the orphanage in Mexico.

The data I collected in Mexico indicated that my program (which at the time consisted of 15 sessions) resulted in significant increases in life satisfaction and global self worth. Since that initial program I have revamped the structure so there are now 10 two-hour sessions that combined games, worksheets, discussions, and thoughts for the day. The first thought for the day and the overarching theme of the program is *control the controllable*. Either within the first session or as homework between the first and second sessions, I ask participants to list six things they can control and six things they cannot control. Across a variety of marginalized groups, participants typically find it easy to think of things they cannot control, but struggle to think of anything they can control. By the end of the program they are all able to list numerous things they can control (e.g., thoughts, activation levels, responses, goals, images, attention). I think that it might be this enhanced sense of personal control that results in the increases in life satisfaction and self worth.

I have used the 10-session program with teenagers living in poverty in two towns in Mexico, groups aged 7-21 in the slums of Buenos Aires, adolescents (ages 12-18) in a large group home in another area of Mexico, and ex-gang members (ages 15-29), also in Mexico. The purpose of this chapter is to describe some of the games, how and why I use them, and how they are received by the participants. You will notice that only minimal equipment is needed for these games, allowing them to be used in communities or organizations where resources may be limited.

TYPES OF GAMES

There are different types of games, and the order in which they are played is important. I slowly build up the amount of communication, trust, and problem solving required. One could consider the sequence of games to have four levels:

a. **Icebreakers** provide nonthreatening interactions and can be accomplished with little frustration. Icebreakers are designed to help participants get to know each other, get used to interacting with each other, and begin to develop rapport. An example of a simple icebreaker game is what I call the Three Cs. Individuals identify their favorite color, cuisine, and cartoon character (*color, comida, caricatura*) and then are given a few minutes to try and find as many people as they can who have at least one C that is the same as theirs. The challenge is to remember who had what that was the same. At the end I ask for a show of hands regarding who found at least two people with one C in common with them (or one person with two Cs in common), then three, four, etc., until there are no more hands. I then ask the person (or people) who identified the most Cs in common to say what their Cs were and identify the other people who had the same Cs. I then ask if there was anyone else with these Cs, and usually find that there are. I also ask if there is anyone who did not find anyone who had a C in common with them. If there is, one of three things typically happens, stated here in order of frequency: (a) there actually is someone in the group with a C in common, but the person never spoke to that individual, (b) there is no one with a C in common, but the individual was too specific with the Cs (e.g., indigo instead of blue, chicken tacos instead of tacos; note—this outcome can be avoided by providing examples at the start of the activity), or (c) the person has unique favorites, in which case I lead a brief discussion on celebrating uniqueness and how boring life would be if everyone was exactly the same. This activity gets people moving around and talking to each other about nonthreatening topics. There are no winners or losers, and in most instances participants feel a small connection with someone else, even if it is something as small as having the same favorite color.

b. **Deinhibitizers/energizers** are similar to icebreakers, but offer a little more challenge or risk and often require more vigorous physical activity. An example of a deinhibitizer/energizer is link tag. In link tag people are safe from being tagged when they have linked arms with someone else. There is a maximum of two people per link. Someone trying to avoid being caught can link onto a pre-existing link, forcing the person on the opposite side to let go and become fair game. Two unlinked people are not allowed to form a new link. Linked individuals must remain stationary. At the start of the game the facilitator chooses an individual to be It, and specifies certain individuals to begin the game linked (I usually pair up about one third of the participants and spread them around the playing area). Individuals cannot relink to the pairs they just left. The multiple options for linking and being safe allow participants to take a quick breather while still being involved in the game (and can be helpful for unfit individuals and those with mild physical disabilities). During the game people come into contact with almost everyone in the group, learn that it is okay to get help from others, and begin to make physical contact with people in a safe environment.

c. **Trust and empathy games** include physical and/or verbal interactions that require the support and cooperation of group members. These activities are fun, but do involve some level of fear because of the need to rely on others for physical or emotional safety. Through my program I discovered that although the focus of these games is on trusting others, the results frequently also involve increases in self-confidence. An example of an introductory trust activity is pendulum. In groups of three people of similar size, one person (the pendulum) stands as straight and as stiff as a board, feet together with arms crossed over the chest. The other two participants, the catchers, stand on either side of the pendulum, with one foot pressed up against the side of the pendulum's foot and the other foot back to provide a stable base. When both catchers are ready with their hands up, the pendulum gently falls to one side or the other and is caught on the shoulder and upper arm by one of the catchers who then gently pushes the pendulum to the other catcher. The person in the middle (the pendulum) can ask the catchers to gradually move apart so the distance to fall slowly increases. If needed, a sense of greater security can be created by the catchers maintaining contact with the pendulum at all times. As the facilitator I need to remember that the level of perceived threat in this activity varies from person to person. For some, there is sometimes a need to begin by standing just an inch or two from a solid wall and start by allowing themselves to be "caught" by the wall. This seemingly simple action can be challenging for those, who through difficult circumstances, have learned to rely entirely on themselves—their fierce independence being related to a need to always be in control.

d. **Initiative activities** provide participants with the opportunity to effectively communicate, cooperate, and solve problems with each other. These games are designed to be challenging; multiple attempts are usually needed to achieve success, providing great opportunities to see how they deal with failure and frustration. An example of an initiative activity is electric fence. The goal of electric fence is to get everyone from one side of the fence to the other without touching the fence. The fence is a piece of string, either held by two people or tied off at one end and held by one person (never tie off both ends of the string, because it is important to be able to let the string go if someone is caught up on it). As a rough guideline I put the string at the height of the armpit of the shortest person in the group. If anyone touches the string, everyone must begin again. If the group is athletic, there is sufficient space, and the ground is soft or mats are available, I require all members of the group to get over the string. Otherwise, I indicate that all but one person needs to get over the string. (I also use this option if there is one member of the group who is notably larger than the rest of the group or who is injured or pregnant.) It is highly unusual for groups to succeed at this task on their first attempt. If they are successful the first time, I tend to have them do it again, but this time with the string higher, or with no talking, or with the person going over the fence being blindfolded. With one group I increased the challenge of the activity by not allowing them to swear. If anyone on the team swore, they all had to start again (a great activity for increasing their awareness of what they said).

No matter what the level or type of game, the main premise of using games is that games are fun! People like to play when given the opportunity. Even when I have run workshops with adults—psychologists, coaches, business and finance officers—the majority voluntarily participate and enjoy themselves. The marginalized adolescents with whom I have worked in Latin America are no exception. Perhaps they may be even more interested in playing because of their limited opportunities. Few have had access to coaching and many have not even had physical education classes. Outside of orphanages and group homes, I cannot think of any facilities adolescents living in poverty can use, not to mention equipment, instruction, or the organization of competition. If they can find a soccer ball (or a substitute such as a plastic drink bottle), these kids tend to kick it around until there is nothing left to kick. In some slums any activities take place in narrow dirt lanes, children competing with stray dogs for the "ball" while at the same time keeping an eye out for possible danger (e.g., a rival gang). I've found that adolescents (and adults) who have been living in poverty or have been underserved in some other way jump at having the opportunity to play and being introduced to new games.

I know the majority of the games I use are perceived to be fun because the children, teenagers, and young adults (a) willingly participate, (b) ask to repeat games they have already played, (c) continue to show up, and (d) are smiling and laughing. When I ran the program at a group home in Mexico, a colleague took photos and then put them to music. When the video containing the photos was shown to people who worked at the group home, they all commented that they had never seen the participants smiling so much (staff also reported goose bumps and tears while watching the video). Even people who have never been to Mexico (and obviously don't know the stories of the individuals) echoed the staff members' sentiments by commenting on how much the participants are smiling in the photos. I think these unsolicited comments support the conclusion that the participants enjoy themselves while playing the games. More direct evidence that they enjoy the games is that in a qualitative evaluation of the program, Mexican orphans indicated that the games were what they liked most (with personal successes and achievements, and sharing with the group reported as the second and third most liked aspects of the program).

BENEFITS AND PURPOSES OF GAMES

Having fun could be a useful result in and of itself, but there are many benefits to the games in my program in addition to having a good time. Games can help develop cooperation, problem-solving skills, communication, trust, and leadership skills. When I asked a group of participants what, if anything, from the program they would use in their daily lives, the two most popular responses were skills related to self-confidence and how to work effectively in groups. Participants also reported that they have learned patience and tolerance during the program, possibly in part because I regularly change the groups with whom they are participating (i.e., they don't get to stay within their social cliques).

I naively assumed that in an orphanage of less than 200 adolescents, they would all know each other; after all, they live together (sometime 40+ sharing a large room with bunk beds), eat together, and go to school together. I was wrong. Most of them stuck to their own cliques, with little or no contact with those who were not part of their small exclusive groups. One activity I used to help them get to know each other is Have You Ever. . .? In this game all but one of the participants form a circle roughly arm's distance apart from each other. I then use chalk to mark the place of each person in the circle, with another X marking the center of the circle. The extra person begins in the center and asks a question that begins "Have you ever …?" (e.g., Have you ever scored a goal in a soccer game? Have you ever eaten chocolate with chili in it?). The question must reflect something the questioner has actually done, should not be potentially embarrassing, and should be something that not everyone has done (e.g., avoid questions such as, "Have you ever eaten lunch?"). All of the participants who are standing in the circle who can honestly answer yes to the question must leave their spot, move to the inside of the circle, and then quickly try to find another spot vacated by someone else. The person who asked the question also tries to find a vacant spot. No one is allowed to return to the spot they just left. The person who is unable to find a vacant spot remains in the middle and asks the next question. If no one can answer yes to a question, the person in the middle asks another question. I have learned a lot about groups with whom I have worked by listening to the questions asked. This activity is also useful because it gets individuals used to sharing information about themselves, setting the foundation for later in the program when they share information about their aspirations and discuss issues such as confidence.

An activity that is useful for getting people from different groups (e.g., cliques, teams, classes, gangs) to realize that they have similarities is Ten Things in Common. I divide the participants into groups of five or six (intentionally splitting up any known subgroups), where one person in each group elects to be scribe. As can probably be guessed by the title of the activity, each group then needs to list 10 things they have in common with each other. The challenge is to list things that are true for everyone in their group, but that are not true for at least one participant in the other groups. For example, "We all have two eyes" is presumably something that is true for all participants, meaning it would not count as a correct response. Once a group thinks they have 10 correct items on their list, I call for everyone's attention and read out the list item by item. I ask participants to raise their hands if the item is NOT true for them. If at least one person raises a hand, the item counts. If no one raises a hand, I stop reading the list (because the group does not have 10 correct items) and encourage all groups to keep working. This process continues until a group has a list of 10 things that they have in common but are not true for at least one person in another group. Although there is no prize for being the first group to create a list of 10 things in common, the groups tend to be engaged and competitive with each other, being excited and relieved when everyone is given more time to work on their lists after an incorrect response by another group. This activity not only allows people to recognize they have things in common with others, but again encourages the sharing of personal information. This activity can be beneficial whether or not the participants already know each other. In a program I ran with ex-gang members, one group was strategic by focusing on what they know about people in other groups and then creating their list from that knowledge (e.g., they knew that one person in another group disliked chocolate, so they then quickly checked to see if everyone in their group liked chocolate). Taking advantage of what they already knew about others allowed them to work quickly.

In the program, I tie in games to the mental skills being introduced or discussed. For example, when talking about optimal activation, I might have them engage in two different types of tag, one that mainly involves balance (e.g., Nose and Toes) and another that has greater cardiovascular requirements (e.g., Knee Tag). We then discuss which game required a higher or lower level of optimal activation. In Nose and Toes individuals are safe from being tagged when standing on one leg holding the toes of one foot with the opposite hand and their nose with the other hand. If they hop or put the other foot down, they need to then take at least three steps before they can try to balance again. A more advanced version is to require that the arm of the hand holding the nose to go under the knee of the leg in the air. If activation levels are too high, it is usually difficult to balance. On the other hand, Knee Tag usually requires a higher level of activation because it requires more speed and agility than balance. Participants pair up with someone of roughly similar height, and then in their pairs try to touch the back of the knee of their partner. They must remain standing (i.e., no tackling the partner and then touching the back of their knee), and no head butting is allowed. I usually say something along the lines of "First to four wins!" (Note: Double or triple taps are not allowed; after one touch participants must disengage before starting again.)

In addition to providing examples of how different activities may require different levels of activation, I also use tag games as a way of increasing activation, particularly between relaxation exercises. If I have just finished an abdominal breathing exercise, participants are usually relaxed. It is rather pointless to then introduce them to progressive muscular relaxation if they are already relaxed (it is difficult to learn how progressively tensing and relaxing muscles leads to relaxation if they are relaxed to start with). Throwing in a tag game before the progressive muscular relaxation exercise raises activation levels, so they can then actively work on decreasing activation using progressive muscular relaxation.

Sometimes I just use quick games as energizers when participants have been sitting too long or are starting to lose focus. The quickest game I use is All-In Tag where, as the name suggests, everyone is It. Once tagged (by anyone) a person must crouch or sit and not leave that spot. Tagged people, however, can keep tagging others if they come near them. One thing I like about All-In Tag is that unlike most tag games, the quickest person may not last the longest.

Another example of using games to promote understanding of mental skills regards the topic of attention and concentration. I explain that attention is not something that is just on or off. Our attention can be on a range of factors. If a coach yells, "Pay attention!", my immediate response is "To what?" Our attention can be on our own thoughts and feelings (i.e., internal) or on other people, objects, or the environment (i.e., external). In addition, attention can be narrow (i.e., focused on one thing) or broad (i.e., focusing on a variety of things). I have participants create a 2x2 grid showing four types of attention: broad and internal, broad and external, narrow and internal, and narrow and external. I then ask them to provide an example of when it would be beneficial to have each of these types of attention. Although not an answer I'd ever received from athletes with whom I have worked, "looking for possible escape routes when running from the police" indicated that one of the ex-gang members understood the concept of broad/external attention. Games I use to broaden external attention include Mirror and Twenty Questions. In Mirror, two people stand shoulder-to-shoulder facing a third person. The person who is alone must mirror the arm actions of the other two. I've found it useful to emphasize that only arms can be moved, that the movement cannot involve covering the eyes, and that rude gestures are not allowed (I've discovered that with teenagers it is better to pre-empt these actions than it is to wait until someone thinks they are so clever as to be the first person to think of it). After a minute or two I then have the two people take a step away from each other without allowing the third person to step back. The challenge for the individual doing the mirroring is to try and see both moving arms through peripheral vision rather than switching the focus back and forth between the two arms (i.e., working on developing broad and external attention).

Twenty Questions requires participants to list 20 questions that require one or two words answers. Yes/no questions should be avoided, as should potentially embarrassing questions, or existential questions such as, "What is the meaning of life?" Example questions include "What is your favorite flavor of ice cream?" and "What color shirt are you wearing?" I then have participants form groups of four. For one to two minutes one person answers questions from the other three. It is important that those asking questions continue to ask questions. They should ask one question, pause briefly for an answer, and then ask another question. If an answer for that question was not forthcoming, then the same question should be repeated. All three people are asking questions at once. The challenge is to try to attend to all three at the same time rather than answering questions in turn, again working on developing broad/external attention.

I also use activities that require individuals to block out external distractions. I usually do these activities in groups of four or five, with one person in the spotlight at a time. The job of those not in the spotlight (i.e., those not attempting the activity) is to do everything they can, except touch the person, to distract her or him. One activity involves picking a number greater than 2,000 and then counting out loud, backwards by sevens (a useful distraction can be calling out other numbers). Another activity requires the person in the spotlight to go through a variety of preset motions on one leg, trying to maintain balance for the duration (a useful distraction for this activity is to make eye contact with the person and then slowly fall to one side—they tend to fall with you). Anyone who has previously tried to do an arabesque or walk on a balance beam with eyes closed already knows that closing one's eyes to block out distractions is not the solution when trying to maintain balance.

I also use games as a way of exploring self-talk and the effect it might have on motivation, confidence, and performance. For example, in Toe Tapper, partners face each other and place their hands on the shoulders of their partner. Arms are straight. The objective is to try to lightly step on the toes of the other person without letting your own toes get stepped on. It may be useful to emphasize that the name of the game is Toe Tapper and not Toe Stomper! After a few minutes of playing (and perhaps changing partners), I ask the participants to reflect on what the little voices in their heads were saying while they were playing. Were they focused on how bad they were at the activity, not getting stepped on, constructive strategies for potential success, or unrelated matters such as what they might eat for lunch? We then discuss which types of self-talk may be more or less helpful.

I sometimes extend the conversation to include the effects of what others say to them and what they say to others. A game such as Push to Stand can be ideal for this discussion. In Push to Stand I begin with two people who sit back to back with legs bent and feet together. Partners link arms and then push against each other to reach a standing position. The activity can be made more challenging by doing it without linking arms and/or by doing it in progressively larger groups (the largest group I have seen succeed is 17). Strong and fit individuals can also try to stand using only one leg. Particularly when larger groups are attempting Push to Stand and not immediately succeeding, it can be useful to observe what they are saying to each other and how they are conveying these messages. Sometimes things are said out of frustration without much consideration of how others may feel, and even statements said with the intent of encouragement may be perceived as being bossy. It is useful to discuss what individuals find to be helpful or harmful in terms of motivation, strategy, and confidence. After discussion it is always important to then either repeat the game or engage in another team-based game so they have the immediate opportunity to put into practice what they discussed.

An activity that focuses specifically on communication is Minefield. (When working with refugees who had experienced trauma, I avoided calling the activity Minefield.) To set up Minefield I scatter a variety of objects (e.g., chairs, ropes, shoes, water bottles, branches) around a defined area, making sure that there are no obvious clear straight paths across the area. Participants are then paired, with one person in each pair blindfolded. The task of the person who is not blindfolded is to verbally guide her or his partner to the other side of the minefield without touching any objects or other people. The guide is not allowed into the minefield. If something or someone is touched, then the person needs to take off the blindfold, return to the start, and begin again. The purpose of this activity it to work on communication (including listening); it is not to memorize and then follow a predetermined route. To avoid the latter, I move objects around during the middle of the activity.

Some strategy is needed for success in Minefield. If people don't think ahead they can end up directing their partners to dead ends or to running into other participants. Another game that requires strategy (and communication) is Chain Tag. In Chain Tag one person begins as It, tags another person who then becomes part of It by joining hands. It continues to grow as a chain until there is only one person left free. Only the two people on the end of the chain are allowed to tag. The chain can only tag people when completely joined up (i.e., if the chain breaks and people are then tagged, those people are still free). No one is allowed to go through the chain or duck under arms. Tactics are an important part of this game. It may be easy to tag a slow person, but having a slow person in the chain may hamper future success. In addition, the chain needs to communicate and work together. Games such as Chain Tag and Electric Fence are sometimes the first opportunity some adolescents living in poverty have to creatively work or play together with peers with a shared objective.

BEING THE FACILITATOR

To facilitate means *to make easier* or *to assist the progress of;* it does not mean *to solve* or *to take over.* Game facilitators try to enable the process to run a little better or help the participants understand their thoughts, feelings, and behaviors. In addition to asking questions or making comments that stimulate discussion, thought, or action, facilitators play many roles:

- **Initiator** sets up the games and instills interest and humor.
- **Safety enforcer** monitors physical and emotional safety.
- **Arbitrator** monitors and restricts conflict.
- **Encourager** supports, cheers, and gives confidence.
- **Observer** takes a step back and notices levels of participation, influence, engagement, and success.

As the facilitator of the program, I need to be flexible. If some games are too easy, I need to think of ways to make them more challenging. If the games are too difficult, I need to decide if I should make them less challenging or allow the game to finish without success. (I usually only choose this option if I know I will be able to revisit the game in a future session.) If one or two people are taking over and not allowing input from others, I either blindfold them or mute them, giving them a different experience and allowing others take on the role of leader.

Facilitation can involve debriefing, which is actively seeking participants' opinions, responses, feelings, and ideas to reflect on the process of the game and to articulate individual and team learning. In debriefing, experiences from the games are shared and then related to everyday life and/or to the relevant environment. The aim of debriefing is to help participants understand and internalize the meaning of their experiences.

Debriefing techniques are varied and can include simple ratings of thumbs up, down, or sideways; quick go-arounds, with each person providing a one-word or one-phrase descriptor; journal writing; or more complex discussions. A discussion might follow a sequence such as "What happened?", "How or why is that important?", and "Now what?" or "How does that apply to your current situation?"

Nevertheless, unlike traditional adventure-based learning activities where debriefing is a major component of every activity, I find it helpful to run some games without any formal debriefing. I think that if I formally debriefed after every game, the adolescents would lose enthusiasm, become less involved in the process, and begin to repeat answers or even disengage. Too much debriefing can also limit the fun atmosphere of the program. I also think that sometimes facilitators don't give enough credit to the natural abilities of many individuals to reflect and process information for themselves. I've found that some teenagers learn by stealth. They take part in the program, actively participating in the games, but not offering much in terms of observations or experiences. Near the end of the program, when asked to review a component of the program or evaluate the program as a whole, they come up with insightful learning experiences beyond those that were ever discussed in the group. For example, with one group of adolescent girls in Mexico, a participant reflected on the concept of controlling the controllable. She went well beyond the idea of controlling attention, motivation, thoughts, and mood. She clearly articulated that she could control what she allowed herself to do with boys or what they did with her. In an environment where teenage pregnancy rates are high, she unmistakably indicated that she was in control of whether or not she put herself in a situation where she could become pregnant. Her community was infused with machismo, and women's rights were rarely (if ever) a topic of conversation. Without any directive debriefing, she was able to reflect on the process and learn from it, underscoring that although debriefing can be an important part of the program, it does not need to accompany every game and activity.

In their evaluations of the program, participants have indicated that they learned things from the program in addition to the preplanned mental skills (e.g., attention, confidence, relaxation). For example, participants in the program I ran with ex-gang members stated that they learned to confide in others, be patient, use more strategies if the first one doesn't work, accept failure and keep trying, and to listen and combine the ideas of others to get a good result. None of these points were directly mentioned in worksheets or discussions. I think these learning outcomes are the result of participating in the variety of games in the program.

CONCLUSIONS

When I ran the first program at the orphanage, I ran it on my own, with no input from locals. The second time I ran the program I invited social workers and psychologists to come along, with the idea that they could then continue to use my program after I left the area. I think their involvement may have increased the chances of sustaining the program, but I treated them as participants. Eventually, I came to understand that I should not only take advantage of the expertise of people living locally, but also invite them to alter or improve the program. The most recent program that I ran with ex-gang members included five individuals who, although ex-gang members themselves, were currently working for an organization to help more people to get out of the gangs. Although they were participants in the program, I met with them for 30 minutes before each session to discuss any issues and answer any questions. During this program I also had local university students who ran sections of the program (often providing better local context than I could) and participated in the games with the ex-gang members. One of the students took detailed notes of the program, which we hope we can eventually turn into a manual (using some photos to aid explanations of some games). Both the five ex-gang members working in the organization and the university students received copies of the daily outline of activities and all handouts. I have yet to realize my dream of locals taking over the program, making it their own, and training trainers to expand the program. I'm not sure if this dream will materialize, but in the meantime I'll continue to try to adapt my program to different populations. I'm also running workshops on games to encourage others to understand the fun and value of games and to see that games are definitely not limited to children. I've run games workshops in six countries, but with my passion for travel and games, I expect that number will increase in the near future. What follows are a few takeaway reflections:

1. The sequence of games used with groups needs to be carefully considered, beginning with icebreakers, moving to deinhibitizers/energizers, progressing to trust and empathy games, and finally building up to initiative activities.

2. All games should be fun!

3. Participation in well-structured group games can lead to the development of cooperation, problem-solving skills, communication, trust, leadership, patience, and tolerance.

4. Games can effectively demonstrate the role of various mental skills and be an arena in which those skills can be practiced.

5. Most games can be modified with extensions or variations that make them more (or less) challenging.
   - Game facilitators serve the roles of *initiator, safety enforcer, arbitrator, encourager, observer,* and *debriefer.* They do not play the role of solver or dictator.
   - Debriefing involves actively seeking participants' opinions, responses, feelings, and ideas on the process of games and how they may relate to everyday life and/or the relevant environment.

Stories from the Basement: Narratives on Disability

9

Tamar Z. Semerjian

The mobility clinic of our university is ironically located in the basement of the student health building. Participants navigate their way through the milling students waiting for appointments and past examination rooms to find the elevators hidden in the back of the building. From there they take the elevator down to a room with no windows. Not infrequently we consider what we would do if we had five wheelchair-bound individuals and there were an emergency, and the elevators were shut down. We hope for previously undemonstrated strength to help assist everyone upstairs. Despite the challenges of our basement space, the atmosphere in the clinic is typically jovial. The undergraduate students look forward to the arrival of the participants they are going to work with, and over time many of them have struck up friendships. The sign on the door says "Mobility Clinic," and the space looks like a gym, filled with exercise equipment that is accessible for individuals with spinal cord injuries (SCI). Most of the equipment allows them to wheel in, or to transfer into, relatively easily. There are adaptations for individuals with weaker grip strength, and each participant works with a student. There is a gait trainer, which allows people with SCI to walk on a treadmill. The treadmill is located in another building, and the participants and trainers have to make their way over there during the exercise session. Nearly all the participants comment on the personal attention they receive, particularly from the students. And yet, the atmosphere is different from the clinical environments they have been in before. They are working with students who are not cynical clinicians who tell the participants not to be too optimistic. Rather, the students are still learning, open to the prospect that with exercise will come increased function, strength, and possibilities. The students learn from the participants, and the participants seem empowered by this relationship. They are not patients, they are partners.

The project started the way many research projects do, through a bit of serendipity. I was in my first year of teaching at California State University, Los Angeles, and had been hired along with Dr. Ray de Leon, a neuromuscular physiologist who was interested in the recovery of gait patterns after SCI. In all his previous research Ray had worked with rats. I was hired as a sport sociologist; my recent research was with older adults. As an undergraduate I had worked with rats in a muscle physiology laboratory, but had since turned my attention and studies to sport and exercise psychology and sociology, working exclusively with people. Ray called me over the summer with a grant opportunity to work on a project that considered the impact of using accessible exercise equipment for people with SCI. He wanted my expertise to consider the psychological and sociological implications of having access to exercise equipment that was actually designed for use by people with SCI. How did people feel about using this equipment? What were the outcomes of a 10-week exercise program? I knew nothing about SCI, but I started reading. We submitted our proposal to the U.S. Department of Education and were funded for five years through a grant from the National Institution on Disability and Rehabilitation Research. In the meantime our department had hired a physical therapist, Dr. Jesus Dominguez, and we had him working on the project as well. When we were notified that we had been awarded the funding, I was excited, but also recognized that I had committed myself to a lot of work over the next five years. Ray, Jesus, and I each had our challenges as we approached the work. Ray had done little work with people, and both Ray and Jesus were new to the psychological and sociological theories that I was interested in investigating. Together, however, we made a strong interdisciplinary team, and we were interested in learning more about each other's disciplines. At the heart of the project was a desire to increase the access individuals with SCI had to equipment that was designed to be easy to use and would lead to increased functioning. The equipment we had included a standing frame, which allowed individuals to stand up and also allowed the legs to move by moving handles with the arms; two weight training machines designed to be easy to use; two upper body cardiovascular machines that allowed participants to either perform a cycling motion or a back-and-forth motion; an adjustable stretching table; and the prime draw of our program, the gait trainer. For most participants the opportunity to walk using this apparatus was the reason they had come to us.

All the participants agreed to be part of a research study that considered the impact of exercise on their physical, psychological, and social well-being. Once word got out about the program, there was interest from people who had been searching for places to exercise, but had been struggling to find settings that were accessible, affordable, and run by people who knew how to work appropriately with their disability.

Each participant we worked with had a different story. One of the women we met had been walking down the street when she was hit by a car. Others were in car accidents, some in accidents they had some part in and others in accidents as passengers. Some people acquired their injuries participating in sports, and some had made decisions that they were not proud of while they were under the influence of alcohol or drugs. Some of the participants had doctoral degrees. Some came from families with financial means who could support them; others had few financial resources, and money was a constant worry. While some lived in homes that were accessible to them, allowing them to move freely into and through their homes, others were constrained in homes where the doorways were not wide enough to accommodate their wheelchairs, preventing them from using rooms of great importance, like the bathroom. One woman could not get into her home without being carried in by a family member or friend. There were stairs but no elevators, and she had no way to get in and out of the building by herself. The experiences that the participants had were shaped by their educational level, financial status, and race.

There were clear differences between some of the experiences of the participants, but also clear similarities. The meaning that exercise had for all the participants was hope. Nearly every person we talked to discussed their hope that exercise would result in a positive change: a better body image, the ability to move more, the ability to feel more, and for some, but certainly not all, the ability to walk again. Early in the analysis of the interviews, I was discussing the transcripts with Ray, and he was shocked that the participants did not all have a strong desire to walk again. He had assumed that this would be everyone's ultimate goal. For some it was. There were participants who would not participate in wheelchair sports because they were waiting to play "for real" when they regained their mobility. Two of the participants had restored the motorcycles on which they had had their accidents, because they were confident that one day they would ride again. From a research perspective we were fortunate, as we had a diverse group of people who participated in the study—men and women, people as young as 18 and as old as 58. We had participants who were White, African American, and Latino, and who represented a variety of ethnic and national backgrounds. The participants in our study reflected the overall population of individuals with SCI.

From the interviews and the time we spent with the participants there were several themes that recurred throughout the stories that relate to social justice and exercise. The first was the hope that exercise provided them, hope that had been taken away when doctors and healthcare practitioners told them that they had to live with less. Hope that was taken away in a society that assumed that having a disability meant that you had to expect less. Incurring the injury had left all of them with less: Less mobility, less opportunities for employment, and fewer relationships. Exercising, especially with students who had few notions about the limits of what could be accomplished, gave them hope for more: More relationships, more mobility, and more possibilities. A second issue that came up for nearly everyone we talked with was that having access to equipment that was designed for them was an empowering experience. Having equipment that they could use—and having student assistants who knew how to properly assist them—was meaningful because it was unusual. Unless they were willing to pay significant amounts of money for treatment in specialized clinics it was impossible to exercise, and most of the participants could not afford such treatments.

In the remainder of this chapter I would like to share the stories of some of the participants in our study, and as much as possible do so in their own words. I use pseudonyms to maintain their confidentiality. I have chosen some stories that were unique to these individuals, but for the most part I have tried to share stories that were told over and over again by different people. They were the stories that became familiar after five years of working with this group, and so are the stories that are likely the most important to tell.

LORENZO

One of the participants in the study was Lorenzo. I found Lorenzo to be a man of few words. In the clinic he usually had little to say to me, although it became clear that he and the students he worked with chatted quite a bit during his workouts. He had a motorized wheelchair because his SCI had impacted the functioning of his hands and arms, and he wore braces to help support his wrists. Lorenzo always wore a Raiders' baseball cap, the brim completely straight, set to the side, typically baggy jeans, and a t-shirt. In speaking with the students, conversation usually turned to the topic of sports, and football was often the center of the discussion. When it was time to interview him I was a bit concerned. He had said so little to me in the time he had been exercising in the clinic, and I worried he would not have much to say. I was wrong. Lorenzo not only had a lot to say, he was willing to share quite a bit of his life story and talked about how important the exercise program had been to him.

Hope

In the interviews, I asked everyone how they felt about exercise, and nearly everyone talked about the hope that exercise gave them.

I had been wanting to exercise ever since you guys called me. I like exercising. I always have, that's what I used to do before I got hurt. My job was hard, so pretty much I like doing hard things. I used to do construction. Put up dry wall, frame up walls, and stuff like that. So I never liked school and office work, that's not for me. I like outside jobs, you know. I like doing something that's hard.

The physical thing, I could say it gave me a little bit of hope. You never know. Maybe if I exercise enough something might move. I just like being physical. I used to play football and I used to take on the bigger guys. I just love it. And like I said, it just gives me a little bit of hope. You never know. I mean that's how come I wanna do it. I'll try anything. If it's gonna help then if I don't do it then I won't get better. That's why I like coming here a lot. When they ask me, "You wanna try this?" It's like yeah, I'll try anything. Don't matter. If it takes work to do it, I'll do it. The harder the better, you know. Don't get me wrong, I'll tell you I can't do it if I can't, but I'll try anything once. I really like it. But I used to be able to bench press 250 pounds. Now I can't even do 30 pounds. That really affects me sometimes. It's kind of depressing. I like to exercise here, and I feel good and everything, but then it gets me. That's the only thing that bugs me, not being able to move my hands. If I had my hands I know I could do way more.

Motivation

I asked Lorenzo if he would have other places to exercise if he were not coming to the mobility clinic. He said that he knew there might be other places, however, he would not have investigated them. He found out about our program from promotional fliers we had sent out through a rehabilitation clinic in the area. It also became clear that not only did exercise make him feel better, it had also led to changes in other health behaviors. His comments also indicated that without the unique relationship with the students he may not have been motivated to exercise or continue coming to the program.

If I wasn't exercising here, the way I am, I don't think I would ever find it. If you wouldn't have called me I would be stuck at home doing nothing. Watching sports and going around the block. That's pretty much it. If you hadn't called me I wouldn't be doing nothing.

The first time I came the student trainer was like "How come you couldn't do this before?" I go, "Fool, man, 'cause the day you guys called me I smoked like half a pack of cigarettes." I don't know how many blunts I smoked. I'm like I wasn't even ready for this. Like on Sunday I'll drink a little you know. I'll drink a little on Saturday, smoke, you know, whatever. Sunday, I'll stay clean, 'cause I know I have to come and exercise and if I smoke I'm not gonna be able to do nothing. You know especially with the little hand bike. It gets you tired, man. So that's why I stay clean. I like being here, man. I like chillin', bullsh**ing with people and talking. That's what I like the most. I like talking to people. Exercising and talking to people. You know, like with Paul [one of the student trainers], we talk about sports. And exercise … it woke me up, I know that. 'Cause I used to be lazy. And now I get up, I get up early. It just makes you feel better. Like if I leave right now my dad says, "Are you tired?" I'm like, "No." My arms feel heavy, but physically I feel like I can stay up all night. I feel good.

Life Changes after SCI

Lorenzo began to share how much his SCI had changed the trajectory of his life. While he said he usually "suppressed" thinking about how much his life had changed, it occasionally crept into his thoughts.

One night I was out with a friend, watching a football game, and I came home and my mom started in on me. She's all like, "What would you be doing if you were alright?" You know that negativity gets in your head, you know. You start feeling down. Then you start thinking, damn, what would I be doing? I used to live in Alabama when I … like I suppressed that so far back in my head that I don't even feel like I even left L.A. at all.

I had to leave here because things weren't going too well. I was doing too many drugs and the week before I left, me and my friend, we got jumped by a couple of guys and we almost got killed. So I looked at it and I thought I needed to do something different. If I don't leave I'm gonna end up dead or I'm not gonna end up doing nothing with my life. So I left. Then when I left, everything worked out pretty good. I was in Alabama for four or five years. I decided I was gonna straighten out, get a job, and I started working. Got a girl. Got married. That was it.

After his accident his wife's family placed a lot of pressure on her to leave Lorenzo, since they felt he could not take care of her any more. He returned to Los Angeles so that his family could help to support him.

So I just came back here and ever since then it's been pretty good. And I know I wouldn't have had all the help that I have here if I had stayed there. Like all this [the mobility clinic], like coming to the university for the exercising thing. My dad wants to check out what they do for me here. He comes every day to see. The one thing I regret the most is that he's seen me as a mess-up. He followed me to every jail that I went to. He never saw me when I was a man, when I was taking care of my business. I told him that I regret the most that he didn't get to see me when I was doing what he wanted me to be doing.

Race and Perceptions

Lorenzo was one of the first men to comment that his race had an impact on how he was perceived by others. This was later echoed my nearly all the African-America men and some of the Latino participants. White participants rarely acknowledged that race had an impact on the lives of people with SCIs, although some recognized that it probably did, they just could not imagine how. Lorenzo did not have to imagine how. His analysis of the situation was compelling.

I got into a car accident, and the car flipped over. Everyone thinks I was drunk or on drugs. I was sober. I was sober driving. I don't know. I never thought I looked like a gang banger. I mean before, yeah I did, because I shaved my head and all that, but now I let my hair grow. I never wore a hat and now I wear hats. But everybody thinks the same thing. Everybody, even when I go to the emergency room for an infection and stuff like that. You know, whatever. That's the first thing they ask me, "You got shot?" Naw fool, I got into a car accident and it kinda gets annoying you know. Cause you're judging me from my appearance.

Once they see, you're brown, you're bald, you must be in a gang. You're in a wheelchair, you got shot. I don't care if you want to ask me what happened. You know what I'm saying. I don't care if you ask me what happened. I'll tell you my whole story from when my car flipped, what happened, I'll tell you the whole thing. Just don't judge me. That's one of the things I hate. I don't judge people. Don't assume what you don't know. Ask me anything. What happened? I'll tell you. Even the doctors will get annoying. Why'd you get shot? It's like, "fool, I didn't." You see a White guy in a wheelchair, people think "Oh, poor guy he must have got hit by a car, got in an accident." They see me, "Aw look, that guy got shot." Like a family walks by and says to their kids, "Look kids, you're big, you're bad, that's what happens to you. You're gonna get shot like he did." Even my own friends, they have kids and they ask me to tell them this is what happens if you get into a gang. I'm like, "Fool, I ain't gotta tell them sh**."

Feeling Normal

Many of the participants felt that society in general saw them differently. Many people were irritated when able-bodied individuals acted as though they were lacking cognitive functioning, could not hear them, or could not speak for themselves. We had hoped that we had mentored our students to create a more affirming and empowering environment, and Lorenzo and others talked about the ways that coming to the mobility clinic helped them to feel more "normal" both physically and socially.

So then they sent me to a nursing home. So I'm there with a bunch of basically old people. Me and the nurses are the only young ones there. So all the nurses they would talk to me and all that, but every time I would hear that someone had just died and it's depressing. And then it's like they are talking to a retard or something. I'm in a wheelchair, okay, I'll give you that one. At the hospital everybody would talk to my sister. They would ask, "Does he have problems with this?" I'm lying there. At first I'm just looking, but then the person that was gonna be my physical therapist, she starts talking to my sister, and I was like, "Hey, who's gonna be doing the exercising?" She goes, "Oh, well, you are." I go, "So why aren't you talking to me?" She says, "Oh, because I didn't know about your condition." I go, "Well the only condition I have is I can't damn walk. I can't use my hands, but you can talk to me. I have a brain. I can understand what you're saying you know." For one, I could probably even be smarter than you. So don't talk to me like I'm an idiot 'cause I could be smarter than you are. Sometimes it is pretty stupid. Like if I go to the store they'll talk to whoever is next to me. I'm the one who's buying.

I always tell my friends, treat me like I'm the same as before. My one friend, we hang out on Saturday night, and he'll joke around. He'll clown on my chair, and he'll joke around, and we make fun about it. He treats me like if I wasn't in a wheelchair, and that's the way it should be, 'cause there ain't nothing different. I'm still the same person, the only problem I have is I can't get up. You know that's how we're all cool. That's the kind of people I like hanging out with. I don't like being around people that go, "Aw, poor Lorenzo." That's how come I like coming here. It's the same thing, you know. Everybody is hanging out and talking, so it's all good.

Lorenzo talked quite a bit more throughout his interview about his relationship with the students: How they pushed him to improve and how important the social aspect of coming to the mobility clinic was. Although some of the participants had very rich social lives outside of the mobility clinic, others did not. For many, the exercise sessions were the only scheduled activities they had, and they had little social interactions outside. While Lorenzo had a large family who supported him and friends he socialized with regularly, there was clearly something unique and important about the social environment our students created in the mobility clinic.

EVE-LYNN

Eve-Lynn was a confident, up-beat, and spirited woman. The students were all quite drawn to her. She was easy to talk to, positive, and so excited about the exercise program. She took pride in her appearance; her outfits and shoes were always coordinated and were often a topic of conversation. Her daughter occasionally came to exercise sessions with her, and Eve-Lynn often talked about her role as a mother and the challenges she faced as a single mother in a wheelchair. Her injury impacted one side of her body, and as a result she had a very high level of functioning on one side, but on the other side she had weakness in her arm, hand, and leg. Eve-Lynn was quite loquacious, both in the everyday exercise setting, and in our interview. Like Lorenzo, she shared stories that resonated with what many others had to say.

Feelings about Exercise

Eve-Lynn felt exercise was critical to her mental and physical well-being. When asked about how she felt about exercise she had a lot to say.

It feels good, especially for someone who can't just get up and walk. Prior to me having my accident, it's probably a feeling that I had all the time. But you are so used to it you don't notice it. It's when you actually are in a wheelchair and you're sitting down that you realize that by someone actually helping you move, or by you moving more, that you say, "Oh, my god, that feels good." It just makes me feel, I would say, a cool feeling all over and that's the only way that I can describe it, and it feels really good. It's also very relaxing. There is nothing I don't like about exercise. I wish that I could get more of it. I really love the program that you guys have. I really feel the patients' needs are incorporated into the program here. I feel really bad for people who don't have a chance to experience what

I'm experiencing. I'm really happy when I'm getting better, but I always want to share my happiness with someone else. So, I am happy to be part of a study that other people can benefit from. Hopefully when the results are in, more hospitals will realize that this will really help people. And it's kind of commonsense, because if someone's exercising me, you get less health problems. The only thing I hate about it is that I can't do it by myself. I need assistance and I wish I had more exercise, not just two days a week. Not to be ungrateful, that's the only thing. I just wish I had more.

Having the opportunity to be in this program is the best because they are actually able to isolate my movements. A lot of physical therapists would tell me that I should isolate my movements, but they never explained or showed me how. And I guess the message from my brain and my spinal cord was going to my strongest muscles so I would get this weird little, I'm trying to move my finger, but I am moving my arm instead. At the exercise program here, the way they hold me, there's no way I can move other muscles. It goes straight to the area that they want it to go to. So instead of the people yelling at me all the time, like "Isolate it!" I feel like if they had done it the way they do it here, they would have gotten better results. It's like they don't understand I can't isolate it, that's why you guys are helping me. I don't know if they meant to do this on purpose, whoever developed this program, but I'm getting three different things. I am getting control of my muscles because they are holding me, I guess what they call it, sensory input, because they are touching me, they are telling me which muscles I need to be using. That's really important when you have lost that connection. I don't know why other people don't realize this. To me it's common sense. After they do it 10 or 20 times I have a chance for my body to go, ok, I know how this feels. So I think it's wonderful. And in my experience that is not how it usually happens. Physical therapists—I have had them move my fingers once, and then go, "Okay, now you try." When I couldn't they're like, "Okay, she couldn't do it." I see them writing it in the notes. And I'm like, that's too early. Maybe if you tried it repetitiously, and I guess they don't have enough time, because they have a high case load, but I feel that you have to work smarter not harder, and I feel like you guys are working smarter. They are touching the person, they are doing it repetitiously, and then they are giving the person the chance to do it themselves, and they don't discourage the person if they don't do it on that first time. It's like "Okay, we'll just do it next week or tomorrow."

Hope

Hope was the most common benefit that participants talked about in our program. Both that through exercise they had hope that they would improve and that the students were optimistic about their progress. I have wondered about why the experience with our students was so different from what they had experienced in other clinical settings. I often think it is that our students were as excited as the participants about what was happening. This was a new experience for them, and they were not constrained by their previous experiences. They were eager to try anything and had no expectations about how far the participants could improve.

In the past I feel as if I was more positive than my doctors. The very last experience I had with a doctor being negative was when I told them I wanted to walk. I explained to my doctors that the physical therapists were giving up on me. I asked them, "What can we do?" And I had two doctors look at me as if I was delusional. Really, they actually sat me down, I think one of the doctors exact words were, "Ma'am, I wouldn't lie to you. You're not going to get better. It's been two years since your injury. You are making it harder on yourself by having this feeling that you are going to walk. It's easier if you just face it. You need to get an electric wheel chair. If you want to drive, you need to get a minivan, and that's it. You need to stop with all this trying to get better. Just face it. Life will be so much easier for you if you just accept that you are not going to get better." And I went home crying, and I called my friends. So my friends reminded me, "You've been told this before, and you've proved them wrong, so don't let this man get you down." And he meant well. I'm not angry at him, and I haven't gone back to him since I've gotten better.

I am waiting for my insurance company to approve more physical therapy. Meanwhile, I'm with you guys, getting better. If I didn't have you guys, then I would be just sitting at home waiting. In your mindset, if you're depressed or if you have low self-esteem because of your disability and if you don't have the endorphins working for you during exercise, you're going to fall into depression. Exercise gives you hope. But if I wasn't coming here, I know I would be very frustrated and sad. I've been the one that's tried to be so positive, and I get tired. So you guys have kind of taken the baton from me so I can rest. And now somebody else is being positive for me and it feels good. Now things are happening so fast that I haven't had a chance to just sit back and go, "Oh my god!" But I know the other day whenever I tried to reflect on all the things you guys do, I started crying. You guys have just saved my life. It was amazing. You guys are so positive, and it really hurts me that other people don't have this opportunity to work with you guys, and it's not like you guys are lying to me and promising that I am going to get better. But we have the same goal. It's, "Let's see if we can do this," instead of, "This is not going to happen based on what I've seen."

While Eve-Lynn had been told she should give up her desire to start walking, after 10 weeks in the exercise program and gait training, she was able to walk independently on the treadmill, then over ground with a walker, and eventually a cane. Our program was not an intensive gait training program, so her progress indicates a high level of functioning and work on her part. The fact that she was able to walk after she had been told so vehemently that she never would made a significant impact on Eve-Lynn's perspective on her injury and the future.

Reconnecting with the Body

Acquired disabilities can leave individuals feeling disconnected from their bodies. While this was not the case for everyone we worked with, many indicated that since they could not feel or move certain parts of their bodies, it felt like they were not a part of them. We had hoped that exercise would reduce the pain that participants felt as a result of their SCI, but what we found is that for some individuals the pain increased, while for others it decreased. Whatever the direction, everyone perceived this as a positive change, because it indicated neural growth or healing. Many people, including Eve-Lynn, remarked that the exercise changed how they viewed the parts of their bodies affected by their SCI.

The exercise is sending messages to my body like saying "This side exists!" I used to neglect my left side early on. My best friend told me I would call my affected side "it." And she said it would really freak her out, it would really scare her. She like, "It's not an 'it,' it's your body!" But I remember in my mind at that time, and saying to her, "Well, it doesn't work, so why should I call it mine? It's not doing anything." Now that I'm better, it seems totally ridiculous to say that, but I remember feeling that at that time. I really felt like I reconnected totally that very last time I was on the treadmill. That's what it was, it felt like my body was one whole body now. I couldn't figure out a way to explain it, but that's it. That's it.

Several other participants made remarkably similar comments, and nearly all who felt a reconnection, or increased innervation of their muscles, attributed it to walking on the treadmill.

PAUL

Paul was our oldest participant. He was injured at 19 in a sports accident, and at the time we worked with him was 58 years old. Paul was funny and charming, and the students were always drawn to him. Because he had lived with his disability for so long he seemed to have a different perspective than those who had been recently injured. His goal was not to walk again, but to have the best quality of life possible. He was socially active and independent. At one point in his interview he commented that he often forgot that he had a disability; it was only when he wheeled by a window and saw his reflection that he was reminded that he was in a wheelchair.

Standing Tall

Because Paul had been wheelchair bound for so long, I was curious as to what his first experience on the gait trainer was like.

The first time, it's hard to explain, you know, because I'm about six feet tall, it's really kind of surreal, it's very strange, even now that I've done it about, what, five, maybe six times. The weirdest thing is looking down at my feet. I can't believe my depth perception. I'm 39 years removed from that, so I just can't believe my feet are that far away from my head, from my eyes. Do you know what I mean? Seeing myself in the mirror, to me it's just cool. I try not to get too excited about it, 'cause nothing's working, but I'm standing up. It's like the astronauts. I try not to get emotionally wrapped up in these little things because it's such a huge journey to go from the earth to the moon. You know, it takes so much to make that happen, just like for any of us to be able to go from where we are, to walking normally, these little things. It can't be a big deal. I don't mean to minimize it—it's still a huge thing to get up. It's fun, so I look forward to getting up to see how much more my body can take and what else we can do and all that. I think the first time I just had a great sensation in my legs, almost like they were buzzing. I was driving home, and it was just, my body feeling revitalized. I just felt like it was charged. It's hard to explain, 'cause I didn't have sensation, but I could feel like there was something going on. I just felt like it was buzzing, and I kind of like that. You want to go back to more of that. That's one of the pull-ins to the exercise. I don't really like the other stuff, but walking on the gait trainer is a good motivational incentive plan.

ANABELLE

Anabelle was incredibly upbeat and positive. She was petite, young, and attractive, and highly conscious of her appearance. She was always motivated to exercise, driven to improve her strength and physical abilities. Her injury was sustained in a car accident. She was driving with friends, one of whom died in the accident and others of whom escaped without permanent injury. After working with people with SCI over the years, the research team was keenly aware of issues of accessibility. To this day I always take note of whether or not a building is accessible, how one would cross the street when curb cut outs are not at every corner. When I enter a public restroom I wonder whether someone in a wheelchair would have enough space. Anabelle, however, made clear that accessible public spaces were the least of her worries.

Accessibility

As Anabelle told this story I was struck at how profoundly not having access to either her boyfriend's or her mother's home affected her daily life.

I would like everything to be accessible, you know? Like a ramp to come in and out of the house. 'Cause at my boyfriend's it's a one story, but there are stairs and no ramp. My mom's place is upstairs so that is not working at all. My brother has to carry me up there, or whoever is around that could help me. At my boyfriend's either he or his dad have to carry me up, and then my chair. And the restroom door frame isn't wide enough for my chair. Just having the bed level with my chair, then I could get in and out on my own and then I'd be fine. 'Cause then I can get up, get ready. I can lounge around if I want to, leave if I want to, come back when I want. But there's times where I will leave and he's at work and I'm like, oh, I can't get in. And there are times when I'm out and I did what I had to do, but I have nothing to do. So I'll just find something to do, but there's times where I just want to go and relax. Before, I worked a full-time job, so that's eight hours of my day. I had to run errands. I was a busy person, but I wasn't always out and about. Now I have a lot of free time on my hands. If I don't come here at this therapy place, it's only Tuesday and Thursday, then after I leave here I'm like, "Where do I go? What do I do?" So I'll find something to do, then I spend money 'cause I go to the mall 'cause I have nothing to do. It's like I don't need to be doing those things. I need to buy a new wheelchair, I need to save money.

Independence

Like most of the participants, Anabelle saw exercise as a way to gain independence. Ironically, Anabelle worked out at the same time as a man quite a bit older than herself. He had a hard edge, was covered in tattoos, and was one of the men who planned on riding his motorcycle again. When this man found out that Anabelle had a driver's license, he was a bit taken aback, because he did not have his. Within a few weeks he came back reporting that he now also had a driver's license and was having his truck modified so that he could drive. These two confided in one another and provided each other with support, and motivation, and together they worked fiercely towards becoming more independent.

By exercising I become more independent. The more exercise, the more better I can get, the more independent I will be, and the more I can do for others. And that's gonna make me feel so much better with myself, it makes a big difference to be volunteering for others. Knowing that you can do for yourself and not have to ask for other's help. Within the time that I started this program, I don't know if it is because I started, but that's when I caught all the changes. I'm confident within myself to move around. Since I started the program I'm transferring in and out of the car, using the restroom on my own and, actually the public restroom. And placing the chair by myself in the car, that's not an easy movement.

CONCLUSIONS

Getting the phone call asking them to be part of our research study was a memorable moment for many of the participants. Often they had completed the physical therapy covered by their insurance and could not afford the other fee-based programs offered in the area. One participant lived 300 miles away, but found a way to relocate temporarily so that he could join us. It was clear that for many this was a tremendous opportunity and that after the 10-week session was over they would once again be left without a place to go to exercise. I had conducted intervention studies before, and I knew that this was always the reality. I also knew that we had given people an opportunity and that we could offer the resources and referrals we had available to help them stay active. At the end of one of our first 10-week cycles I was struck when Ray expressed that he was concerned that now that the study was over, the participants would be left without the benefits of the program we had offered to them. He said, "When I finish a study with rats, they are sacrificed, and I collect my data. But with people, I just feel bad that we let them go. What will they do now?" In establishing the mobility clinic Ray had already created opportunities for university students and community members to come take a class where they could exercise on accessible equipment with trained students. We made sure that the study participants knew that they could come back. Unfortunately, this would take some money, as participants would have to register as students and pay tuition. For some it was still an excellent opportunity, but for others who did not have the ability to pay for the class, they were once again left without. The disparities highlighted what we had already learned from the study. Individuals with money could afford therapies, equipment, and assistance that could help keep them healthy, fit, and feeling good about their bodies and their health, and those without money could not.

Throughout the process of writing this chapter, I have reflected on how social justice comes into play in the stories I heard and have told, and for me it is salient in many ways. First, the fact that the mobility clinic was in the basement speaks to the position of people with disabilities in society. The challenges of simply getting to the bathroom are centrally important to quality of life, but for the able-bodied folks who make decisions about room selections, doorway sizes, and the accessibility of buildings, these are not always issues thoughtfully considered. I am glad to say that after our project was complete there were renovations on campus and Ray's lab and the mobility clinic are now above ground, in a new and accessible building. A second issue is that there are very obvious ways that having money makes life simpler. Having an SCI impacts every aspect of one's life, from how one gets out of bed and, eventually, out of the house, to how one sees one's body. Having access to a more technologically advanced and newer wheelchair, a car one can drive, and the ability to modify one's home are all important to the daily lives of people with SCI. Third, race matters. Men of color, particularly African American and Latino men, are seen as gang members, shot in the course of their criminal lives, not as people who acquired their SCIs through the same random events that befall White people. The constant assumption that they were complicit in their injuries by their imagined participation in a gang affected their interactions with their friends and the people they saw on the streets, in the malls, and even in healthcare settings. Finally, what was spoken of most clearly, and most often, is that people with SCIs are often told by their healthcare professionals that they will not walk, that they should resign themselves to the "fact" that they will be in their chairs forever. But we learned what most of our participants knew, that through exercise, through attention to their bodies, and by making their bodies stronger and more able to function, they gain hope. I leave you below with a few final thoughts and reflections:

1. *Accessibility matters.* Social equity and justice for individuals with disabilities can only occur in environments where there is access to spaces that allow for a life unconstrained by physical barriers. From a sport and exercise perspective this means that sport and exercise spaces need to be accessible and have equipment that can be used by people with a variety of physical disabilities.

2. *Money matters.* Many of the inequities that individuals with disabilities face can be addressed and resolved through financial resources. Being able to afford the right wheelchair, sport and exercise equipment, ramps, modified cars, and assistants can all make life simpler. Without money the barriers that prevent participation in the activities people want to engage in, particularly sport and exercise, can be insurmountable. For individuals with disabilities and whose capacity to use their bodies in ways that are seen as conventional in mainstream society is limited, opportunities to be physical and increase strength and functioning are critical to maintaining a positive sense of self and quality of life.

3. *Race matters.* The ways that race and disability intersect are rarely discussed, but it is clear that for men of color the perception that they were responsible for their injuries has a significant influence on their interactions with others. A critical awareness of racial stereotypes and biases and how they intersect with stereotypes regarding disability needs to increase.

4. *Hope matters.* The most significant way that participation in an exercise program and the use of accessible equipment impacted the participants was that it gave them hope. Working towards increasing strength and functionality gave people hope that the possibility for improvement existed. And at the end of the day, we all hope for possibility.

It Takes Several Northern Communities to Raise a Reflexive and Effective Sport Researcher

Audrey R. Giles

Sport for development is a contemporary term for practices that have a long history, particularly in Canada's north and especially with Aboriginal peoples for whom the region is home. Most sport and recreation programs are founded on Eurocentric understandings of youth development: that youth should participate in such activities because they are good for them; that they will improve their educational attainment, leadership abilities, health, and their proclivity to become productive members of society; and that this will help them to avoid any number of socially undesirable behaviors, such as drug and alcohol use, teen pregnancy, and criminal activities. As Aboriginal youth are stereotypically understood as being particularly at risk for such problem behaviors, they are often the targets of sport-for-development programs. In this chapter, I examine my 13-year involvement in sport and recreation in Canada's provincial and territorial north, specifically with residents of the regions. In particular, I use personal stories to trace how my understanding of both my efforts and the programs with which I have been involved have changed over time, how the youth and communities I was supposed to help "develop" ended up instead helping me to develop into a more reflexive and effective scholar.

Though I trace my interest in the North to an outstanding junior high school geography teacher who taught his students about communities in northern Ontario, it is embarrassing for me to admit that my initial interest in the North was equally piqued by what we now know to be largely fictional texts by the Canadian author Farley Mowat. My young and emerging sense of social justice was deeply troubled by the depictions of marginalized communities in the North that were largely abandoned by the Canadian government in times of need. While most young teens want to spend their holidays at beaches or amusement parks, my twin sister and I begged our mother to drive us up to exotic locations like Kapuskasing, Moosenee, and Moose Factory, all in northern Ontario, so that we could gain first-hand exposure to the provincial North. My sense of social justice was further shaken when I realized there was a correlation between where the roads in northern Ontario became unpaved and rutted and where the houses became dilapidated: This was my introduction to First Nations reserves. As a White, middle-class Torontonian, I was shocked to see such poverty. When we finally made it to Moosenee and Moose Factory after a journey on the famous train, the Polar Bear Express, I was further shocked to encounter hostility from the locals. I remember children giving us obviously erroneous directions and laughing at our expense. I felt uncomfortable and out of place, yet something about that trip remained with me for many years; the feeling that there was a huge disconnect between my comfortable life in the South and the lives of many individuals in the North was something I could not ignore.

CAPE DORSET, 1998

After several years of having a summer job as waterfront staff at a camp in the Muskoka region of Ontario, I was ready for a new challenge. With a year of undergraduate studies towards my goal of becoming a sport psychologist under my belt, a still-growing social conscience, and an overdeveloped sense of confidence in my abilities to change the world due to my newfound academic knowledge, I decided to apply for a summer job in the Arctic. The fact that there were swimming pools and waterfronts across the Northwest Territories (which at that time included what is now Nunavut Territory) did not surprise me. I firmly believed that every child should learn how to swim and that I had the necessary skills required to teach northerners the importance of breaststroke, a strong flutter kick, and the dangers associated with water of every description. That I learned these skills in swimming pools in Toronto and that I had taught them for years in the context of a private swim school that operated out of one of the nicest facilities in the city and also in a lake at a summer camp did not deter me. I did not question the transferability of my skills. I packed my ABBA Gold and Elvis' Greatest Hits tapes and dreamt of the aquafit classes I would teach in the facility that I imagined would be a small-scale version of the multimillion dollar pool in which I taught lessons in Toronto.

My sense of panic began to set in once I was at the Montreal airport. Waiting for my First Air flight to depart to Iqaluit, I noticed that most people at the gate were Inuit, wearing parkas, Sorrel boots, and, most alarmingly, speaking a language that was completely unfamiliar to me: Inuktitut, a language that I had erroneously assumed few people would speak. After landing in Iqaluit, where I would have to remain overnight before heading to my final destination, Cape Dorset (population 1,200), I realized that one of the difficulties with the wonders of modern air travel was that one can fly, for example, from one's home in the toasty 30°C humidity in southern Canada to the snowy Arctic in the span of only a few short hours. There was little time to adjust to my new surroundings. The next day, I boarded another flight and headed to Dorset, as the locals call it. I had called ahead and described what I looked like to my boss so that he would be able to pick me out at the airport. My description was met with a chuckle and, "Don't worry, we'll know who you are." Upon being picked up at the airport, my overflowing suitcases and I were packed into the Hamlet of Cape Dorset's suburban transport. My co-worker nodded at the weather outside and said something in Inuktitut, which I decided (given the flurries) roughly translated to, "Wow, is it ever cold out there." I nodded in agreement. He then rolled down the window. Indeed, what he said actually translated to, "Wow, is it ever warm today." The airport was a great introduction to life in Cape Dorset: I would not fit in easily and my thinking often proved to be the polar opposite of the locals'.

The pool was not a small version of the pool where I had worked in Toronto. It was a small, shallow water pool that had been retrofitted into a curling area. It was also missing key pieces of safety equipment, like straps for the spine board. My pool assistants did not know how to swim. Finally, despite the fact that it was a seasonally operated pool and thus had no water in it, there was a rumor that the pool water was contaminated. I was not off to a good start at developing local aquatics leaders, which was my mandate.

My summer in Cape Dorset was not one that was particularly successful. I was convinced that local people would finally come around to doing things "the right way" at the pool; all I had to do was to make residents aware of the excellent programs I was offering and they would finally start to show up, for instance, for swimming lessons at 9:30 a.m. In the end, only a small handful of children took swimming lessons, though many more would use the pool later in the day. Rather than learning from the community members that life in the land of the midnight sun means that kids stayed up very late and slept in equally late, which made morning swimming lessons next to impossible, I instead thought that I could change the community. I thought that programs and policies that worked in the South would work in the North, that northerners would adapt to an approach that worked so well in Canada's largest city. I was young, naive, and wrong. In the end, not a single community member came to join aquafit, and I did not manage to certify anyone as a lifeguard.

When I left Dorset at the end of the summer, I felt a sense of relief. I had no intention of returning to the North. I would return to Queen's University and life would go back to normal for me. It turned out, however, that normal had shifted. This first became apparent to me when I attempted to go shopping at a mall. I was overwhelmed not only by the number of people there, several times the entire population of Cape Dorset, but also by people's fixation on how they looked (why were they so dressed up for the mall?) and their rushing around (it was the weekend—why such a sense of urgency?). I also realized that no one returned my attempt to make eye contact and smile. I left the mall after 15 minutes. Normal in the Toronto sense had started to feel wrong after a summer in the Arctic.

My shift in normal also began to be reflected through my views of what I was learning in my undergraduate classes. When professors would make statements about certain phenomena in Canada, I would raise my hand and point out that they were really talking only about the part of Canada that borders the United States and, in particular, its non-Aboriginal inhabitants. I began taking classes about Aboriginal peoples, and I started to make every assignment that I had somehow touch upon the North. Perhaps most importantly, I began to reflect on my summer in Cape Dorset and why it had been less than successful. I realized—to my horror—that I had behaved a lot like others who had acted as colonial forces: in short, I had insisted that the southern Canadian way was the right way. The "right" way also happened to be the White way.

Having attended what was at the time the most multicultural high school in Canada, I had honestly never really thought of myself as White. I was, like the vast majority of my classmates, a first generation Canadian. I had never thought of the privilege that being the daughter of White, British immigrants brought me. My backpack of privilege, as some feminist scholars call it, had not yet been unpacked. It was only after going to Cape Dorset and having the experience of being an ethnic minority that I realized how much of what I did and how I understood the world related to my cultural background and the unquestioned supremacy of Eurocanadian ways of life.

SPUNC, 1999-2001

My twin sister, Sarah, had also worked in the NWT during the same summer that I was in Cape Dorset. She ran a waterfront in a tiny community (about 100 people at the time) above the Arctic Circle, Colville Lake. After returning home, we compared notes and realized that we had both been saddened to see that children in the communities in which we had worked had very little in the way of sports equipment. Initially, our thought was that we should gather up the skates that we had sitting idle in the attic and send them to the kids that we knew in the North. We then thought about all the other people we knew who had sports equipment collecting dust in their basements and how their equipment could be put to similar use. What started as a tiny idea grew into Sporting Partnerships of Universities and Northern Communities (SPUNC), a nonprofit organization that my sisters and I ran as volunteers. We paired universities across Canada with communities in the North. With the help of several airlines and a trucking company, we were able to organize equipment drives and send over 3,500 pounds of new and used sports equipment to northern communities over a three-year time span.

My sister and I wanted northern children to be able to have the same opportunities that we had had. In SPUNC's early days, we asked the Territorial Sport Organizations in the Northwest Territories and Nunavut to decide which communities would receive the equipment. Over time, we realized that we could respond to some of the nagging critiques that we made of our own efforts (who are we to tell them which sports they should play?) by asking the communities to come up with wish lists of equipment, so that we could try to better meet their needs.

Through my involvement in SPUNC, I learned several important lessons (not the least of which was that one should avoid inadvertently naming an organization after a slang term for ejaculate, but I digress). Perhaps most importantly, I learned that simply providing sports equipment was a band-aid solution that would not lead to long-term change. I had fallen into the classic donor-recipient relationship that typifies development paradigms and is critiqued so heavily by development scholars. I began to wonder if by donating sports equipment, we were actually perpetuating the problem as, to a small extent, it alleviated the need for others to address the fundamental inequities that caused a shortage of sports equipment in the first place. To facilitate change, a different approach was needed.

WABASCA/DESMARAIS, ALBERTA, 2000

After my third year of university, I decided that I was ready to go back up North. I accepted a job with Alberta's Future Leaders Program (AFL). AFL is a program that places university and college students, who are employed as Youth Workers or Arts Mentors, in First Nations and Métis communities, many of them in the Provincial North. Throughout the summer, the Youth Workers and Arts Mentors are to develop sport, recreation, and arts programs and through doing so are to help First Nations and Métis youth develop their leadership potential. Ideally, each community is involved with the program for three years, after which it is hoped that the community will be self-sufficient in terms of the provision of sport, recreation, and the arts. I felt that it was an ideal situation for me to put my new-found knowledge from my time in Cape Dorset, with SPUNC, and through my university courses to use. I also secretly hoped that it would be a chance for me to redeem myself.

Unlike the pool program in Cape Dorset, where I was given no training and was basically thrown the keys to the pool and told to go to work, I received a week of training through AFL. During workshops, lectures, and group activities, we were encouraged to build relationships with community members and told that our job was to help to create "happy, smiling faces." I felt quite prepared and incredibly optimistic when I headed up to Wabasca/Desmarais, Alberta, home to the Bigstone Cree Nation. I made myself several promises before that summer started, but the most challenging one was that I would build stronger relationships with people for whom the community was a permanent home. In

Cape Dorset, it had been easy to make friends with the RCMP, teachers, and nurses—individuals who, for the most part, came from southern Canada and who longed to return there after they gained experience or had made enough money. While I certainly valued my friendship with these people, I found that they often viewed their time in the North as a sort of purgatory: they were often there "killing time," waiting for better opportunities to come their way. I was tired of hearing complaints about the North and northern cultures. I wanted to be around people who saw the North as home, not a temporary stop along the way to a better life in the South. Permanent northerners, however, were harder people to befriend. Having watched a steady stream of people come and go from the North, they wanted to know that I had a commitment to their community and that I wasn't just going to leave. By the time I had taken the job with AFL, my commitment to the North was easier to demonstrate. My new plan was to conduct graduate studies pertaining to sport and recreation in northern Aboriginal communities. That information, in addition to the credibility that a summer on Baffin Island and SPUNC gave me, made it easier for people in Wabasca/Desmarais to believe that I wasn't there to just make money and leave.

My work partner for AFL, Jennifer, and I worked really hard in Wabasca/Desmarais to create a sport, recreation, and leadership development program that worked for the community, rather than one that worked for us. As it was the third summer that AFL had been in Wabasca/Desmarais, we saw it as our task to work ourselves out of our jobs—to help the community to coordinate its resources so that AFL did not take such a prominent role.

The foundation to our approach in Wabasca/Desmarais was consultation, the very thing that was missing from my time in Cape Dorset and which was really only an afterthought in SPUNC. Prior to planning any programming that summer, we surveyed all the youth in the local schools and asked them what activities they wanted to participate in over the course of the summer. Some of the items on the list were unsurprising. Wabasca/Desmarais was a volleyball powerhouse, so we helped to ensure that the school gym was open for biweekly volleyball nights. Due to the proximity to Edmonton, a trip to West Edmonton Mall and its various attractions also made the short list. To me, the most surprising activity in which the youth wanted to participate was golf. Neither Jennifer nor I had any expertise in golf; as a result, we took several groups of children to Slave Lake, the nearest urban center, for golf lessons.

Further, with very few exceptions, our programming all occurred in the afternoons or evenings. While our social lives certainly suffered, as we were working while most other community members were off work, the programs that Jennifer and I offered were generally very successful, largely because we learned from the community that mornings were not the youths' favorite time of day to participate in sport, recreation, and arts programming. While there were definitely times when we drove around the reserve in a truck, yelling out the window to tell children about the day's activities so that they remembered that they were occurring, we did not take that as a sign that we had failed. Instead, we took it as a sign that we had adapted to the ways things worked in the community. We expected ourselves to adhere to the community's norms. I had learned to let go, for the most part, of my belief that the community should adapt to the programming format and content that I thought was best. While I certainly had professors (mostly women's studies) who had argued that community consultation was a beneficial practice for developing any program, I was given very few examples of how that might actually work and what it might look like. AFL gave me the opportunity, time, space, and resources necessary to become a better, more culturally appropriate sport and recreation practitioner.

One of main points of AFL is to develop strong youth leaders within the communities with which AFL works. I must admit that I think it was much more successful in helping me to become a better leader than it was in terms of helping me to build leadership on the reserve. The idea that primarily Eurocanadian university and college students from urban communities have a great deal to teach First Nations and Métis youth about leadership is, to me, laughable. There is no doubt in my mind that the youth taught me more than I taught them. I write this not as some warm and fuzzy platitude, but because I believe it to be true. While the programming I offered in Wabasca/Desmarais was successful in terms of the number of participants who came out to programs, in hindsight I am unconvinced that the best way to promote leadership development in typically marginalized youth is by bringing in AFL Youth Workers and Arts Workers, who are meant to act as mentors. The problem with that model is that the youth teach the Youth Workers how to become culturally competent leaders, and then the Youth Workers deliver programming that is supposed to help build the leadership skills of the very youth who taught them how to lead in the first place. I would argue that the leadership skills we were seeking to develop in the youth were already there and that successful Youth Workers and Arts Workers were the best evidence of that.

FORT SIMPSON, NWT, 2000

During the summer between the completion of my undergraduate degrees and the start of graduate school, I again took a job as a swimming pool supervisor in the Canadian North. This time the location was Fort Simpson, NWT. By that point I had spent many summers in the North, had completed two undergraduate degrees, had run a nonprofit organization, and had learned to take direction from community members. The impact of these experiences showed. In contrast to Cape Dorset, the swimming pool in Fort Simpson was incredibly popular in every way. After consultations with community members, my Assistant Supervisor, Kathleen, and I built on successes from previous summers of pool programming in Fort Simpson by devising a schedule that offered a variety of programs. There were over 60 children enrolled in swimming lessons (which, due to their popularity, started in the late morning and continued into the afternoon), we had a young staff of eager local youth, we had a swim team—and even women who came for aquafit (that featured Top 40 hits, not Elvis). By the end of the summer, we had had thousands of visits to the pool, five local people became certified lifeguards, many youth were well on their way to becoming future lifeguards as a result of their participation in lessons, and I was run ragged. I felt that my co-workers and I had finally run the perfect pool program.

After starting graduate school, I thought my days as the "pool girl," as northerners often called me, were over. What I had not anticipated were the ways in which an interaction in a grade two classroom in June in Fort Simpson would nag at my conscience for years and, in the end, shape my career as a professor. When I had arrived in Fort Simpson, the building in which the swimming pool was housed had a problem with paint peeling off the walls and ceiling. As a result, there were five weeks during which time Kathleen and I had to find work to do because of the repairs that were being done to the building. With no water in which to conduct programming, Kathleen and I went into elementary school classrooms and taught boat, water, and ice safety.

I remember very clearly being in front of a classroom with Kathleen and discussing the dangers of the mighty Mackenzie River with grade two students. We reminded them that the water was dangerous and that they should stay away from the banks of the river upon which their community was perched.

"You can't tell them it's dangerous," the teacher snapped at us afterwards. "It's part of their culture."

I was unmoved. As a water safety *expert,* I felt that I knew what was best. Children can drown in a few centimeters of water—telling them that water was anything but dangerous struck me as completely ridiculous and ill advised. Did the teacher not realize the danger of her words?

Upon reflection, it was me who did not realize the danger of my own words, of the ways in which they reflected a Eurocentric bias—the belief that there was only one way to view water and to develop water safety practices, and that was a fear-based approach. I had failed to recognize that the lessons I offered were steeped in a particular set of beliefs, ones that were at odds with Dene beliefs that water both gives and takes life and, as a result, must be respected. Many Dene peoples will offer tobacco to the water before going on it or taking something (like fish) from it. They recognize it as an important spiritual force, not just a source of anxiety concerning water safety, which was very much the lens through which I saw it.

Another vivid example of the failings of Eurocentric water safety was brought to my attention in the same school. In a different classroom in Fort Simpson, Kathleen and I were teaching boat safety. We asked the children what they should bring with them when they go boating or things that they should do prior to going out in a boat. We based the "correctness" of their answers on the Department of Transportation's Pre-Departure Checklist. Upon asking the question, many children's little hands shot into the air, eager to provide a response. I selected one boy and asked him for an answer.

"You need to bring a gun," he replied. A gun was not on the Checklist. I told him, no, that was not the answer we were looking for. With the benefit of hindsight, it's clear that the child was absolutely correct. Even the youngest residents of Fort Simpson knew that it was of vital importance to take a rifle with you if you are going out on the land, both for protection from bears and in the event that one gets stranded and has to hunt for survival. Why, then, does the Checklist not include this information? The obvious answer is that Aboriginal peoples' cultural practices are marginalized in the face of Eurocanadian, southern "expertise."

I became more familiar with Dene culture during my doctorate, which focused on Dene women's involvement in Dene games in the NWT. While conducting my research, I heard more about cultural practices concerning water. The more I learned, the more I questioned the ways in which I had run programs in the North and tried to develop aquatic leaders. I became convinced that aquatics programming in the North could be used as an example of the ways in which colonial practices can be rooted in and expressed through attempts to develop sport and recreation in the North. As a result, upon becoming a professor at the University of Ottawa, the first grant for which I applied concerned that very topic.

RESEARCH INTO AQUATIC PROGRAMMING IN THE NORTH, 2005 – PRESENT

The drowning rate in Canada's north varies between 6-10 times the national average. Further, Aboriginal people drown more often than non-Aboriginal people. Past research has explained these findings as being due to several factors: cold water, time spent on the water, distance from help, a failure to wear lifejackets/floater suits, the use of alcohol while boating, and a lack of access to swimming lessons and water safety. Based on my experiences, I had a hunch that these findings missed a few very important points: that the water safety taught in the North and Aboriginal communities was based on Eurocentric approaches to water safety; messages concerning aquatic-based risk communication are culturally inappropriate in many northern communities; and the source of water safety messages (i.e., southern-trained, typically Eurocanadian summer students) is problematic. To paraphrase that grade two teacher from Fort Simpson, water is part of northern Aboriginal cultural practices and water safety practitioners were (if you will excuse the pun) missing the proverbial boat.

After receiving funding, my students and I spent four years working in seven NWT and Nunavut communities. Rather than looking for ways in which community members failed to follow mainstream safety practices, we took the time to ask community members how they and their ancestors had stayed safe in the past; we asked about the messages that they had been told as children in order to stay safe around the water; and we asked them about the content that they believed would be important in water safety programs. We did not assume, as my 20-year-old self had in Dorset all those years ago, that the problem was a *lack* of aquatics programming and people choosing to make risky decisions. Instead of viewing northerners as being the problem, we viewed Eurocentric aquatic programs as the potential problem.

Over the course of my research, I was met with a great deal of skepticism. One well-known national newspaper columnist even devoted an entire blog entry to the apparent stupidity of my research. There was, she insisted, no such thing as "northern" water safety—the swimming lessons that she took at summer camp should be good enough for any Canadian child. The comments on her story ranged from people calling into question how I could have possibly earned a doctorate to others saying that I should be left on an island with all the other "left-wing academic kooks." To me, the reaction to my research showed the extent to which Eurocanadian cultural supremacy is so engrained in many aspects of life in Canada that it becomes difficult for many to imagine alternatives.

The alternatives that community members offered to mainstream water safety programs and messages were ingenious and, of course, tightly linked to their understandings of their own culture, environment, and needs. During about 120 interviews, northern residents told my students and me about the ways in which they had stayed safe in the past. For instance, participants from Taloyoak and Pangnirtung, Nunavut, told us about caribou skin's flotation properties. We were told stories of children who had fallen overboard but who floated—not because they were wearing mainstream personal flotation devices, but because they were wearing caribou-skin coats. We were also told that sealskin boots, if inflated and tied at the top, could be used as a flotation device. The inclusion of knives on boating trips was deemed to be very important, too. Interviewees told us that knives could be sunk into pieces of floating ice, which are common in summertime in some bodies of water in the Arctic, and then used to pull oneself out of the frigid waters if one were to fall in.

Oral traditions, too, played a role in community-based approaches to water safety. Inuit participants recounted stories about *Qallupilluit,* female sea monsters who take children who go too close to sea ice down to the bottom of the ocean, where they will live for the rest of their lives without ever seeing their parents again. Many participants recalled hearing such stories as children and how they were absolutely terrified by them. Indeed, this oral tradition was particularly effective in keeping Inuit children out of risky situations involving ice.

Northern traditional technologies and oral traditions have played important roles in aquatic-based safety in the past and they continue to do so in the present, but knowledge about these technologies and oral traditions is marginalized in mainstream water, boat, and ice safety programs. Instead, the assumption—which was so clearly articulated by the aforementioned newspaper columnist—remains that Eurocanadian-based programs and messages are superior to those used by Aboriginal peoples since time immemorial, and that the only people qualified to teach water, boat, and ice safety are those with formal qualifications (like my 20-year-old self), even though they potentially have absolutely no experience on arctic waters or ice.

Importantly, none of the northerners I interviewed advocated for the complete abandonment of Eurocanadian technologies; indeed, most thought that survival suits and personal flotation devices were of vital importance when boating. What they argued instead was that there is room for both Aboriginal forms of knowledge and Eurocanadian knowledge—that if the strengths of each approach were combined, aquatics-based injuries and fatalities might be reduced. In one community in which we conducted research, Pangnirtung, Nunavut, we did exactly that. We took the Department of Transportation's Pre-Departure Checklist and augmented it with items that local people deemed necessary, like hooked harpoons, knives, rifles, and ammunition. Community members told us that if that list were printed on thermoses, an item frequently taken on boating and snow-mobiling trips, then they would be likely to see the list each time they participated in an aquatics-based activity. Following their guidance, we thus printed the message on thermoses in both Inuktitut (the Inuit language) and English and had them distributed. Of all my attempts at collaborative research, the thermos is the one of which I am most proud. To me, it illustrates the power of meaningful partnerships and the ways in which research can be used to meet northerners' self-defined needs in the area of sport and recreation for development. Rather than seeing Aboriginal northerners as the ones in need of "development," the thermoses highlight how two bodies of expert knowledge can be brought together in a way that emphasizes the strengths of each and allows for a strong exchange of knowledge. When these forms of knowledge are combined, I would propose that the results reflect the best possible outcome. My previous attempts at conducting collaborative programs and research in the North, where I was mostly gently, though sometimes aggressively, challenged to examine my own assumptions, prepared me to do collaborative work about which I can feel proud.

CONCLUSIONS

Though at times painful (for both myself and Aboriginal northerners), I fervently believe that my spectacular failings in my previous work in sport for development in the Canadian North taught me a great deal about the ways in which sport-for-development programs—whether geared towards drowning prevention or sport and recreation leadership development—need to be rooted in local people's cultures. While this is certainly not ground-breaking insight, it has taken me many years to learn about the extent to which my own White, middle-class upbringing in Canada's largest city influenced my ability to design, implement, and later conduct research on sport and recreation programming with Aboriginal communities in the Canadian North. Indeed, I am still learning.

As a professor, I try to share the stories of both my successes and failures with my students in the hope that they (and the communities with which they work) will face less steep learning curves than those upon which I both climbed and tumbled. Nevertheless, I can only teach from my own perspective, which has inherent shortcomings. It is thus my strong desire that Aboriginal peoples from the Canadian North will become professors in greater numbers so that they can continue to challenge the ways in which non-Aboriginal peoples understand the development of sport and recreation in our diverse country. Their voices are critical in the development of more reflexive—and thus I would argue effective—sport-for-development researchers and practitioners. I leave you below with a few thoughts and reflections:

1. I always tell my graduate students, "first, do no research." Indeed, I believe you will do your best work if at first you do not focus on the work itself. Your initial job should be building relationships with community members. You may actually be doing your best work when you are sitting and sharing tea with community members, volunteering in a classroom, or popping into someone's office so that you can learn about his or her job. In so doing, you will build yourself a network that will enable you to be far more successful in the work that you have been hired to do.

2. Northern Aboriginal peoples are experts on their own lives. Many Eurocanadians assume that formal education and qualifications equate with expertise and will equate with job success in the North. Such an approach is problematic in that it marginalizes those who have not been afforded opportunities for such formal recognition, and it also ignores the expertise that can be accrued through life experience. Northern Aboriginal peoples have an excellent understanding of what will and will not work for their communities; indeed, their communities have experienced the results of others' attempts—both successful and unsuccessful—at research and sport and recreation programming. Any attempt to create programs without their meaningful input will result in programs that are less likely to be successful. If you allow yourself to be vulnerable by admitting that you can only be successful by learning from them, particularly about their culture, and that you do not have all of the answers, you will be better able to build not only successful programs, but also relationships based on cooperation and trust.

3. Non-Aboriginal peoples can play important roles as allies to Aboriginal peoples and in learning from Aboriginal communities. Such allies can bring that knowledge back to their own communities to help to increase everyone's cross-cultural competence.

4. My final recommendation is to take a strengths-based approach. Currently, many sport-for-development programs seek to identify and then address deficits (e.g., drug use, teen pregnancy, delinquency). A strengths-based approach, by contrast, is one that assumes that an individual or a community has strengths, and not just deficits, and that the recognition of these strengths can result in people being better positioned to bring about self-defined positive change in their own lives. Such an approach takes the emphasis off the importance of external resources and experts, and instead focuses on community members' talents and capabilities. Without a doubt, the northerners with whom I have worked and conducted research are the strongest, most resilient people I have ever met.

SPORT FOR PEACE AND SOCIAL JUSTICE

More than Just Medals: Athletes' Storied Experiences with Sport for Development and Peace

Erin Cameron, Ann Peel, Marko Begovic, and Scott Sandison

For this chapter, we, four elite athletes, endeavor to use storytelling methodology to explore our experiences in sport and sport for development and peace (SDP). In an effort to move beyond Western notions of scientific inquiry and ideas of objectivity, we employ storytelling to acknowledge our presence in the relationship with our ideas, and the processes through which these ideas were formed. Herein, we share our sport experiences, on and off the field, and how these experiences fundamentally changed our ideas in, of, and about sport. Finally, we draw from our experiences in order to build an argument for the important role SDP has played in our development as athletes and as human beings. We conclude with a call for amateur sport systems around the world to consider bridging athlete development with SDP. By sharing our different stories in sport and SDP, we not only hope to breathe meaning into our lived experiences, but we also hope to promote reflexive narrative as an approach that creates space for others to reflect and share their own sport and SDP experiences.

ANN PEEL: THE PROCESS OF BECOMING

A blonde, lean Canadian woman (Glenda Reiser) wins the 1,500m at the Universiade in Moscow, Russia, in 1972. A blonde, lean 11-year-old girl, her very being swelling with patriotic pride as she watches, decides who she will be: a runner, a runner who wins gold for her country.

I grew up an outsider. The daughter of a Canadian Foreign Service officer specializing in Eastern Europe, I was raised in Ankara, Madrid, Prague, Moscow, and Vienna. I was an active kid, always playing. An early memory is of a teacher in Prague once commenting that it was the first time she had seen me without the scabbed knees and scrapes of active playground life. I always won the ball kick and triumphed in school sport days. Self-identification as an athlete came early.

Self-identification as different arrived concurrently. You cannot grow up an outsider and be unaware of what surrounds you and of how you are not connected to where you are. I struggled with relatedness. Sport gave me a sense of belonging, and fed my overwhelming need for autonomy, perhaps itself an assertive response to that sense of difference. I have always enjoyed huge personal energy and a sense of destiny. Together they made for an accomplished, yet isolated, child.

As I struggled with my sense of difference, I also spent my formative years in places where people put their beliefs on the line. We were closely involved with dissidents in both Prague and Moscow. In Prague they were writers; in Moscow, artists. They were people of ideas and intellect. Their lives were difficult, their stories immensely powerful, and their circumstances dreadful (the Russian government would permit non-Soviet art as long as the artist agreed to spend three months of every year in a mental institution to acknowledge that to paint anything other than official art was an act of personal insanity). Not surprisingly, early experiences taught me that one must be prepared to fight for one's beliefs, that greatness lies in moral courage and in creativity.

On our return to Canada for high school, I was completely lost. Children in the Canada of the 1970s, a place I had romanticized and longed for, didn't know their geopolitics, turned their noses up at kebabs and moussaka, had never read Solzhenitsyn, and had no interest in the ballet or opera. They'd never even ridden the metro. I was a freak.

Desperate, I turned to what I knew best and lost myself in dance and running. At the offer of a classmate, I joined a track club and competed for my school in track and Nordic skiing. Fortunately, our teams were good. We won Ontario Federation of School Athletic Associations competitions consistently, and five of us ended up on national teams. Those successes created an appetite for excellence that has never been satiated.

I also discovered race-walking. In grade 12 I headed off to the World Cup of Racewalking and finished seventh. With a series of great, committed coaches, a supportive track club, and the company of teammates, I felt part of something bigger than myself for the first time. No longer an outsider, I was at the center of an endeavor to build track and field in Canada. It felt great.

Because of the experiences in my early years, I think I was always aware of myself as a member (or not) of society. I did not see myself in isolation, just as different. I always knew that one had to contribute, to be part of the larger world, and that to do so was good for the self as well as for others.

As I gained stature in race-walking, I learned there would be many times when my willingness to fight for fairness would be put to the test. The first was in 1980 when, after winning the Nationals, I was told there was no women's Olympic race-walk. I returned to university, to a class with Bruce Kidd, an activist and runner extraordinaire, who immediately challenged me to do something about it.

Raised to believe that what mattered was effort and merit, despite all evidence to the contrary, I had no idea that women had been so excluded from sport. Bruce sowed the seed for a lifetime of activism in sport to support the rights of athletes, women, and more recently, to expand the opportunities for children in Canada and overseas to discover the immense personal and societal power of sport. Sport is my way of building a stronger world. It is my way of reconciling my passion with my difference. Sport gives all people a way to belong.

Bruce helped me run a worldwide campaign for a women's Olympic race-walk. We succeeded in 1988 when the International Olympic Committee added a women's event to the Barcelona Games in 1992. Along the way, I became deeply involved in sport politics. I joined the Board of the Canadian Track and Field Association (now Athletics Canada) as athletes rep, along with many other boards and committees. One cannot change a situation unless one is intimately familiar with the status quo.

The turning point from active participation as an athlete representative to impassioned activist was the moment the Canadian Olympic Association (COA, now the Canadian Olympic Committee) rejected the athlete report to the Dubin inquiry, which had been established in response to the positive doping test of sprinter Ben Johnson.

As the vice chair of the Athletes Council of the COA, in the late 1980s, I worked with other members of the athlete executive committee to establish cross-country groupings of athletes to discuss what we needed to succeed in sport. Overwhelmingly, we had all determined that we needed an independent athlete voice. Additionally, in response to Ben's test, we prepared a briefing for the COA on our views that doping was endemic in sport, and sport in Canada had to respond.

When the COA decided not to include our views in their report to Dubin, the athlete group based in Toronto decided not to wait. In 1991 we founded the independent Canadian Athletes Association (now AthletesCAN). This decision changed the Canadian sport landscape quite radically and is one of which I am particularly proud.

What followed were four years as co-chair and a lifetime of commitment to fairness and equal opportunity in sport. One could not ask for a more rewarding or meaningful passion. It compels me to this day.

ERIN CAMERON: FINDING MY VOICE

I grew up in a small French farming community in the Canadian prairies. I was free to roam, explore the woods, play in the streams, sing as loud as I wanted, and dance wildly. In most of the snapshots taken of me as a little girl I seem to always be moving. I was a spirited kid with a high degree of energy. On our farm, my favorite jobs were to collect the sap from the maple trees in the spring (I knew exactly which trees produced the sweetest syrup) and to look after our animals. Through these early years, I developed a strong connection to place, community, and moving as a way of being.

When I was 6, the same year I started school, I started taking skating lessons. I fell in love with skating immediately. I loved flying around the ice as fast as I could; it made me feel like I could fly. This wasn't the case with school. In school, I would count the minutes until recess or gym and struggled to understand why we had to sit to learn (wasn't moving integral to learning?). Over the years I excelled in anything that involved moving the body. I participated in every school sports team I could throughout junior high and high school while maintaining my first love, skating. By the time I was 10 I was skating six days a week and competing provincially and nationally.

In grade eight I had my first injury (stress-fractured vertebrae), so I began cycling for cross training. Despite returning to skating a few months later, I continued to cycle in the summers. In 1996, I was inspired by fellow Winnipeg cyclist Clara Hughes, watching her win two bronze medals at the Atlanta Olympic Games. I remember thinking "I'm tall and have red hair. I want to be like her!" I liked the idea of a sport with an objective finish line so I traded in my skates for a bike.

As I excelled in cycling; I saw my actions being watched by younger athletes. I remembered how Clara had been a powerful role model for me, and I wanted to do the same for others. It was for this reason that I joined a British Columbia motivational speaking group called *The Esteem Team*. With them I had the opportunity to speak to school classes of all ages and all sizes about goal setting and my experiences in sport. I shared my dreams of becoming an Olympic athlete and would direct the question back to them: "What are your dreams?" Often it was the students sitting in the back row, those you least expected, who would speak up. After one presentation I had a teacher approach me to say thank you for reminding her that despite their resistance to schooling, each and every kid has dreams and that he or she should not give up on some of them so quickly.

With growing confidence in my abilities to engage and empower audiences, I started publishing a weekly sports column called "Gearing Up" in *The Carillon,* a rural Manitoban newspaper. I endeavored to share my experiences gearing up for the Olympics with my community. To my surprise I started hearing back from the community, and in one "Letter to the Editor" one community member wrote, "Erin, I thank you for your candor, your perception and for your open mind." It was through these experiences and hearing back from my community that I began to think about the privilege of athletes, the role of athletes in society, and the development of athletes. In other words, I was beginning to see that while athletes learn to internalize everything (failure, performance, success), they are not immune to their contexts and are shaped by the systems and communities that surround them. As the saying goes, "It takes a community to raise a child;" I also believe it takes a community to raise an athlete.

It was during this time, as I reconnected to my community, that injury plagued me again, but this time it would inevitably change the course of my athletic journey. While it took sports specialists from across the country over a year to diagnose my problem, I began to seriously explore who I was outside of sport and who I was outside of being an athlete. This questioning continued as I finished my undergraduate degree and lived for a summer in Pangnirtung, an Inuit community on Baffin Island, Canada. I had grown up listening to my grandfather tell stories about being a Hudson's Bay fur trader in the North. I had always wanted to go there someday. I spent almost three months in the Arctic learning to speak Inuktitut, listening to Inuit elders share stories, and organizing summer youth activities. It was there that I learned the true power of sport to connect, innovate, and educate. But it wasn't me doing the educating; I was being educated by the youth. They taught me many lessons for which I am indebted, and they continue to be voices in my head, reminding me about the true meaning, culture, and context of sport.

After having surgery, I decided not to return to cycling and instead began working in the field of communications and actively advocating for a different kind of sport. I developed, organized, and spoke at a Development through Sport workshop at the 2006 Annual AthletesCAN Forum designed to engage athletes in dialogue about their roles in society. I became politically involved and was elected by my peers to sit on a number of boards, including AthletesCAN, the Coaching Association of Canada, and Sport Manitoba. I pursued a master's degree to explore what I believed to be a shifting ideology towards a social consciousness among the athlete population. I wanted to better understand why other athletes were giving back. In listening to athletes share their stories, it became evident that not only did responsible citizenship have a positive impact on an athlete's performance and continued participation in sport, it was vital to the athlete's human development.

Through my research and other activities I have become aware of the historical, social, political, and social contexts of sport, and with this lens I feel I have a lifetime of passion ahead of me for advocating meaningful change in sport and SDP.

SCOTT SANDISON: CHANGE MYSELF TO CHANGE THE WORLD

The year 2003 was to be a great year for me. We had the Indoor World Cup in February and then the Pan American Games in July. It was supposed to be the year that I stepped forward to prove myself as a top-level international field hockey player, while booking my ticket to the Athens Olympics. Things didn't quite go according to plan.

I struggled at the Indoor World Cup and the team finished sixth, when a better performance could have easily led us to the semifinals. The Pan American Games were not so straightforward, and I saw my contribution in playing time significantly reduced from the year before. Still, it's a team game and we were on course for our Olympic berth as we took on Argentina in the finals. Only the gold medal winners would make their way to the Olympics. It was a hard-fought battle; Canada vs. Argentina always is in men's field hockey. This time we came out on the short end. We lost 1-0, and with that, our Olympic dreams ended.

I was very disappointed, to say the least. It had been the focus in my life over the previous four years to compete at the Olympics, and now I didn't know what to do with myself. After some serious self-reflection, I decided I needed to get away. I looked into Canada's International Development Agency's youth abroad program. They sponsored several nongovernment organizations and funded their placements of interns in developing countries. I applied to a few placements and found myself heading to Botswana with Commonwealth Games Canada's International Development through Sport Unit.

This was another experience that didn't go according to plan, as the day before I was to travel to Botswana I received a phone call saying the partner organization that was to host me was no longer prepared to do so. That translates roughly into no job, no idea, and no plan. Commonwealth Games Canada was extremely supportive of my needs, though, and together we decided that I would head out to Gaborone and work with other partners they had connections with.

I lived in Botswana for three and a half months working with their Field Hockey Association, with an agenda to increase the number of youth participating in hockey around the country. Roughly two months into my stay I traveled to Namibia to take part in a training workshop run by the Kicking AIDS Out! Network. It was a weeklong course in combining sport and play with HIV/AIDS education. Taking part in that course helped to open my eyes to the breadth of the diversity of sport options. I left inspired and wanting to incorporate HIV/AIDS education into everything I was doing.

Through that experience an opportunity arose in South Africa to work with an organization called SCORE. They were working with diverse populations and communities in South Africa, Namibia, and Zambia, helping to bring sport and play to areas in need. I continued working with Kicking AIDS Out! through SCORE and found myself running activities in several places. South Africa was, and still is, the country with the highest number of people infected with HIV. The work we were doing there was of great benefit. I can remember running Kicking AIDS Out! activities in Khayelitsha (a township on the outskirts of Cape Town) during World AIDS Day, where the games helped lead to some very frank and straightforward discussions with the youth who were taking part. Their enjoyment in the games, combined with their obvious learning, reaffirmed to me that there was merit in this approach.

Before the end of that year I would run the first ever Kicking AIDS Out! trainer workshops in Malawi and in the Caribbean, helping to increase the knowledge and awareness of sport for development in those regions. Working with community and youth leaders in these areas was really inspiring, as they all shared their positive experiences of sport.

When I finished my internship at Commonwealth Games Canada, I returned home to decide what path I would pursue. Having had such a powerful experience in Africa, it was not so easy for me to return to life as it was before. I spent a fair amount of time debating what I was going to do with my future. I returned to the national team, but I also applied for a few international jobs. I was really close to taking a sport-for-development job in Sudan, but decided that my sporting career had a limited window of opportunity, and so, I made the choice to once again compete full time and attempt to qualify for the Olympics.

It was a difficult transition—playing sport at the Olympic level requires everything you have, but I always did my best to remain involved with sport for development whenever I could. I ended up on the board of AthletesCAN, a Canadian-based organization for all national team athletes, and in 2006 at the Melbourne Commonwealth Games (after competing), I ran a workshop open to athletes using their status as national team athletes to create change in their communities.

Then in 2007 we won the Pan American Games and qualified for the Beijing Olympics. The dream had finally come to be reality. We finished 10th at the Olympics, not what we were aiming for, but we put in some good performances and showed that we could handle ourselves with the teams at the top level.

Post-Olympics I had always thought that I would retire from international competition, but somehow I ended up playing another two years. As things started winding down on the field, off the field I started looking at more ways to get involved with sport for development.

The biggest step for me came when I retired from the national team and moved to London, England. I moved there to play with and coach a hockey club, with the intention of getting another job on the side. In searching for work I found my way to Right to Play. As the world's biggest sport-for-development charity, reaching 1,000,000 children on a weekly basis around the world, I was very excited to start working with them. I began in their education team doing mostly school outreach and have since moved into working with other athletes in promoting the cause. High-performance athletes are uniquely positioned, not only to be fantastic spokespeople because of their status in the public eye, but also because they understand the benefits sport and play can yield. As well as being involved with Right to Play, I worked as a program director for World at Play, a small sport-for-development charity that takes international volunteers abroad to work alongside local caregivers to offer sport and play opportunities to children in need. For example, traveling through the Balkans was a real highlight, as I was able to be hands-on and deliver programming. It reinvigorated me, and I saw that sport and play truly are languages in their own right.

MARKO BEGOVIC: A DEEPLY CONTEXTUAL EXPERIENCE

After WWII, the development of sports in Eastern Europe was heavily supported and regulated by the state. This resulted in the emergence of Yugoslavia as a powerhouse in a number of individual and team sports worldwide. Montenegro reaped the benefits of this development as it gained independence, while at the same time it encountered a lack of institutional support for the growth of sports. In the last 25 years, the Montenegro society has changed dramatically. Capitalism was introduced, yet the country easily slipped back into a bloody war and living standards plummeted (salaries averaged $5 per month). Within this context, it has been impossible to create a sustainable sport system. Even within elementary schools, high schools, and universities, sport suffers from a lack of prioritization, equipment, and physical education specialists. According to the available data, only 4% of students are involved in organized university sport events. Even if our government says that practicing sport and physical activity is open to everybody, from an investigation of the sport infrastructure in Montenegro, it is obvious that there is not enough "space" for recreation and amateur sport.

In Montenegro, sport is seen only through the prism of professional sport, namely the results. Management structure in most sports organizations can be primarily defined as maximization of infrastructure that is renting the courts and equipment for wealthier citizens. Not enough space is left for developing sports systems to enable the integration of a larger population into specific sports. The strategy for the allocation of state funds is not well defined, and it is unusual for funds to get to where they are most needed.

While I have no formal data to support this, I am privy to information due to my involvement in many formal meetings. I regret that a number of Montenegro athletes are becoming social problems after their careers. Essentially, they have no fallback plan, no skills outside of athletics, and no social, medical, or any other type of insurance. This is in part due to a system that fails to help athletes develop the necessary knowledge and skills for careers after sport.

In response to this climate, and as an athlete who sees the potential of sport, I was inspired to create an SDP platform, primarily for reaching the UN Millennium Development Goals through sport, with a specific focus on education of youth, promotion of gender equality, environment protection, partnership building, and creating a sustainable sport system. The platform, Game Set Peace, has been warmly welcomed by the general population and formally adopted by the United Nations Development Program in Montenegro, the Montenegrin Olympic Committee, the Prime Minister, the Ministry for Minority and Human Rights, the Ministry for Finance, the Ministry for Tourism and Sustainable Development, and the University Sport Federation.

Since we have been experiencing a social crisis for more than two decades, youth, especially orphans, are being discriminated against and excluded from society. The Game Set Peace program created a project to organize camps for kids from the only orphanage institution in Montenegro, with the specific mission of creating an environment for these kids to gain life skills (responsibility, motivation, and hard work), work towards developing healthy habits, and developing individual skills based on their own strengths. Mr. Igor Vušurovic (winner of an Olympic gold medal in volleyball in Sidney 2000) was the ambassador of this project. The program introduced several sports: tennis, soccer, kayaking, running, and PE classes, along with the hosting of various workshops. Furthermore, Game Set Peace organized several university events in tennis and track and field, using different approaches to attract students to participate. Another very important part of this project was the organization of the Special Olympic Day and Women and Sport Day, when five hundred kids and adults aged 5 to 25 participated in several sports on the University of Montenegro campus, with the clear message: Sport is for all, regardless of gender, age, or ability.

Not only were these events organized in line with the highest international standards in environmental sustainability (*leave no trace* methodology), the projects were also used to enlist the participation of girls, and women in sport. This was the first evidence-based research project assessing the current status of girls' and women's sport participation in Montenegro, at all institutional levels. The research identified those who played sport in Montenegro, and the factors (family, education, economic, gender stereotypes, and so on) that contributed to, or limited, girls' and women's participation. It was found that women comprise only 10% of all individuals in sport at the national level; they hold only 8.8% of coaching positions; only 13.3% of national-level referees are women; and there are no female sport delegates at all. This revealed an overall gender inequality in sports in Montenegro. As a result, Games Set Peace has since organized for girls and women a number of sports camps, two trial soccer camps (30 female soccer players), and a trip to the United Arab Emirates to play in an international tournament.

I believe one of the biggest successes of the Game Set Peace program has been its focus on partnership building. Through its efforts it has created an environment where a community and athletes are connected. It has initiated informal links between local authorities, commissions, and ministries along with international institutions, to introduce sport in Montenegro as a way of striving for a healthier state through various national projects.

While I am happy with all that Game Set Peace has been able to accomplish, I believe we still have a long way to go. For example, I believe we are still missing fundamental research that would help guide governmental stakeholders in creating strategies for schools, health and recreation, and persons with disabilities. To create these strategies there needs to be a change in the philosophy of sport, one that shifts focus from professional sports to sport for all. This transition from professional sport to a sustainable sport system would require the involvement of several governmental institutions, such as the Institute for Public Health, the Ministry for Education and Sport, the Ministry of Science, the Finance Ministry, and the Montenegrin Olympic Committee.

All those individuals working in the Game Set Peace program are driven by the belief that the time for change in sport is upon us. Montenegro, a young country with an unclear domestic policy and foreign policy, will fail to lay the foundation of a sustainable sport system if it does not respond quickly to the current situation in sport. Improving the system of sport in Montenegro will not only change the philosophy of sport within our country, but it has the potential to improve the health and well-being of our youth, communities, and country.

DISCUSSION

While each of our stories varies in context and content, all four of us have experienced the power of SDP to change our perspectives in, of, and around sport. Through our experiences in SDP, we became more than just athletes; we became athlete-citizens. We engage in the world. But as we will argue in this section, and as our combined stories suggest, none of our SDP experiences were inspired by sport, but rather, because of sport. Due to sport-related encounters with frustration, identity crisis, individual failure, and national failure, we each went beyond the current sport models of athlete development to find our own ways to continue to develop as athletes and citizens inside and outside of sport.

A SHIFT IN IDEOLOGY: ATHLETE SOCIAL RESPONSIBILITY

While sport's influence is undeniable, much has been written about the influential role some athletes have played in sport and society. Consider for a moment athletes like Billie Jean King, Jackie Robinson, and Muhammad Ali, all of whom were athletes and activists. These examples not only challenge the pervasive paradigm that athletes must have a singular focus and devote all their time to athletic (physical) performance, but they also indicate that athletes can be committed to athletic excellence while developing as human beings and active citizens of the world. While there has been growing attention toward the role and responsibility of professional athletes in society, amateur athletes are often discouraged and even punished by the amateur sport system for engaging in such activities.

One of the most well-known examples is when US athletes Tommie Smith and John Carlos, medalists in the 200 meter event at the 1968 Olympics, were stripped of their medals for their deliberate actions to expose racism in the US sport system. While it was accepted that countries were using sport as a political platform (for instance, the Olympic boycotts of 1980 and 1984), it clearly was not okay for the athletes to do the same. While amateur sport systems have sustained the belief that athletes should focus only on sport, athletes themselves are demonstrating that this needn't be true.

Consider also the actions of Canadian speed skater Clara Hughes, who after winning gold at the 2006 Torino Winter Olympics, announced that she was donating $10,000 of her own money to Right to Play, an international humanitarian organization that uses sport and play programs to improve health, develop life skills, and foster peace for children and communities in some of the most disadvantaged areas of the world (rightto-play.com). That same winter, Canadian Olympic skiers Thomas Grandi and Sara Renner launched Play It Cool, an innovative environmental program that teams elite athletes who are concerned about global warming and are committed to making life changes to reduce climate impact with the David Suzuki Foundation (davidsuzuki.org). While these examples are both Canadian, the movement of sport development is international in scope. For example, prior to the 2008 Beijing Olympic Games, amateur athletes around the world formed an international coalition to raise awareness about the crisis in Darfur, Sudan (teamdarfur.org).

So we ask, what is inspiring these athletes to act beyond themselves? While more research is needed in this area, Erin's 2009 master's thesis offers a place to start. What emerged from her study of 15 elite Canadian athletes engaged in social and political activities was the athlete social responsibility (ASR) framework. This framework highlights four common phases of an athlete's development toward a strong sense of responsible citizenship in sport and society: *narrowing, defining, opening,* and *redefining.* Athletes indicated that early in their careers sport provided discipline, direction, and purpose (narrowing). They indicated that sport began to define who they were (defining), but at some point this changed (opening), and they found that becoming socially and politically active outside of sport was instrumental to their personal development, improved performance, and continued participation in elite sport (redefining). They voiced frustration that the current sport system had done little to encourage such engagement throughout their athletic careers and claimed that sport needs to do a better job of supporting both an athlete's physical and psychosocial development. They articulated a need for sport to merge the defining and opening phases of an athlete's development through facilitated guidance and intention. Arguably, if the amateur sport system were to bridge the relational distance between the physical and the psychosocial development of an athlete, it would not only benefit athletes, but it might also help to raise the social consciousness of the sport culture.

While research has supported the belief that athletes begin sport for self-interested purposes, the emerging shift towards responsibility offers sport directions for the future. By athletes experiencing other dimensions of sport, the value of sport moves beyond the field of play and embeds the experience into community and society. It provides athletes with an opportunity to maintain a balance between a singular pursuit of athletic excellence and contributing to a strengthened civil society. As such, amateur sport systems would do well to consider the role of SDP within athlete development models.

CONCLUSIONS

We have explored our experiences within SDP and, as a result, have witnessed the current model of athlete development that privileges the development of performance over people. We propose that early exposure of young people to the power of sport as a tool for engagement would help to change their view of, in, and about sport. We propose that young athletes would benefit from early exposure to a robust view of sport's power in society. We hope that through our stories you have been encouraged to think about ideas in, of, and about sport and its role in the world.

Drawing from our experiences, here are a few more specific suggestions for sport scholars, leaders, administrators, coaches, and athletes:

1. More research is needed that explores SDP and athlete development models (such as the long-term athlete development model) that would serve to inform best practices in sport.

2. Sport leaders, coaches, and administrators need to acknowledge the benefits of an athlete's performance on and off the field. For example, the recognition that athletes might also enhance their performances by engaging in community-building initiatives, would allow sport leaders (including coaches, administrators, and others) to consider the impact and implications of such activities.

3. More discussion needs to take place at decision-making tables about the role of sport in society.

4. We need to offer the National Coaching Certification Program Level 1 Community Coach (which is connected to long-term athletic development) to all members of provincial and national teams on a complementary basis. This would ensure that they are qualified to coach kids in multiple sports and can become involved in sports camps in their communities.

5. Provincial sport organizations (PSOs) could offer athletes and former athletes priority for coaching positions at training camps and summer camps with which they are affiliated.

6. PSOs and national sport organizations (NSOs) could connect with funders (such as the Jumpstart Foundation of Canadian Tire) to create coaching opportunities for their athletes in the community at JumpStart-affiliated events and programs.

7. PSOs and NSOs could connect with organizations such as Right to Play or Play It Cool, to create volunteer opportunities in the community for their athletes.

8. If athletes belong to speaker bureaus or mentorship programs, connect these programs with ongoing opportunities for working with young people.

9. Encourage athlete participation in governance by ensuring that athlete representatives are elected fairly by all member athletes and by supporting their learning to be effective leaders by enabling someone on the board or committee to which the athlete is elected to act as the athlete's mentor.

10. Recognize athlete participation in the community on the PSO/NSO website.

Fortunate Tales of a Decent Sociologist, a Failed Footballer, and a Reluctant Peace Maker

John Sugden

I finished my undergraduate education in 1974 and left university with a thirst for knowledge and a passion for my sport of choice, Association Football (soccer). Like many of my peers I also had wanderlust. I would partially satiate this by spending a year as a volunteer in Africa's Sudan followed by five years as a postgraduate in the USA. If upon graduation I were to have been be asked, "Is there anywhere you don't want to go to?", my answer would have been quick and unequivocal: "Northern Ireland and Israel/Palestine." In both cases this response would have been fuelled by the media's presentation of these hazardous places. The fact that I was destined to spend 14 years living and working in the former—where both my children were born—and spend almost as long leading peace-building programs in the latter, was, with hindsight, fortuitous. I have learned so much and met and been befriended and mentored by so many wonderful characters—the kind of personalities that only a lifetime of struggle against adversity can produce. What follows is my attempt to show how my continuing personal journey has influenced the way I think more generally about the role of sport in conflict resolution and peace building in deeply divided societies.

BELFAST UNITED

"Remember, remember the fifth of November" is a well-known phrase and part of a short poem dedicated to the memory of the "Gunpowder Plot" in 1605. On that day a group of dissident Catholic aristocrats, led by Guy Fawkes, failed in their attempt to explode a bomb beneath the Palace of Westminster with the aim of assassinating the pro-Protestant monarch, King James I of England. This was but one manifestation of the often bloody conflict between Catholics and Protestants that was a defining feature of the political climate that prevailed across Europe in the 16th and 17th centuries. This kind of sectarianism faded almost everywhere in the ensuing centuries as political and sometimes military conflicts within and between nations; however, for historically specific reasons, it continues to define the contemporary contours of social and political divisions in a few regions. Nowhere was this more pronounced than in Ireland, where a centuries-long struggle for national self-determination by the Irish in the face of British imperial rule continued to be articulated behind the banners of the two different versions of Christianity: Roman Catholicism and the Church of England. Irish independence in 1921 may have brought a temporary resolution to the national question, but it did so only through the creation of a British condominium in Northern Ireland. The fact that a British loyalist Protestant majority persisted in the face of a significant Irish nationalist and Catholic minority set the stage for further sectarian conflict and bloodshed.

Which is why I remember, remember the fourth of November. The year was 1983 and that was the day that my engagement with sport and peace-building really began. I had just taken up my first full-time lecturing post at what was then called the Northern Ireland Polytechnic in Jordanstown on the outskirts of Belfast. Before that I had spent five years at the University of Connecticut, USA, studying for a master's and a PhD in the then-fledgling subdiscipline of sociology of sport. I had an undergraduate degree in politics and sociology and, as a postgraduate, had trained in physical education. To be offered an academic scholarship in the United States that would enable me to bring the two areas together was too good to turn down, but I had an agreement with my partner that as soon as I had finished my studies in the USA we would return to the UK and I would take the first job that came along. In the early 1980s academic posts in the UK were hard to come by, particularly in the infancy of the niche area that I had chosen. Thus when the post came available in Northern Ireland I had to apply, despite the sectarian conflict there. Known depreciatingly as the Troubles, the conflict bordered on an undeclared civil war, and it was peaking in the early 1980s, with shootings, bombings, rioting, and various acts of paramilitary gangsterism and state-sponsored retaliation and retribution occurring routinely.

Nevertheless, under impoverished circumstances I was delighted to be offered my first proper job, which I accepted without a moment's hesitation. The news was not so enthusiastically received by my partner and even less so by my late father, who at the time was working as a police detective for Special Branch with a particular brief for Irish-related terrorism, thus making his Belfast-bound son a potential target. Unperturbed, I arrived in Jordanstown for my first meeting with the senior course tutor who oversaw the BA honors in sports studies. At that meeting he gave me two memorable pieces of advice: first, he warned against having any intimate and amorous relationships with any of the students, and second, he counseled me not to bring local politics into the classroom. To begin with I obeyed both pieces of advice, but after November the fourth I decided that I could no longer follow the latter. On that day I was scheduled to be lecturing to a group of about 30 undergraduate students on the relationship between sport and politics. The students were a mix of Protestants and Catholics. The two different ethnoreligious groups only shared an educational environment because they were part of a small minority who had made it into higher education, which came as a bit of a shock to me. Otherwise, the physical and social sectarian geography of the Province kept them in separate neighborhoods, going to separate faith-based primary and secondary schools, and, of course, attending separate churches. Higher education was the first place these students shared a common curriculum. Perhaps ironically, the theme of that day's lecture was the role of sport in South Africa, another deeply divided society that, at the time, was mired in a racially defined struggle between pro government and antiapartheid movements and factions, within which sport played a significant role. I was in mid-sentence when—BOOM!—my voice was drowned out by the sound of a massive explosion that caused the blast-proof picture windows to vibrate. Students scattered to huddle against the far wall of the classroom. I looked out towards the adjacent teaching block and saw smoke and fire bellowing from a top-floor classroom, the remains of which seemed to be raining down from a hundred feet in the air. I remember rather pathetically asking nobody in particular, "I don't suppose that was the chemistry department?"

Of course, it wasn't the chemistry department. It was just another teaching room like mine, but instead of regular undergraduates it was full of Royal Ulster Constabulary police officers, who were taking a criminology examination as part of a course they were studying at the college. The Provisional Irish Republican Army had gotten wind of this gathering and decided that for them it constituted a legitimate target. They planted in the classroom ceiling a series of plastic-explosive bombs, which detonated to devastating effect. Three serving officers were killed and many more were seriously wounded, including the lecturer, who would never walk properly again. Thus, despite the wishes of the senior course tutor and out of no choice of mine, local politics had let itself in with a bang that could not be ignored.

Retrospectively, I can review this event as a kind of Damascene moment, but in reality it merely accelerated what had already become a growing area of concern for me. It is said we are what we eat. I prefer to say that as a sociologist steeped in the traditions of C. Wright Mills, I am where my sociological imagination takes me. That is to no small extent determined by where I am, whom I'm with, and what happens to me. So long as I was living in Northern Ireland, it was inevitable that the seismic social and political events that characterized the 14 years I spent there (1982-96) would shape my agenda both as a researcher and as an activist. Taking a leaf out of the book of the Chicago School, I turned Belfast into a living sociological laboratory as I used my critical sociological imagination along with an ethnographer's eyes and ears to map and interpret the city's sectarian geography in relation to its sports cultures.

While I had been employed to teach the students, they were also teaching me. The students were required to take part in a common curriculum, which included a full spectrum of practical and sport-related subjects, but during my first year it became clear that on certain subjects some students were voting with their feet and not attending. This was particularly the case with Gaelic Games, in which a significant number of Protestant students refused to take part. When confronted about this, they explained to me that for them this tradition of sports was emblematic of Irish nationalism, and they felt that in taking part they were betraying the embattled Loyalist cause. This was a fascinating revelation, and it triggered in me a curiosity that led to an extensive new research agenda. I wanted to unravel the complex relationship between sports participation and fandom and identity politics in Northern Ireland; this agenda generated several books and many research articles, written with colleagues. Despite the claims of sports administrators and related public officials, who insisted that sport offered a nonsectarian, neutral haven and escape from the Troubles, the broad conclusions we drew at the time suggested that, at best, sectarian divisions were reflected in the Province's sport culture and, at worst, sport exacerbated sectarian tensions.

At the same time I was also actively participating in sport and developing my credentials as a soccer coach, first for the college's men's football team, then for the combined Northern Ireland Universities representative XI. Ultimately, I coached for the all-Ireland student team that represented Ireland at the World Student Games in Japan in 1996. Once more I learned a huge amount from these experiences. To begin with, unlike Rugby Union, a game played almost exclusively by Protestants in Northern Ireland, or Gaelic Football, largely the preserve of Catholics, Association Football was played by both communities and at the college level the teams were quite mixed. As such, as I coached at the various levels, I noted that one consequence of successful exercises in team building that I undertook was that strong cross-sectarian bonds and friendships that developed, many of which endure to this day. Despite the pessimistic conclusions drawn in the previous paragraph, this taught me that if sport could be organized and delivered in appropriate ways, and if it could be prepared for and contested within a selected framework of antisectarian principles and values, then it could make a positive contribution to interpersonal and intercommunity relations.

Could this be done outside of higher education in ways that would expose less privileged sectors to sport's community relations potential? It was another atrocity that provided the trigger for me to attempt to answer this question. On March 16, 1988, in my role as coach and manager of the combined Northern Ireland Universities Football Team, I was driving a group of student footballers to a training session I had scheduled at the playing fields of Queens University in South West Belfast. It was a particularly tense period in the history of the Troubles. A week before, an IRA active service unit in Gibraltar was preparing to blow up an Army marching exercise when they were ambushed and killed by members of the British Army's elite SAS regiment. The three bodies had been returned to Belfast for burial that day, and little did I know as I approached the ring road below West Belfast's Milltown Cemetery that the funerals were underway. Suddenly, as if from nowhere, dozens of heavily armed British soldiers appeared in the middle of the road, causing me and fellow motorists to skid to a halt. I looked farther down the road and saw what appeared to be a mob chasing a man who was running towards us. This man turned out to be the rogue Ulster Defense Association gunman, Michael Stone, who moments before had infiltrated the funeral, throwing hand grenades and unleashing a hail of automatic gunfire into the crowd of mourners, killing three and injuring more than 60. I was witnessing his attempted escape. Responding to the urging of the military, I spun the car around, exited the ring road and sped off via an improvised route to the university playing fields. Thus I found myself sitting in stunned silence in the changing rooms amidst a mixed group of Catholic and Protestant footballers as we struggled to come to terms with what was happening around us and what we had just witnessed. As my emotions swung between helplessness and anger, I determined that from that point forward, rather than simply criticizing from the sidelines the role played by sport in the Province's fractured community structure, I needed to find a way to combine my contextual knowledge and coaching experience to make a positive contribution to building peace.

As stated, through my university sport experience I had learned that in relatively neutral settings, given a common cause and goal, a shared set of values, and committed mentors, a sport team was an excellent crucible within which to nurture intimacy and mutuality. I did not see why this experience had to be limited to groups that might be described as the relatively elite in Northern Ireland—people who were university educated. To this end, in cooperation with colleagues at the Institute of International Sport at the University of Rhode Island, USA, we developed the Belfast United concept. Using mainly soccer but also basketball, this was a sport program for Catholic and Protestant teenage boys drawn from some of the more entrenched and mutually hostile Belfast neighborhoods. Ethnoreligious mixed teams were shaped in the neutral setting of a university campus before being taken on playing and coaching tours of New England in the USA, where they were hosted in mixed pairs (Catholic and Protestant) by American families.

It wasn't always easy managing these groups. At the best of times, packs of teenage boys can be hard to handle, but sometimes out of adversity comes unexpected success.

One particular Belfast United tour featured a match between the Northern Ireland team and an all-star varsity X1 at the University of Rhode Island in front of a crowd of about 200 people. It was literally men against boys as Belfast's 15- and 16-year olds bravely went head to head with young athletes up to four or five years older than themselves. Trailing 1-0 with five minutes to go, Belfast United's 5'8" right back made a lung-bursting run and found himself one on one with the 6'2" URI goalkeeper. He slightly overran the ball and the big keeper scooped it up, only to find himself barged to the ground by the onrushing fullback, who himself was upended by the furious goalkeeper. Punches were thrown and then all hell broke loose as both teams, including both benches, converged on the URI penalty box to fight on the side of their respective champions. I looked on in horror as Protestant and Catholic boys from East and West Belfast fought side by side against their Yankee hosts. The URI coach ambled over to me and said, "Well, John, I guess this proves that your project's working!"

Weeks later, when I was back in Belfast, I got a call from the same coach who told me he wanted to offer the transgressing fullback a full college scholarship to study at URI and play soccer for the team. The lad in question took up that offer and played with distinction for the university for four years. After graduating he went on to complete his master's degree at the same institution.

In addition to anecdotes such as this, accompanying research and evaluation demonstrated that Belfast United did have a measurable, positive impact on the young people who participated. Although initially small in scale, Belfast United also helped to inspire larger and much more ambitious cross-community residential sport festivals both in Northern Ireland and the USA, and generally contributed to the emergence of the sport for development and peace movement.

Importantly, this intervention was not done in isolation from my other ongoing avenues of research and critical scholarship. On the contrary, applied knowledge about the structure, process, and politics of sport in Northern Ireland in general was used to inform and shape Belfast United and related grassroots interventions. At the same time, information emanating from research and evaluation of these interventions fed into a growing corpus of critical scholarship that in turn began to have an impact upon the policy community for sport in the Province—clusters of government, private, and voluntary stakeholders, as well as pressure groups that shaped the wider institutional agenda for sport in a given region. By the time I left in 1996, the Sports Council for Northern Ireland had developed and introduced a community relations policy for sport, while most local councils and sport governing bodies had employed dedicated sport and community relations officers. This was all part of a very complex interaction of social, economic, political, and civil society initiatives that were giving momentum to a peace process in the region. It is impossible to say precisely how much the combined critical interventions in sport in Northern

Ireland that I have had a hand in have contributed to the peace process there; however, I like to think that, in some small way, a more progressive, proactive, and politically sensitive approach to sport has contributed to making Northern Ireland a more peaceful and prosperous place to live, work, and play.

FOOTBALL FOR PEACE

The knowledge and experience gleaned from my days in Northern Ireland travelled with me when I took up a new post at the University of Brighton in 1996, but I had no conscious intentions of developing this line of work in my new surroundings. On the contrary, one of the main reasons I had changed positions was to work more closely with Alan Tomlinson, with whom I was collaborating in an investigation of politics and corruption in the International Federation of Association Football, football's world governing body. This new research venture would eventually yield three co-authored books and lead to another monograph based on undercover investigative research in the shadowy world of global football's underground economy.

These ventures, along with a full-time lecturing post, meant I had little room for much else. Thus, it was with some reluctance that in 2000 I agreed to meet with a group of well-meaning, nonaligned, private citizens who were frustrated with nightly news bulletins filled with scenes of conflict and violence in Israel and Palestine. They wanted to do something to contribute to the faltering peace process there. They believed football could be used as a vehicle to help overcome mistrust. One of them, Geoffrey Whitefield, a retired Baptist minister, had connections with the local universities and began asking around to find out if the local academic community could offer any advice or help. As someone who had experience in developing and directing sport-based community relations projects—albeit in a very different setting—I was invited to sit in on one of their meetings.

The meeting was chaired by David Bedford in his London office. At the time, David was the race director of the words largest mass-participation sporting event, the London Marathon. He had been an elite athlete himself and at one time had held the world record for the 10,000-meter run. In his mid-50s, David's longish, graying hair and bushy Pancho Villa-style moustache made him instantly recognizable.

As I sat in the meeting, I realized the group of individuals meant well, but had neither the knowledge base nor the "raw materials" to advance their good intentions. They would need access to resources, facilities, equipment and, above all, a professional staff and a reservoir of qualified volunteers. My work place at the University of Brighton is the Chelsea School of Sport, a dedicated sports department that, among other things, specializes in training physical education teachers and sport coaches at undergraduate and postgraduate levels. I realized that this fledgling endeavor, the group meeting in David Bedford's office, which had been given the rather grandiose and immodest working title of The World Sport Peace Project, could benefit greatly from our involvement.

Given my already crammed schedule, I sat through that first meeting determined to say as little as possible. However, as time wore on, I became more and more enticed by the potential of the project, first because of the level of operational complexity and, second and most importantly, because of its sociological challenge. One of the main reasons I had stayed in Northern Ireland for 14 years was that it offered so much in terms of sociological and political richness.

At that time I had only a limited understanding of the contextual detail and power relations and dynamics that inform the wider conflict in the Middle East, particularly issues specific to Israel and Palestine. I did, however, know enough to realize that there was a lot more to know. My experiences in Northern Ireland had taught me that those intent on engaging in this kind of sport-for-development work, if they are not to be perceived as clumsy and patronizing neocolonialists, need to do their homework.

The more I delved into the social and political context, the more fascinated I became. As my sociological understanding grew, I felt better informed to help to guide and develop the project through its various phases. Thus, when I was invited to the next meeting, not only did I go along, but I began to open my mouth and, more than 10 years later, had talked myself into being the overall director of the more modestly entitled Football for Peace (F4P) project.

What began as a relatively modest intervention involving one staff member and half a dozen volunteer coaches from the UK working with approximately 60 children from one community in Northern Israel, grew year by year until by 2010 over 50 volunteers were working on a series of parallel projects incorporating more than 40 Jewish and Arab communities and attracting around 1,000 children from all over Israel. F4P has since also launched development programs in Jordan and experimented with a project in Bethlehem in the Palestinian Authority's West Bank.

F4P's fourfold aims are to provide opportunities for social contact across community boundaries, promote mutual understanding, engender in participants a desire for and commitment to peaceful coexistence, and enhance sports skills and technical knowledge about sport. In order to achieve these goals, a dedicated values-based teaching curriculum has been developed, along with a coaching style through the modeling of which participants are encouraged to demonstrate appreciation of the basic qualities of good citizenship, namely respect, trust, responsibility, equality, and inclusivity. In summary, a series of cross-community sports partnerships (CCSPs) have been established, involving small clusters of Jewish and Arab towns and villages. In these CCSPs, over six consecutive days at alternative Jewish and Arab community venues, children are coached in mixed groups (Arab and Jewish), growing into teams and taking part in end-of-project football and multiactivity festivals. Parallel to the football training there is an off-pitch program of trust-building, recreational, and cultural activities. In respect for local traditions and customs, one project is for girls only and is staffed entirely by female coaches. In addition, F4P has biannual training camps—one in Europe and one in Israel—during which volunteer coaches from Israel and other countries are schooled in the methodology of F4P prior to helping with the delivery of the program during the summer months in Israel itself.

The philosophy underpinning the F4P programs in Israel and neighboring countries emphasizes social justice and human rights as the moral principles that underpin and guide the search for equality and peaceful co-existence among different ethnoreligious communities and political factions. Central to our modus operandi is the view that Israel will be better placed and more willing and able to move towards a peaceful settlement with the Palestinian Authority and with its neighboring Arab countries once it has developed equitable and harmonious relations with the 20% Arab and 80% Jewish populations living within its existing boundaries. We are not doing this in support of the status quo there, and neither are we involved in the business of normalization. Instead, we see our bridge-building work between Arab and Jewish communities inside Israel as part of a broader challenge to influence progressive social and political change in the wider region.

Specifically, F4P aims to use values-based sport coaching as a structure upon which to build bridges between neighboring Jewish and Arab towns and villages in Israel, and in doing so, make a modest contribution to the peace process in this most troubled of regions. We hope to make pragmatic and incremental grass-roots interventions into sport cultures, helping to build bridges between otherwise divided communities, while at the same time contributing to political and policy debates around sport in the region.

While helping to forge bonds of friendship between children and young people—the next generation of leaders and followers—has always been at the center of our endeavors, as the program has endured, the growth and durability of the fraternal relations between adult community volunteers and key figures from the network of institutional partnerships that have grown up have become more and more important. Indeed, the development of a network of partnerships has been crucial to the success and continuing growth of the project. First, there are the community partners: the dozens of Arab and Jewish towns and villages that willingly provide their children as well as volunteer coaches and leaders to work alongside their European counterparts. Second, there is a growing list of key institutional partners, including the British Council, the Israeli Sports Authority, the English Football Association, the German Sport University, the London Marathon, and the University of Brighton. In complementary ways all of these organizations have helped with the planning and resourcing of the program, as well as providing important moral and intellectual input.

Building on the lessons learned in Northern Ireland, engagement with and expansion of this embodied stratum of influential institutional players has dramatically enhanced the potential impact of F4P, having a ripple effect that connects relatively microscopic community-level interventions with the wider policy community for sport. In doing so, F4P promotes social change on a much larger scale. For instance, the British Council, the English Football Association, and, most importantly, the Israeli Sports Authority have all adapted and developed their own approaches to community relations work with sport through engaging with and learning from F4P.

For me these network partners are more than just impersonal organizational titles on a list; they are a roster of embodied relationships, evocative of warm and enduring friendships among dedicated and committed individuals who, though they have different backgrounds and vantage points, all share a passion for building peace through sport. In this regard those of us at the center of this fraternity have come to view F4P as an extended family.

Of course, through more than a decade working in one of the world's most troubled regions, there have been pitfalls, reversals, and occasionally family fallouts. Indeed, the inaugural project in 2001 almost never happened, as shortly before we were scheduled to send a handful of volunteers to Northern Israel, the Second Intifada erupted in the West Bank. The conflict spilled over into Israel and sparked violent confrontations between Israeli security forces and locals in Arab towns and villages in the Galilee, where we were scheduled to be working. Fearful of the deteriorating security situation, the Jewish partner community, which had been lined up to work in cooperation with the Arab village of Ibilin, withdrew its support. Having built up local expectations in Ibilin we decided to proceed, albeit cautiously. We thought that at least this would allow us to do some generic community development in the Arab town, as well as give us a chance to see if our structural delivery plan and accompanying logistics would work. As it turned out, we did end up running a cross-community program because, unbeknown to us in advance, there were significant divisions within Ibilin itself between Muslim Arabs and their Christian counterparts. This proved to be a valuable lesson, as in subsequent years we expanded the program in the region, learning all the time that Israel's demographic and ethnoreligious social geography was far more complex than a simple equation between Jews and Arabs. This had to be accounted for and nuanced into the design template for each local project.

More than a decade after this first venture, Ibilin remains involved as one of F4Ps outstanding foundation community partners, along with its Jewish community partner, Misgav, which joined the following year. At our training event at the German Sports University in Cologne in 2010 I was delighted to be introduced to one of that community's latest volunteer recruits, Shukri, who told me that he had first participated in F4P 10 years earlier when he was a child, during our first project. He is by no means the only F4P volunteer to begin his engagement with the program this way, and throughout the country there are many young local volunteer coaches who started out as child-participants. This bodes well for the project's sustainability and longevity.

There have been other setbacks. On July 7, 2005, the day after the 2012 Olympics had been awarded to London, the F4P team and volunteers were scheduled to gather at the city's Stanstead Airport. A series of bombs exploded across the city center's commuter network during the morning rush hour, killing 52 innocent civilians and the four suicide bombers, as well as injuring more than 700 others. Despite the ensuing chaos and last-minute panic attacks by student volunteers and their parents, we managed to assemble the entire group and fly to Tel-Aviv. This is more than can be said for the 2006 program, which had to be abandoned altogether, as only a matter of days before we were scheduled to start, what began as a relatively minor skirmish on Israel's northern border with Lebanon between the Israeli Defense Forces and Hezbollah developed into a full-scale war.

I was in Jerusalem making final preparations for a program that was scheduled to finish with a national F4P festival to be held in the Teddy Kollek Stadium, the home ground of the Beitar Jerusalem football club. This was a coup for us, as at the time Beitar fans had the reputation of having Israel's largest anti-Arab following. Bringing F4P there would have sent a powerful antiracism message. However, as missiles began to rain down on some of our partner communities in the Galilee, it soon became obvious to all concerned that F4P could not safely go ahead. Instead, I had to call other F4P staff, who once more had assembled 50 volunteers at London's Stanstead Airport, to tell them not to board the flight to Tel-Aviv. It is said that out of adversity there comes strength, and once the war was over and the missiles had stopped flying, we were implored by the local communities to come back to Israel later in the year and run a three-day residential program for 300 children in a small town less than 10 kilometers from the Lebanese frontier. We successfully delivered this project, and not only kept the forward momentum, but along with our local partners we were also able to show to ourselves and others that when at all possible we would not allow the terrorists, politicians, or military strategists to set our agenda. Despite such setbacks, generally speaking, F4P continues to steadily meander along its progressive journey towards peace, and until that journey is complete, so long as I can still kick a football, if invited, we will keep going back.

CONCLUSIONS

Looking back at the rocky road to peace in Northern Ireland and the contemporary Israeli-Palestinian situation, it is clear to me that a multiplicity of factors, including forms of violent resistance, state-sponsored responses to such violence, economic sanctions, international political pressure, passive forms of resistance, and intercommunity civil society interventions, all play some part in the cessation or escalation of conflicts in troubled regions. Positive outcomes cannot be repeated formulaically, as all contexts of division and conflict are different, but lessons can be learned, the chief one being that paradigmatic social and political change has multiple causes, both negative and positive, all of which will have to be accounted for in the final reckoning.

Another way of visualizing this is to think of the current peace process in Israel/Palestine as an unfinished 10,000 piece, three-dimensional jigsaw puzzle made additionally challenging because each piece is yet to be finished and no picture came with the box. For me, F4P is one of the pieces under construction in that box. At an unspecified time in the future, as happened in South Africa and Northern Ireland, it is to be hoped that patterns will emerge and the pieces will come together to finish the puzzle. While more positive civil society interventions will neither be so prominent nor so important as political and economic initiatives, when peace does come to the Middle East, programs like F4P will form a small piece of the completed jigsaw, and as such, in my view, they are invaluable.

Drawing from personal experience in the field and ongoing critical self-reflection, this chapter has attempted to provide an insight into my way of thinking about, planning for, and doing sport-for-development work that is neither idealistic nor simplistic: one that is justified from a humanitarian perspective, accounts fully for the local context, engages with and empowers local actors and partners, and connects with wider national and regional policy processes. I have attempted to show here how a fully informed sociological imagination, in combination with practical engagement and local contextual emersion, work best together in strategic planning and project implementation.

In invited lectures I have often finished a presentation on this subject by invoking the words attributed to the 18th century political philosopher Edmund Burke, the unofficial patron of F4P: "The only thing necessary for the triumph of evil is for good men to do nothing." It is to be hoped that the adoption of a critically pragmatic approach to sport in the service of conflict resolution and peace can provide activists—including sociologists— with both the reason and method for doing something positive.

A number of reflections can summarize my view on the contribution of sport to the development of the individual:

1. Residential setting and experience have the potential to become a living sociological laboratory for the sport sociology researcher. He or she can use their critical sociological imagination along with an ethnographer's eyes and ears to map and interpret the given geographical area and unique atmosphere in relation to the sport culture.

2. If sport could be organized and brought to the community in appropriate ways within a selected framework of anti-sectarian principles and values, then it could make a positive contribution to inter-personal and inter-community relations.

3. In relatively neutral settings, given a common cause and goal, a shared set of values, and committed mentors, a sport team can also be an excellent crucible within which to nurture intimacy and mutuality among players from conflicting cultures.

4. Sport programs developed for individuals from different or conflicting cultures should aim at making pragmatic and incremental grassroots intervention into sport cultures, helping to build bridges between otherwise divided communities, while at the same time making a contribution to political/policy debates around the topic of sport in the region.

From the Laboratory to the Field: Working with Soccer Players from Conflicting Cultures

Ronnie Lidor

Since completing my PhD studies at the University of Florida in 1991, I have been a member of the faculty of the Zinman College of Physical Education and Sport Sciences at the Wingate Institute, Israel, heading the Motor Behavior Laboratory. The Zinman College has the largest physical education teacher preparation program in the country, in terms of both the number of students enrolled and the number of staff members teaching in the program. In fact, this is the only college in the country that offers preparation programs solely for teaching physical education.

My areas of research have focused mainly on (a) sport psychology preparation in (1) beginning athletes involved in early phases of talent development and (2) in elite athletes who have reached an international level of competition (e.g., competing at the Olympic games or being members of Israeli national teams), and (b) cognitive aspects of motor skill acquisition (e.g., the use of learning and coping strategies in learning and performance of self-paced sport tasks). Since 1991 I have been involved in conducting research projects in these two areas, as well as in teaching undergraduate and graduate courses associated with my research interests. Most of my undergraduate and graduate courses have been composed of students coming from different cultures—Jews, Arabs, and students whose families have immigrated to Israel from countries as diverse as Ethiopia and Russia. Some of the students became involved in my research projects, so I came to know them better than the other students. As I will elaborate upon later in this chapter, the research and teaching work I have done in these two fields of interest have also stimulated me to be involved in the area of sport development (SD).

Before explaining how my involvement in the area of SD was initiated and how I perceive my experience in this field, I would like to provide some background on Israel, my country. This background is strongly related to the way I perceive SD, and particularly to the work in which I have been engaged with athletes from conflicting cultures: Jewish and Arab basketball and soccer players.

The state of Israel was established in 1948 and today is a multicultural society composed of more than 7 million residents, among them about 5.5 million Jewish citizens, 1.5 million Arab citizens, and 500,000 immigrants, mostly from Eastern Europe and Ethiopia. The Jews, Arabs, and immigrants are spread out all over the country. In the large- and medium-sized cities, such as Jerusalem (the capital, located in the center of the country), Tel-Aviv (the most populous city in the country, located in the center of the country), Haifa (located in the northern part of the country), and Ashdod (located in the southern part of the country), you will find Jews, Arabs, and other immigrants, although mostly living in separate neighborhoods.

Israel is surrounded by Arab countries: Egypt, Jordan, Lebanon, and Syria. It has diplomatic relations with only two of these countries: Egypt and Jordan. Concerning Lebanon and Syria, relations with Israel have been characterized by hostility and instability. In addition to problematic relations with Lebanon and Syria, Israel has an ideological-political conflict with the Palestinian population, living mainly in Gaza and the East Bank. The difficult relations with our Arab neighbors as well as with the Palestinians have negatively influenced relations between the Jews and Arabs who live in Israel, mainly by elevating the political-social tension between the two populations. In spite of this long-term tension, many Jewish and Arab citizens in Israel have been struggling to find the most expedient ways of living peacefully together. Most of the governments that have been elected in Israel have aimed at developing mutual understanding among the Jews and Arabs in the country.

There are not many areas in Israel where the Jewish and Arab populations can regularly interact. One of the areas in which Jews and Arabs are able to get to know each other, cooperate, and interact is sport, and particularly soccer. The game of soccer is one of the most popular sports in Israel, particularly among the youth population. Soccer presents a rare situation in Israel where young individuals from conflicting cultures—Jews and Arabs—can spend time together interacting with each other and enjoying an activity together. Since the two groups mostly live in separate neighborhoods, they have little opportunity to get to know each other and do activities together. In this regard, soccer provides a unique opportunity in Israel for individuals from all parts of the population to spend time together for a number of hours on a daily basis. In this way soccer can serve as a mediator for fostering relationships and increasing mutual understanding among its participants.

HOW DID I BECOME INVOLVED IN SD?

As indicated before, I was a laboratory person. Most of my data were collected under laboratory settings. It is true that some of my studies were undertaken in the field, such as physical education classes and practice sessions, but most were carried out under controlled laboratory conditions. How did I initiate my involvement in the area of SD? How did I find myself working outside the laboratory, in a field setting, observing how Jewish and Arab soccer players interact with one another? How did I replace laboratory conditions with authentic environments such as the soccer field?

A number of years ago I began working with my colleague, Dr. Boris Blumenstein, an experienced sport psychology consultant also from the Wingate Institute, on the development of sport psychology consultation programs for Israeli athletes, both beginners and experts. Together, Boris and I developed the theoretical and applied foundations of the program, which are briefly outlined in the following part of this chapter, and we created specific interventions for each player/team, finally assessing the contribution of the program to the actual success of the player/team. However, Boris was the one who worked practically with the players/teams and implemented the interventional strategies.

In our multiyear collaborative work, we developed sport psychology consultation programs mainly for soccer and basketball players. In this chapter I focus on our work with Jewish and Arab soccer players. Typically, elite soccer teams in Israel are composed of 22 players: about 15 Jewish players, 3-4 Arab players, and 2-4 foreign players (players who were not born in Israel and are not Israeli citizens). During the initial phases of our work, we developed psychological interventions aimed at improving the psychological readiness of the players for practice sessions and games. For example, we focused on improving the players' abilities to focus attention, to imagine specific situations, and to self-talk, all psychological techniques that have been found to enhance performance.

However, after some time working with the soccer players, we discovered that we could use the sport psychology program not only to facilitate psychological skills in our players, but also to foster relationships between the Jewish and Arab players who were playing on the teams. That is to say, we shifted our consultation emphasis from a solely psychological one to a combined psychological-social one. We felt that our sport psychology program could provide the players with opportunities to interact with one another and to increase mutual understanding among them. This was the first time in my academic work that I adopted a cultural perspective when developing interventions in sport psychology. Boris and I felt that through the psychological interventions we had developed over the years, we could also contribute to creating a better atmosphere among Jewish and Arab players playing on one soccer team.

The sport psychology program that we developed for Jewish and Arab players was not the only framework where I was exposed to the area of SD. I was also exposed to

SD through my involvement in Mifalot, the largest and most diverse organization in the Middle East that promotes the use of sport for fostering development and peace. Through my association with this organization, I realized how the game of soccer can contribute to fostering relationships among young Jewish and Arab players. In this story I describe my experiences working with Jewish and Arab soccer players through (a) the implementation of our sport psychology program and (b) my involvement with Mifalot. I will also present my own reflections on this involvement, as well as reflections of the Jewish and Arab players who took part in our sport program and the programs offered by Mifalot.

THE SPORT PSYCHOLOGY PROGRAM: WORKING WITH JEWISH AND ARAB PLAYERS

There are six main foundations of our psychological program for elite athletes in Israel: (a) The sport psychology consultant should be one of the members of the professional staff that works on a regular basis with the individual athlete or the team; (b) the sport psychology consultant should discuss his or her psychological plan with the coaching staff; (c) the sport psychology consultant should meet on a weekly basis with the coaching staff in order to exchange ideas on how the psychological program can contribute to the athlete's or the team's success; (d) the psychological consultation should take place in three settings: (1) laboratory settings (controlled and sterile conditions), (2) practice settings (authentic and actual conditions), and (3) home settings (quiet environment); (e) the sport psychology consultant should be willing to consider any request from the coaching staff, the individual athlete, or the team during the time he or she provides the consultations; and most central to this story; (f) the sport psychology program is provided to each individual athlete, regardless of his or her gender, race, or ethnicity.

The most popular session used by Boris when he worked with the Jewish and Arab players was small-group meetings (as opposed to meetings of the entire team together). The main objective of these meetings was to bring together a small number of players (2-4) from the two conflicting cultures in order to increase mutual understanding and foster relationships among the participating players. In these meetings, Boris used various psychological-sociological approaches to increase the mutual understanding among the Jewish and Arab players. For example, he asked the players to talk about themselves and their families: their hobbies other than sport, their academic interests, the names of their family members and the meaning of the names, the occupations of their parents, and how their families perceived their sport career. This communication was essential, since the Jewish and Arab players had few opportunities to socially interact, and therefore had little knowledge about one another's way of life. In order to increase mutual understanding among the Jewish and Arab players, confidence and trust between them had to be established. Informal verbal communication about themselves, their families, and their way of life was the first step in developing confidence and trust among the young Jewish and Arab soccer players.

In addition, Boris focused each time on one issue reflecting the diversity of the players. Among the topics were food, clothes, native language, music, and customs. He decided to focus on the diversity of the players because he assumed that the players would be interested in understanding the unique characteristics of their teammates and a discussion of these would attract their attention. He wanted the players to (a) listen to one another, (b) accept the fact that different players on the team had different preferences, and (c) respect the other regardless of his or her culture and religion.

When the players talked about the food they liked to eat, they not only had to provide information about the food but also to bring a sample to one of the meetings, so that the other players could taste it. In another instance, Boris talked with the players about their native language (i.e., Hebrew and Arabic). Although all the players spoke Hebrew, the Arab players spoke Arabic at home. He prepared a list of words in Hebrew, such as *soccer, sport,* and *music,* and asked the Arab players how to say these words in Arabic. These actions were conducted by Boris in order to enable the players to become more familiar with different aspects of their teammates' culture. As indicated before, Boris wanted the Jewish players to learn about the unique characteristics of the Arab players, and for the Arab players to learn about the unique characteristics of the Jewish players.

In our informal assessment of the contribution of the psychological program to foster relationships between the Jewish and Arab players, we were pleased with the verbal interactions that occurred among the players when they were talking about subjects such as music, food, and clothes. All of the players were about same age and were attracted by the same topics, despite their different cultures and religions. Boris stressed to the Jewish and Arab players that although their style of music or type of clothes may differ, most of them liked to listen to music and to be dressed stylishly. That is to say, despite the diversity of the players, they shared common interests.

Through the use of small-group meetings with the Jewish and Arab players, we attempted to provide the Arab players with the feeling that in this case they were not a minority. We assumed that a small group of players composed of two Jewish and two Arab players could create a great deal of intimacy among the participating players, and therefore the players would feel more comfortable when interacting with each other. We felt that the small-group meetings were the ones preferred by the Arab players. The players on the teams—both Jewish and Arab—were motivated to take part in these meetings and only rarely missed sessions. They opened up to each other, felt comfortable with each other, and did not make a big deal about their different cultures. This observation strengthens our assumption that by the use of appropriate sport psychology consultation sessions, not only psychological skills can be improved, but also the social climate among the participated individuals.

MIFALOT'S SPORT FOR EDUCATION, DEVELOPMENT, AND PEACE PROGRAM

The assumption that sport can foster relationship among athletes in conflicting cultures, such as that of the Jews and the Arabs in Israel, has been adopted by several nonprofit organizations in the country. Since the game of soccer is considered to be the most popular sport activity among both the youth and adult populations in Israel, one of the main objectives of these organizations has been to use soccer as a mediator to foster mutual understanding among young Jewish and Arab players. This objective has been achieved by the development of soccer programs aimed at gathering Jewish and Arab players to practice and play together on a regular basis.

Mifalot is the largest and most diverse organization in the Middle East that promotes the use of sport for fostering development and peace. Founded in 1997 by the owners of Hapoel Tel-Aviv (a major sport club in Israel), the vision of the organization is to take full advantage of the potential and power of soccer in order to build more active, compassionate, and cohesive communities, and to support the sustainable development of a more open, just, and engaged society. The primary objective of this organization is to serve the educational and social needs of children and youth throughout the region. Mifalot has over 300 programs that use soccer to teach life skills to children with special needs, promote the integration and inclusion of newly arrived immigrants, create bonds of friendship between Israelis and Palestinians, and provide much-needed assistance to children living in at-risk, disadvantaged, or isolated environments. About 20,000 children and youth across the region participate in Mifalot's programs throughout the year.

Mifalot also attempts to engage political institutions, the corporate sector, the general public at large, and the international community to ensure that attention is directed to the most pressing social issues in the region and that resources are provided to communities in urgent need. Rather than being perceived as a marketing ploy or public relations campaign, Mifalot is perceived by its founders, supporters, and partners as an earnest and effective use of sport to promote development and peace. The organization seeks to provide children and youth with any and all opportunities to learn, grow, excel, and participate in the development of their community and their world.

There are four overarching objectives for each of the educational programs offered by Mifalot: (a) to provide equal access to quality sport and educational opportunities for children and youth in need; (b) to teach and empower children and youth with essential life skills and values; (c) to develop local leaders and promote stronger families within partner communities; and (d) to promote peace, inclusion, and coexistence across different cultural, religious, ethnic, and social groups. These objectives are what guides Mifalot's work in Israel, the Palestinian Territories, and around the world.

As an organization committed to solving local issues via local solutions, efforts have been made in a number of development arenas:

a. **Early childhood development and education.** The organization has more than 100 active programs around the region using soccer as a powerful incentive to work hard and do well in school. These educational soccer programs provide the children with the needed tutorial and homework assistance, as well as a safe place for after-school programs. For children living in at-risk or isolated environments, such as children in state-run institutions, the organization fills in the gaps in education by providing unique instructional programs for teaching life skills, nurturing a love of learning, and promoting a healthy and active lifestyle.

b. **Social integration and inclusion.** The organization reaches out to socially excluded groups and uses sport to teach life skills, and works at fostering relationships between different communities. The organization works with recreational centers and schools to provide sport and educational activities designed to help children with special needs, new immigrants, and refugees, and to open new paths for inclusion in mainstream society.

c. **Coexistence and peace.** To foster a culture of peace and coexistence, the organization uses soccer to bridge social, religious, and ethnic divides. Mifalot's peace programs encourage new friendships among children of Arab Israelis, Christians, Bedouins, Druze, Ethiopian immigrants, Jewish Israelis, Kibbutz (small cooperative farming settlements) members, Palestinians, and refugees.

About five years ago I was asked by one of the board members of Mifalot to serve on one of its committees—the one that is responsible for curriculum development. At that time he explained to me that some of the board members of Mifalot thought that they could benefit from my knowledge on talent development and particularly on the use of learning and coping strategies. They stressed that Mifalot has no intention of "producing" skilled soccer players, but mainly to provide Jewish and Arab players with the opportunity to interact with each other on a regular basis for a long period of time (e.g., one year). I was also told that this committee had three objectives: (a) to develop soccer programs that are based on cooperative learning activities among the Jewish and Arab players; (b) to develop academic programs that help the Jewish and Arab players overcome difficulties they may face in school, such as an English program for those having difficulties in learning a foreign language or a leadership program for those who lack confidence on and off the field (e.g., improving players' ability to work with others or their ability to direct others); and (c) to develop instructional-pedagogical materials for the coaches who work in the soccer programs and for the instructors who work in the academic programs. Although I did not have any experience in soccer (I was a basketball coach before entering the academic domain) I was happy to serve on this committee, since I was curious about how young Jewish and

Arab soccer players practice and play together on one team. Indeed, I have had some experience working with elite Jewish and Arab players through my psychological work with Boris; however, I did not have any experience with Jewish and Arab children. Since I had never been involved in any SD program for children from conflicting cultures, I had some doubts if such programs could succeed among children in a country such as Israel.

Upon serving on the committee, I was actually able to observe what SD is all about. I started to realize how sport programs have the potential to foster relationships between young individuals from conflicting cultures. Moreover, I began to realize that the assumption made by Mifalot, as well as by other nonprofit organizations in Israel, that participation in designated soccer programs can increase mutual understanding between Jewish and Arab youngsters, might be true.

There were two events that influenced my way of thinking. The first was visiting soccer practices in which both Jewish and Arab players participate. The second event was a one-day conference organized by Mifalot for its coaches and instructors who worked in the different programs with the Jewish and Arab players, a conference that I helped to organize. In visiting the soccer activities offered by Mifalot, I was amazed at how the Jewish and Arab players practiced and played together. I saw soccer activities in which all the young players performed together without bearing a label that said "I am a Jewish player" or "I am an Arab player." I had never seen such sport activities before, where the distinction between Jewish and Arab youngsters did not play any role. All players—Jewish and Arab—performed the soccer drills together as one unit. All were involved in the activity without paying attention to whom they were playing with on the team. The coaches provided *all* the children with verbal instructions, demonstrations, and feedback. The children were enthusiastic about cooperating with each other as well as with the coaches. If I had not known in advance that the soccer program was composed of Jewish and Arab players, it would not have been revealed to me from the actual activities I observed taking place on the field.

The second event was, as I indicated before, a one-day conference organized by Mifalot for its coaches and instructors, for which I was asked to give the opening lecture of the conference. After delivering the lecture, I did not leave the conference but remained there the entire day. During the coffee breaks between the sessions, as well as during lunchtime, I talked with some of the Jewish and Arab coaches. I knew some of them from when they had studied at the Zinman College of Physical Education and Sport Sciences. A number of them had been students in my own classes. In my interactions with the coaches, I could feel that they were happy with the role they were playing in Mifalot. They understood that they were involved in unique soccer programs that are not often seen in Israel. They realized that what they were trying to achieve with the children, namely to develop trust and understanding among the players, particularly among the Jewish and Arab players, may not necessarily be transferred to real life. They understood that it would be difficult for them to make a big change in the relationships between Jewish and Arab people at large. But they truly believed that some small educational steps should also be taken to foster relationships among individuals from conflicting cultures. They were proud of the fact that these small steps were made in their soccer programs, and felt that they were contributing to a complex and long-term process aimed at increasing understanding among Jewish and Arab athletes in Israel.

While visiting the soccer practices and participating in the conference, I considered myself as part of a group of people who share similar interests. When watching the soccer practices, it was hard for me to distinguish between the Jewish and Arab players, since all wore the same soccer uniforms and followed the same code of behavior. While interacting with the coaches in the conference, I knew who was a Jewish coach and who was an Arab coach. However, this distinction made no difference to me or to the coaches. Both the Jewish and the Arab coaches talked with me about similar topics, such as sport, soccer, instructional strategies, academics, and achievements. In my interactions with them, no political or military issues were brought up. We did not care about them in that framework.

REFLECTIONS AND FOOD FOR THOUGHT

My experience in planning sport psychology programs for soccer teams composed of both Jewish and Arab players, as well as my involvement in different educational programs offered by Mifalot, has taught me a valuable lesson: in Israel, Jewish and Arab individuals can cooperate and work effectively when common goals are shared. Despite the tension that exists between the Jewish and Arab populations in Israel, as well as the tension that exists between Israel and the Arab countries surrounding Israel, sport activities can play a major role in fostering relationship between the two populations. This can happen if one of the main objectives of the sport programs is to offer opportunities in which Jewish and the Arab athletes can learn about one another, learn from one another, respect one another, and find a way to work together.

Jewish and Arab players playing in professional soccer teams in Israel have similar goals: they want to become better players, win games, and be part of a winning team. If all of the players on a soccer team are provided with the required professional-psychological-social conditions to achieve a high level of proficiency, then the relationship between the players from conflicting cultures, such as Jews and Arabs, can be fostered. In our sport psychology program, both the Jewish and Arab players worked together and were happy to attend the same consultation sessions. They cooperated with each other, opened up to each other, and left any political debate out of the program.

The Jewish and Arab youngsters who participated in the soccer and educational programs offered by Mifalot were enthusiastic about spending time together. The attendance rate was high for both the soccer and the academic programs, and only a few participants dropped out from the ongoing activities. Another good indicator for the success of these programs is the fact that many of the participants resumed their involvement in one of the programs in the following year.

In both of the cases I described in this chapter, sport served as a mediator between Jewish and Arab soccer players. It is true that neither quantitative nor qualitative data were obtained and analyzed in order to study the actual contribution of the sport programs in fostering relationships between the Jewish and Arab players. Evaluative studies should be conducted to enable those involved in the programs—sport psychology consultants, coaches, instructors, management members, and policy makers, as well as those who sponsored the programs—to better understand the contribution of the activities offered in each program. Without this objective knowledge the actual contribution of the different programs in increasing mutual understanding between athletes from conflicting cultures cannot be fully assessed.

However, in Israel, any educational initiative that is aimed at fostering relationships between the Jewish and Arab populations should be encouraged. Since soccer is a popular activity among both the Jewish and Arab populations, and since both groups already play soccer together in recreational and professional programs, more effort should be made to gain from this activity in fostering relationships between Jewish and Arab players. More initiatives should be begun to increase the number of Arab players on the roster of professional teams dominated by Jewish players and vice versa. In addition, more soccer programs should be established for young teams composed of both Jewish and Arab players. The potential of soccer to create opportunities in which both Jewish and Arab players will get to know each other on a regular basis is great. Politicians and policy makers should be aware of this potential. Finally, sport (soccer) development should be used as an example for other activities that can offer opportunities for decreasing tension between the Jewish and Arab populations living in Israel.

CONCLUSIONS

Based upon my experience in developing sport psychology programs for soccer teams composed of both Jewish and Arab players, as well as my involvement in Mifalot, I have come to three conclusions:

1. More sport programs in which Jewish and Arab athletes practice and compete together should be developed. It is true that soccer is the most popular sport activity in the country; however, there are other sports attracting the attention of both the Jewish and Arab populations. Basketball, volleyball, and track and field have also become very popular, and therefore sport programs should be developed in these sports as well. These programs should be sup-

ported—ideologically and financially—by governmental bodies such as the Sport Authority and Education Authority in Israel. In Israel, where sport is a very popular activity among the public at large, more efforts should be made to use sport as a mediator to promote peace between the Jewish and Arab populations who live here.

2. The families of the Jewish and Arab athletes who participate in sport programs should become part of the program as well. In order to increase mutual understanding between the Jewish and Arab athletes in Israel, particularly the young athletes, it is not enough to develop programs for the athletes themselves. The programs should offer some cultural or social activities for the parents of the athletes and also other members of the athletes' families could be included. In this way more individuals from the two populations will get to know each other.

3. A multisystem approach should be adopted in order to reap benefits from the use of sport as a mediator between individuals from conflicting cultures. Not only should the athletes, coaches, instructors, and the leaders of the nonprofit organizations that support the sport programs play a role in attempts to use sport as a vehicle for fostering relationships among the Jewish and Arab athletes, but it is also essential that other key figures in Israel be made aware of the existence of these programs. Among these individuals are ministers, politicians, state administrators, and journalists from the written and electronic media. Only a joint and long-term effort by these individuals will facilitate the greatest benefits from the use of sport in promoting understanding between the Jewish and Arab athletes in Israel.

Project Nepal: The Experience of Implementing Life Skills Programming in a Developing Country

14

Tanya Forneris

THE FIRST STEPS

For as long as I can remember I have wanted to travel to and work in a developing country, as I am inspired by those who devote themselves to enhancing the lives of others. My motivation for developing an expertise in community programming and positive youth development came from the desire to work with and improve the health and well-being of individuals and communities. I appreciate that I was fortunate to be born in a country and family that could provide me with the resources, opportunities, and support to grow into a healthy individual. As a result, I strongly believe that those of us that have had such opportunities should work to help others around the world by providing them with opportunities to enhance growth. The purpose of this chapter is to share my experience developing and establishing a working relationship with a Nepalese nongovernment organization (NGO) to implement life skills programming for Nepalese youth.

The opportunity to work in Nepal occurred unexpectedly. The journey began with an email I received from an undergraduate student named Jocelyn in the fall of 2006 when I was teaching at Queen's University in Kingston, Ontario, Canada. Jocelyn was interested in completing a community project under my supervision. The community project course requires the student to work on an independent project that could benefit an organization within the local community. Jocelyn wanted to work with an organization called Basecamp International. This organization provides opportunities to volunteer abroad, which Jocelyn had taken advantage of in the past. During her volunteer work Jocelyn had observed that there were a lack of volunteer placements for human kinetics students. The majority of the volunteer placements were in the fields of education (e.g., teaching English) and medicine (e.g., assisting doctors in hospitals). Jocelyn had learned that schools in developing countries often do not integrate any form of physical activity programming or extracurricular activities into their curriculum. As a result, she wanted to develop a physical activity program. Given that my expertise is in life skills programming, we discussed developing a physical activity-based life skills program. Jocelyn presented her ideas to Basecamp International at the end of the semester and they were immediately interested in implementing the program. Basecamp International decided Nepal would be a good starting point, as they had a house where Canadians could live while volunteering and they had established relationships with local NGOs.

NATIONAL CONTEXT

Going into this project I did not know much about Nepal. I, of course, was aware that it contains Mount Everest and therefore attracts thousands of tourists each year. As I began to research Nepal it quickly became apparent that it is a country that could benefit from a program designed to help youth be active and develop life skills. According to the World Health Organization (WHO), Nepal is one of the least developed countries in the world, with a GDP per capita of only $1,000. On the human development index Nepal ranks 157 out of 187 countries. Furthermore, the literacy rate is very low, with only 63% of males and 35% of females over the age of 15 being literate. Many of these issues are a result of the political turmoil Nepal has experienced, particularly in the past 20 years. In fact, no government has lasted for more than two years since 1991.

Until 1990 Nepal was a monarchy, but during the early 1990s there was a movement by the Maoists, a local communist party, to abolish the absolute monarchy. This movement strengthened, and as a result, the king agreed to political reforms and created a parliamentary monarchy. In 1996 the Maoists, still unhappy, started a violent insurgency. Although a cease-fire was put in place in 2001, turmoil continued with the murder of the king and his family. This led to a new king, who suspended parliament and enforced martial law, which only led to further upheaval. Eventually, in 2006, power was given back to the people. Since that time Nepal has struggled to maintain a consistent government, and there is still doubt that the political parties will succeed in writing a constitution that will satisfy all of the political parties. Having spent considerable time in Kathmandu, it is evident to me that this political turmoil has greatly affected both the people and the institutions in Nepal. There are numerous general strikes known as *bandhs* that shut down the cities, leading to disruptions in transportation and frequent school closures. This political disruption has led many of the Nepalese people with whom I have worked to recognize the importance of developing the youth into strong leaders who are able to work together to solve problems.

In January 2007, I started recruiting undergraduate students to implement the physical activity-based life skills program that we subsequently named Project Nepal. In the end, 10 undergraduate students decided to make the trip. Given that there was no funding in place for this project, the students were responsible for all costs associated with the trip. For that reason, it is to these undergraduate students that I owe the success of Project Nepal. Once the group was formed, Basecamp International linked me with a Nepalese NGO, Environmental Camps for Conservation Awareness (ECCA). ECCA is a leading organization in social mobilization and community development in Nepal that implements various programs to enhance the quality of life of the Nepalese people through wise use of available local resources. One of ECCA's programs is the School Environment Improvement Program. The specific objectives of the School Environment Improvement Program are to increase school enrollment and decrease dropout rates, to improve the health and sanitation of students, and to increase coordination among students, parents, teachers, and administration. ECCA was interested in the physical activity-based life skills program because it supported their mission. They recognized that this program would help the youth learn important skills that could help improve their school work, help them succeed in the future, foster positive relationships among the students, and improve the relationships between the students and the teachers.

In May of 2007, Sidhi Bajracharya, the volunteer coordinator at ECCA, and I started to plan the implementation of Project Nepal. ECCA has a large group of young adult volunteers, typically university students, who help to implement the programs ECCA has developed throughout Nepal. Sidhi suggested that we pair two Canadian volunteers with one ECCA volunteer to implement the program in five different schools. This team-based approach was very effective, as the Canadian leaders were familiar with various physical activity games and active-based learning, while the ECCA leaders, who spoke Nepalese and English, knew the principals, teachers, and students in the schools. The principals asked for the program to be taught in English so the students could practice their language skills. However, as expected, there were numerous occasions when a translation of concepts was needed, and therefore the bilingual ECCA leaders were a key to success.

ARRIVING IN NEPAL

In the beginning of June 2007 we all arrived in Nepal to start the program. The first week was an orientation week; we participated in a Nepalese language class in the mornings followed by afternoon excursions to understand the public transit system and to explore the many historic sites in and around Kathmandu. A team-building session was arranged for the Canadian and ECCA leaders. The Canadian and ECCA leaders led different ice-breaker activities that were popular in their respective countries, and funnily enough, were quite similar. After getting to know one another we made our way to the schools by piling into a microbus, a popular form of public transportation in Kathmandu. A microbus is a 15-seat van, although at any time of day you can find 20 or more people crammed into one. To the Canadian leaders the amount of personal space on public transit was at first quite challenging and was one of the cultural differences to which they had to adapt. To cope with this challenge, the Canadian leaders would count the number of people that made it into a microbus. The record that anyone observed during our trip was 26—quite a feat. To get to the schools we travelled across Kathmandu to Lalitpur, a district just outside the city but still within the Kathmandu valley. Once we arrived in Lalitpur the ECCA leaders led their respective Canadian partners to the school in which they would be working and introduced the Canadians to the principal, teachers, and students. Everyone appeared to be excited by our arrival. Students would run up to us to shake our hands and have their picture taken with us. As soon as the picture was taken they would scramble to see themselves on the digital screen of the camera. It was quite a scene. After a few minutes the students calmed down and we were provided a tour of the school.

The schools in which the program was implemented were government schools that are publicly funded and, consequently, have fewer resources than the local private schools. The schools vary in size but most have one classroom per grade (kindergarten to grade 8 or 9). The classrooms are all open; they have openings for windows and doors but many do not have actual windows or doors. In addition, there is no electricity in the classrooms. The schools also have very little, if any, clean drinking water available to the students, and there usually are only two to three toilets for the hundreds of students in the school. As a result, ECCA is constantly working with the schools to improve the physical environment. We also observed that the students do not have access to any type of physical education or sport, either during or after school. The curriculum in Nepal is primarily based on rote learning, meaning the students are quite passive in their learning process. Hence, we recognized that the life skills program using an active learning approach would offer something new to the students. Although we were unsure whether the students would like the program or whether it would have any type of impact, we hoped that it would help engage the youth and improve the social interactions within the school environment.

THE PROGRAM

The program focused on teaching five life skills (goal setting, cooperation, communication, leadership, and self-confidence) that are consistently found in positive youth development programs. ECCA also believed these skills would be important for Nepalese youth to develop. All students in the sixth through eighth grades participated in one program session per day for 45 minutes, every day, for a period of three weeks. As a result, the youth were exposed to the five life skills (one per day) repetitively throughout the three-week program. It was believed that this format would enable the students to have a positive first experience with active learning strategies, would lead to a greater understanding of the life skills, and would provide increased opportunity to practice the skills.

Each of the 45-minute sessions started in the classroom with a five-to-ten minute overview of the life skill, including a discussion about why the skill was important. This introduction was then followed by 30 minutes of physical activity-based games and activities that allowed the students to practice and develop the life skill of the day. When teaching goal setting, for instance, the leaders would have the students select an activity for which they could set an individual goal (e.g., a timed short run, long jump, skipping), or when teaching cooperation the leaders would use activities like the human knot or knights, horses, and cavaliers. Each session ended with a five-minute debriefing where the leaders and students discussed what they had learned from the activities related to the life skill of the day.

I did not set expectations in terms of program impact, as it was only a three-week program. My hope was that the students would enjoy the program and that ECCA, along with the principals and teachers at the schools, would feel that it was valuable. Although the Canadian leaders were very excited and motivated to be in Nepal, many of them also wondered whether such a short program would have an impact on the youth. Many of us were concerned that the experience of going to Nepal and working in the schools would meet our needs (e.g., the need to help others less fortunate then ourselves) and goals (travel to a developing country) more than the needs of the Nepalese youth. These thoughts and feelings were definitely present in the first week as everyone was adapting to the program. The students were a little hesitant the first few days of the program as the activities were very new for them. It was very different to be outside of the classroom and to interact with each other through games. However, by the end of the first week the youth were beginning to get into the routine of the program, and you could see that they were having fun playing the different games and that they enjoyed getting out of the classroom to be active.

By the end of the second week the leaders observed that the students were cooperating more with each other and were starting to understand what the different life skills were and why they were important. In the third week the leaders shared with me that the students were quite engaged, more interactive with one another, and appeared more confident. This was particularly true for the female students. One of the Canadian leaders shared this in an interview: "Especially the girls, I saw a lot of progression in terms of them becoming less inhibited and voicing their opinions more and going outside of their comfort zone. I saw a lot of progression in a very short amount of time." As stated above, the Canadian leaders had expressed prior to the start of the program their uncertainties regarding the impact of such a short program. They believed the youth would have fun but were unsure if they would understand or develop the various life skills. Yet by the end of the program, the leaders were thrilled to see that the youth were practicing the life skills and were sharing what they had learned with younger students. What I observed to be the greatest difference was the level of cooperation among the students. During their breaks the youth did not fight as often over the soccer ball, basketball, or skipping ropes, but rather they started to take turns or to pass the ball. It was quite impressive, and I, along with the leaders, felt we had made an impact at some level.

The teachers, like the students, first appeared to be quite hesitant about the program. Unfortunately, the Canadian leaders did not have very much interaction with the teachers. Although the teachers were invited and encouraged to participate in the program, many of them took a break during the program sessions. Some of the teachers also questioned whether the students were learning anything from the program and had the impression that they were just playing games. However, as the program progressed the teachers started to appreciate the program more, and some began to participate in the sessions. In each of the schools we attempted to have a teacher training session, but these did not occur due to logistics or the level of interest on the part of some of the teachers. However, since this time we have been able to conduct teacher training related to active learning strategies to enhance youth development in collaboration with ECCA.

On the other hand, from the very beginning the principals were excited to have volunteers from Canada. The principals stated that it was important for the students to meet and interact with people from different countries. They were also happy that the students would be learning skills that could lead to increased school engagement. The principals would often thank us for coming and always invited myself and the leaders to join them for lunch, where they would serve us tea and biscuits.

At the end of the program, each of the schools organized a day of events to show their appreciation for the program. The principals expressed that they wanted us to return again to teach life skills to more of the students. One of the principals commented, "It has injected in them [students] a notion of many good things like goal-setting, confidence building, and leadership development" while another principal shared, "The principles of goal setting, discipline, obedience, communication, determination, leadership, and confidence have been put into practice through various student-centered activities that demand the students' physical and mental skills; this program has had a positive effect on them [students] in that they got to learn by doing different things by themselves. . . not just listening to lectures on the topics but also by performing them on their own." The principals and the Nepalese leaders also shared that in order for Nepal to advance and move past its political instability, these youth—the future leaders—would need to be able to work together, set and achieve goals, and develop into strong leaders.

SUSTAINING LIFE SKILLS PROGRAMMING IN NEPAL

Although the program seemed to have a positive impact on the youth, it was really important to me to find a way to sustain the program. Three weeks was just the beginning, and it was unrealistic to think that these youth would be affected by the program for any great length of time. Prior to arriving in Nepal I believed that to make the program sustainable, ECCA would need to take ownership of the program. I also believed that the program would need to evolve into a Nepalese program instead of just a Canadian program implemented in Nepal. Therefore, as ECCA and I continued to work together, I encouraged them to try new activities that they themselves believed would be effective for the students and to plan and organize their own life skills events.

In May of 2008 I returned to Nepal with three new undergraduate students. Upon our arrival, Sidhi had arranged for us to return to three of the schools. Each of the Canadian leaders was paired with a Nepalese leader, and together they implemented the same three-week program to the grade six through grade eight students. The principals were very excited that we had returned and the students, especially those who had participated the previous year, were excited to have the program again. However, the goal of this trip was to enhance the sustainability of the program by creating a life skills club at each of the schools. As mentioned earlier, very few, if any, extracurricular activities are offered in these schools, but ECCA had been successful in creating nature clubs, where a small group of students worked to improve the physical environment of the school. Therefore, it was decided that we would use a similar model to sustain the life skills programming.

In each of the schools, six to eight youth comprised the life skills club; they were from grades seven and eight and were interested in becoming leaders of life skills activities. The mission of the life skills club was to plan and organize life skills activities and events for the students and teachers. Each week the life skills club would meet to plan and/or implement a life skills activity for the duration of the school year. For example, one week the club would teach one of the life skills to the grade four students and another week they would teach some of the life skills activities to the teachers. Although the students who comprised the life skills club were responsible for the planning and organizing, the ECCA leader who had worked with the Canadian leader oversaw the students' implementation of these activities.

In addition to the creation of the life skills clubs, ECCA began to take more initiative and expanded the life skills programming. ECCA organized a number of life skills days, which involved inviting students from various schools across the district of Lalitpur to participate in different life skills activities and games. ECCA has continued these life skills days and have now developed their own program resources. One of these resources is a Nepalese life skills book. To create this book ECCA integrated activities and games from the original program and also adapted games and activities they had used in the past when working with Nepalese youth. This book is a great resource as it describes a large number of life skill activities and games in Nepalese. ECCA also translated the book into English so that it could be shared with me and any Canadian volunteers that work with ECCA. I was very excited and impressed when I received this book, and it was at this point when I began to see a transfer of ownership take form. ECCA was taking the lead and this to me was a sign of success, as it showed that the program was beginning to be sustainable.

To further enhance the development of the students who had participated in the life skills clubs, ECCA organized a life skills camp at the end of the school year (Spring 2009). The purpose of the camp was to bring the life skills clubs from the three schools together to learn about what they had achieved in their schools, to strengthen the development of their life skills, and to plan activities in their respective schools for the following year. Altogether 31 participants (11 boys, 20 girls) attended the four-day camp. For the majority of the students, this was their first experience being away from home, and thus it was very exciting and there was much anticipation on the bus ride to the camp.

Each day of the camp was packed with organized activities that began at 7 a.m. and ended at 7 p.m. The camp began with introductions through ice-breaker activities, as this was the first time that the students from the different schools were meeting one another. Following the ice-breakers one of the ECCA leaders led a discussion on the expectations of the camp (e.g., the importance of being responsible and networking with other students from different schools). To help enhance responsibility and leadership skills the students were divided into four groups, and each group was given a different task for the duration of the camp. One group was responsible for reporting all of the events that took place at the camp, one group was responsible for evaluation of the camp (e.g., distributing and collecting surveys and feedback forms), one group was responsible for managing the time and the activities, and the last group was responsible for entertainment at night after the activities were finished for the day (e.g., drama show, dance). The first morning ended with the students from the different schools sharing what their life skills club had accomplished throughout the year. After lunch it was time to get to business, and I led a discussion that focused on reviewing the five life skills with the students. We discussed the importance of these skills in life and in school and how they could help the students reach their future goals. I also explained the importance of continuing to practice these skills through activities they lead in their respective schools, as it is through practice that these skills are further developed and refined.

Days two, three, and four all began with a two-hour physical activity session that incorporated life skills. For example, day two started with a hike, and one of the activities to enhance cooperation and communication involved the students taking turns being blindfolded and being led by a partner through the trail. Day three started with a treasure hunt where the students set goals for how much treasure they would find. Day four started with a village walk with students taking on different leadership roles. The remainder of the days focused on learning and playing new life skill games, with three hours devoted to each of the five skills. These sessions started with a review of what the skill was, why it was important, and then a number of activities to practice each of the skills. The format of these sessions was the same as the life skills program that was implemented in each school; however, more time was devoted to learning and playing the different games. The rationale for this was that in order to be able to go back into their respective schools and teach the younger students and teachers about life skills, the youth would need to have had the time to learn and practice the games first.

On the last day of the camp the students practiced applying the life skills to realistic hypothetical problems. The students were divided into different groups and each group was given a situation in which they had to identify which skills were important for resolving the problem or situation and to plan for how they would solve the problem. The purpose of this session was to help the students recognize how the life skills transfer into real life. For example, one was "Your brother wants to be a computer engineer, but he does not like school so he does not do his homework" or "You are a teacher and the students in your class fight with each other and do not participate in class." This session was effective in helping the students make the link between learning about and practicing the skill to thinking about how to apply the skill in real life.

The camp ended by having the clubs work on their plan for life skills activities at their respective schools. The students were instructed to develop a six-month plan, and they then presented this plan to the whole group. After the presentations, a celebration of the completion of camp ensued and all of the students were given a certificate of completion. It was very rewarding and reinforcing when I spoke with the youth about their experiences. Many of the students stated that being in the life skills club and participating in the camp helped them be more confident and that they would work together and become leaders. One student shared, "It is very helpful for my life and career. I have developed self confidence and leadership," while another student said, "Before I used to be afraid even to say my name in front of people, but now I have capacity to say what I feel in front of others." Another student stated, "I feel very proud to be a part of life skill club at my school because I learned many new things and I am able to convey them to others." Overall, the camp was a great success and I was amazed at how much the students developed in such a short period of time.

Throughout 2010 ECCA continued to implement life skills activities, such as life skills days, in schools across the Lalitpur district. In addition, the life skills clubs have continued at the schools. However, I believed that to expand the program and have a greater impact we needed to involve the teachers. Earlier in the implementation stages Sidhi and I had discussed the importance of getting the teachers involved, but up to this point that had not transpired. Then in May of 2010, while at the Teaching Personal and Social Responsibility Conference in Chicago, I met Dr. Doris Watson. As Doris and I conversed, I learned that she had an expertise in pedagogy and had been quite involved in training teachers. As Doris learned about my work in Nepal she expressed interest in becoming involved. As a result we applied for and received a small grant for her to lead a teacher-training workshop in May 2011 using the Teaching Personal and Social Responsibility (TPSR) model. The workshop took place in Nepal over the course of four days and was attended by 16 teachers and 13 ECCA volunteers. The teachers were partnered with the ECCA volunteers who had all participated in life skills training in the past, and therefore could help the teachers better understand the material and recognize how to integrate life skill activities into their lesson plans. In addition, the ECCA volunteers were more fluent in English, and as a result, language barriers between the teachers and Dr. Watson were reduced.

The workshop was considered a success and the teachers reported that the workshop helped them to understand how they could engage their students within the classroom and how they could use the TPSR model in their teaching. To sustain the impact of this workshop, ECCA is now planning a follow-up program that will involve the ECCA leaders conducting school visits to help the teachers integrate life skills using the TPSR model in the classroom. ECCA is also planning to train ECCA leaders how to teach the TPSR model, so that they can go into schools throughout Nepal to train teachers on site to further enhance the sustainability of the program.

CHALLENGES AND LESSONS LEARNED

Overall, the experience of bringing a life skills program to Nepal has been inspiring, and it would not have been possible without the willingness, support, and initiative from ECCA, in particular Sidhi Bajracharya and the ECCA and Canadian leaders. However, this process has not been without its challenges. Some of the challenges we have overcome with time, such as the involvement of teachers, while others continue to persist. The biggest challenge in implementing the life skills programs has been related to the political instability. There were many times when the schools were closed due to general strikes, and this led to cancellations of life skills activities at the school, including sessions during the three-week program, activities planned by the life skills clubs, and a delay in the start of a teacher training workshop. Although such events are out of ECCA's control, these interruptions do and will continue to negatively impact the planning and execution of life skills programming. Fortunately, ECCA has persevered in delivering the life skills programming, as they recognize that developing youth who learn how to work well together may eventually lead to a more stable and peaceful country.

CONCLUSIONS

Project Nepal started out as an independent project for an undergraduate student and has grown into a diverse array of life skills programming (school programs, life skills days, teacher training). It has been an incredible learning experience for everyone involved, and I am thrilled that the life skills programming has been perceived as having a positive impact on the lives of Nepalese youth. I have learned an incredible amount about implementing programs and collaborating with organizations, as well as about myself personally, so much that it is difficult to put into words. The following section will outline the biggest lessons that I learned and that I believe are important to share with others interested in this kind of work.

1. First, never underestimate the impact that undergraduate and graduate students can have on the direction of your work. Students often have novel ideas, can open doors for new opportunities, and are motivated to make a difference in their communities and beyond. This work would not have been possible without the involvement and commitment of students both here in Canada and in Nepal.

2. Second, whether you are a professor, a student, or a professional, if an opportunity to volunteer or work abroad presents itself, take it. For me, as well as all the students who have volunteered in Nepal, the experience has been life changing.

3. Third, when working in other countries it is critical to identify an NGO that shares similar goals, objectives, and vision. It is also important that the NGO is well organized, communicates effectively and consistently, and is willing to invest in the program. From the start I was impressed with ECCA, as they were able to overcome many obstacles to implement the life skills program in the schools, took great initiative to enhance and expand the life skills programming, and are committed to sustaining the programming.

4. Fourth, and in my opinion the most important, is the transfer of ownership. For programs implemented internationally to be sustainable and have a real impact, it is imperative that the NGO take ownership of the program. Given the various cultural differences, programs designed in one country, particularly a developed country, cannot just be transplanted into a developing country and be effective. The program has to be adapted to meet the needs of the youth in the developing country, and transferring ownership to the local NGO increases the likelihood of such needs being met. In addition, transferring ownership is the key to program sustainability. The expanded life skills programming today that started as Project Nepal would not have been possible without the transfer of ownership to ECCA.

The Wheels of Hope

Yeshayahu Hutzler

Some authors argue that the founding of the renewed Olympics by Pierre Coubertin was initially a pedagogical move intended to educate about peace among nations, achieved through the experience of peaceful international encounters between rival nations. The modern Olympics were expected to follow the ancient way of celebrating a sport festival for a period during which competitors, spectators, and officials had safe passage to and from the host city, which was considered an inviolate territory. The principles of fair play and obeying the rules, which manifest the Olympic spirit and the sport culture in general, are the core elements of peace education endeavors, typically merging participants from diverse and sometime hostile ethnic and social origins in team activities under acceptable rules.

In Israel, the experience of peace education is not new. One of the more intensive programs is the development of the Twinned Peace Sport Schools (TPSS) project of the Peres Center for Peace in the Middle East, launched in 2002. The TPSS cuts across traditional and often conflicting national identities and allows the children to interact in a safe, healthy, and fun environment built on principles of equality, diversity, respect, and mutual understanding. The Peres Center utilizes a wide variety of sports, including football, basketball, wheelchair basketball, and cricket to encourage unity and eliminate conflict, with Israeli and Palestinian children always playing together in mixed teams (and not Israelis versus Palestinians).

In this chapter we will uncover one of the unique stories within this framework: of the wheelchair basketball player Asael Shabbo, Reverse Integration Basketball Activity (RIBA), and Twinned Inclusive Basketball and Peace Activity (TIBAPA).

REVERSE INTEGRATION BASKETBALL ACTIVITY (RIBA)

RIBA is based on a program developed 2008-2010 by the Israel Sport Center for the Disabled (ISCD) and the Ilan Foundation supported by the Fund for Special Projects of the National Security Institute with Jewish and Arabic youth with and without disabilities, following the principles proposed by F. M. Brasile, of reversed integration in basketball. The RIBA initiative focused on cooperative comparable participation, which means sharing the activity goals, environment, equipment, rules, and actions among equal status players. The vision of the program was that it should facilitate the self-identity of all participants as basketball players rather than as persons with or without disability who happen to participate in sports. Several teams were established throughout the country, comprising a league where all players played in wheelchairs according to adapted mini-basketball rules. The main adaptations were (a) using a unique point system, classifying players by their functionality, and (b) using the twin-basket principle imported from Japan, where two baskets are used alternatively with a low basket (1.20 m height), which is warranted only for the players with lowest functionality who are not able to reach the higher basket from anywhere in the court. Following these principles enabled players with a variety of functional levels to be equally as effective as players with low functionality (not able to reach the high basket) and to develop a satisfying and successful game activity. Across the first competitive season, these players scored almost the same mean number of baskets per player as those with the highest functionality. Also, questionnaire and interview data revealed positive outcomes while maintaining very moderate rates of absenteeism and drop-off during the first two seasons. Following the principle of creating a social environment applicable for long-term athlete development, a national youth team was selected and sent to participate in international developmental tournaments.

Based on the experiences during the RIBA experience, including data suggesting its impact on participants' and spectators' attitudes, it was concluded that the inclusion experiences gained in this project could also be beneficial within the framework of developing peace and mutual understanding among hostile nationalities—the Israelis and the Palestinians, for example.

THE TWINNED INCLUSIVE BASKETBALL AND PEACE ACTIVITY (TIBAPA)

TIBAPA is a three-year-old initiative providing wheelchair basketball and fitness training, peace education, and joint peace-building activities to Palestinian and Israeli youth with and without disabilities from the communities of Holon, Rishon Letzion, Kiryat Malachi, and Bat Yam in Israel, and Beit Jallah and Bethlehem in the Palestinian Authority. This program, which is supported by the Peres Center, is directly impacting the participants and secondary beneficiaries by breaking down stereotypes of disability and nationality, building self-confidence, improving physical skills, teaching empathy, and offering a safe and meaningful space for dialogue and fun with the "other side."

The TIBAPA is organized jointly with the ISCD in Ramat-Gan, Israel, and the Lifegate Rehabilitation Foundation of Beit Jallah. The participants of the paired club program were recruited from the ISCD, established in 1960, which is one of the most experienced organizations in the world for providing physical activity and recreation services to youth with disabilities, and the Lifegate Rehabilitation foundation, which is a fast-growing service provider, where youngsters with disabilities are accepted and integrated in school and the vocational world. Lifegate initiatives and activities include a residential home for disabled people, an early childhood development center, medical care, and vocational job training. The ISCD activities include recreational and competitive sport-oriented programs focusing on swimming, basketball, tennis, table tennis, judo, and motor developmental activities.

The TIBAPA was developed as a program facilitating regular encounters among youth with and without physical disabilities, who regularly played wheelchair basketball at their home clubs. The activity follows the guidelines of RIBA, utilizing the twin-basket principle and the adapted rulebook.

In order to establish basic knowledge and skills for instructors at the Palestinian club, who were unfamiliar to the RIBA program, coaching clinics as well as followup educational meetings have been maintained, sharing the experiences and knowledge of coaches from the Jewish and Arab sectors in Israel together with the Palestinian coaches of Beit Jallah. The coaching clinics include the basic personal practices, as well as a general rule book and training principles, which are needed by the Palestinian participants, who come mostly from health rather than sporting professions.

The first encounter between the Palestinian and the Israeli children occurred on February 1, 2010. About 25 children and adolescents aged 14-18 from Beit Jalla, Palestinian Authority, and Rishon Lezion, Israel, met at the court of the Israeli team for a joint activity of twin wheelchair basketball. The group included participants with diverse functional abilities, ranging from severe disabilities such as spinal cord injury, cerebral palsy, spina bifida, learning disorders, and hearing impairment to participants without any known disability. All children used the wheelchair as a tool for experiencing an exciting and enjoying competitive and collaborative physical activity.

For the Palestinian group, this was the first encounter with the wheelchair sport environment, and an excellent opportunity for starting an extracurricular sport program. For all of the children this was a first encounter with children from "the other side." Nevertheless, no signs of resistance or avoidance were observed. Almost immediately, participants

mixed and cooperated in the different activities, specially designed to attract cooperative activity, while adapting to the wheelchair environment. Activities followed one after
the other and included wheeling and stopping to shake hands with a partner, passing in
groups, passing and wheeling, shooting at baskets of different heights, and finally, performing the touchdown game, a lead-up activity towards wheelchair basketball. It was
particularly impressive to see the spontaneous and barrier-free responsiveness of the children to each other, using the language of playing and sporting together as a common
denominator. Most striking was the patience and involvement of the able-bodied children
who exhibited open-mindedness and willingness to help where and when it was needed.
At the end of the activity mini bilingual sport dictionaries were handed out. As a result of
the first encounter one of the Palestinian participants said, "I did not know anything about
Israelis before, but now I know that they love sports just like me. I have an Israeli friend
and his name is Noam. I think it is good to have friends."

Bimonthly encounters followed between the two groups for over two years and continued with the same atmosphere of understanding and mutual respect. During the program
several experimental activities were provided, including the setting up of a joint team
composed of a mix of six Palestinian and six (Jewish and Arab) Israeli players, who trained
and competed against teams from several European countries under the joint supervision
of coaches from both partner clubs as well as from the Beer Sheva club in Israel, which
regularly included Arab Bedouin together with Jewish players and coaches. The story of
this unique experiment of the Peace Team is interwoven into the life story of Asael Shabbo.

THE PEACE TEAM

As described earlier, the highlight of the collaborative experience of the Palestinian and
Israeli clubs was when the Palestinian club was invited to join as part of the team that
was expected to attend an international youth tournament in Belgium. This was a practice
initiated two years before as a part of the RIBA project, and there were two alternatives:
one more- and one less-competitive tournament. The noncompetitive tournaments where
teams were mixed for practice and games was preferred, but due to technical constraints,
ultimately the more competitive tournament was selected as the target, and it appeared
that it was attended by youth national teams with a very high experience and performance
level in wheelchair basketball. This situation caused a major barrier to the joint team due
to their inexperience in this kind of activity and their inadequate performance level. The
uneven practical experience, where the Israelis had more experience and a higher performance level than the Palestinians, was a significant threat for normalization and frictionless
integration. Asael, the key Israeli player, explained, "We taught them some basketball and
showed them a different style, you may say, a higher level of basketball than what they had
before." Salim, the Bedouin Israeli coach, said, "A major problem was the competitiveness.

For example, the German team had four players who played on the national team. We intended to include an even number of Palestinians and Israeli players, but the kids wanted to be successful and the differences in performance level were very high. However, we always had at least one Palestinian player on the court, and sometimes two."

Obviously, language was an additional barrier threatening the joining of the young players from the opposing populations. In order to cope with this barrier the coaches tried different practices, particularly during the joint meals or leisure time. The Israeli Arab coach Salim explained, "One of our achievements was that by the end of the tournament they merged together rather than were seated as two different groups. … We were partially successful," he added, "but whenever two friends wanted to sit together, we couldn't disallow it."

Gadi, the other Israeli coach, reported that the Peace Team was a success, saying, "You stay a few days in a row together, and you understand that he isn't your enemy. The fact is that you continue to meet together, travel abroad together, and count on other members of the team when your are playing together, so even if someone says something about Arabs, I am sure it trickles down that there are good people on the other side."

Odeh, the Palestinian coach, was also satisfied with the results, and he summarized: "This project is great because it gave an opportunity for these people to enhance and develop their skills together with the other people. Sometimes their potential was more than ours, so we gained more and more experience from the others."

The experience of the Peace Team was unique, particularly for one of the participants who was the victim of a terrible terror assault.

ASAEL

Asael Shabbo was seriously wounded about nine years ago, when he was 9 years old.[1] A Palestinian terrorist group broke into the family home in one of the Jewish settlements in the West Bank. His mother and three of his siblings were murdered in this attack, and Asael's leg was seriously injured and had to be amputated above the knee. This tragedy doubtlessly left traumatic scars on the little boy's soul.

Losing a leg was not Asael's major problem. The pain, grief, and shock of the terrible moments of losing a major part of his family drove him into a constant state of mourning. The hammering of the fatal shots during those terrible moments resounded repeatedly inside his head. Again and again he saw the fire that broke out in his home and the screaming and agonizing, dying cries of his mother and siblings assaulted his ears.

It was not surprising that Asael became a very sad and solitary child. He kept his distance from those around him and spoke to almost no one apart from his father. When

[1] Some of the following text was used with permission from Moshe Raske's book *Doomed to Glory,* published by Milo Publishers in 2010.

people tried to make contact with him, they sensed his hostility, as if he were angry with them. What he really felt at that time was a maelstrom of emotions—anger, pain, and a desire for revenge. The many therapists working with the child found it very challenging to change his state of mind.

When he was first invited to join the Israel Sport Center for the Disabled (ISCD), Asael's father was not optimistic. He did not believe that sport activities were the appropriate tool to relieve the agony of his little child. However, after visiting the Centre and seeing Asael hesitantly moving a wheelchair and trying to pass, dribble, and shoot a basketball together with other children, his skepticism started to fade. Asael's father hoped that the contact with other disabled children and Asael's desire to play with them would help him counteract his depressed mood. He saw his son playing again—and even grinning when he scored a basket. His family, and especially the father, began to actively encourage Asael to spend time at the Center. Asael trained in swimming several times a week under the supervision of pedagogically skilled coaches, and soon became one of the top swimmers in his age group, winning bronze, silver, and gold medals during national and international competitions. His state of mind improved. Sport activities helped him to grow stronger and perform a variety of activities, which enabled him to live with the pain and the memories.

Through the practice of sport Asael has gained mental strength and renewed his spirit and energies. He became able to smile more often. He has matured into a strong and self-confident young man. In addition to his swimming practice, he also attended a swimming instructor's course and was exposed to the practice of wheelchair basketball. Having learnt about his mental capacity, it was just natural to involve him within the RIBA and TIBAPA programs and select him for the joint wheelchair basketball team representing the twin partners of the peace project. In the following, some statements from an in-depth interview with Asael are provided, exposing an inner glimpse of his experiences within these unique environments:

> I came from knowing nothing about basketball, and I learned very fast and started to train with them. … It was great fun to be with the guys of the team and we went to league games, where I was very pleased. It was a warm atmosphere to which I was very happy to join. I invested a lot and every day I used to come to the court and throw to the basket. I invested time to learn the moves of the wheelchair and learned the basics of basketball. Therefore, I was integrated very fast and became one of the opening five players of the team after three weeks.

Asael specifically highlighted the social support provided by the group activity: "There are another four people together with you on the court and another five on the bench—

about 10 people, as well as a very good coach, and this ties you together and makes you to want to invest even more."

Regarding the Peace Team, he explained, "Every year, two from each club are selected and included in a team that travels to participate in friendly games. There were guys with us from Beit Jallah, and we were six and six. It was not easy to integrate with them because sometimes they don't speak either English or Hebrew, but the coaches speak English, and I speak fluent English."

The joint traveling and playing with the Palestinians was a surprise for him. He soon accepted the idea and commented to us, "I learned to know them in Belgium. They are not bad people. Their coaches are very funny. At the end I enjoyed being with them, and this is something I was not expecting. It was not a bad experience." It was even an important experience, because according to his perception, "Today they are everywhere; queuing up at the supermarket or bus and you learn to know that not all of them are bad—just like not all the Jews are good. They are here and live with us and one needs to face it. You talk to them and see a different culture, different clothing, and different communication—less courteous, more aggressive." Nevertheless, due to his experience in the Peace Team he concluded, "I learned that not all the Arabs hate us! Everywhere you find bad people, but most of us are good people who try to help and assist each other."

Even though Asael and other members of the Israeli team have maintained their right wing political beliefs, the joint activity during the Peace Team "made them understand that on the Palestinian side there are people like them, not only terrorists," as one of the Israeli coaches elaborated.

CONCLUSIONS

Sustained peaceful interaction with "the other side" is an essential practice by which individuals revise their understanding of the other's perspective, as well as their own assumptions and prejudices. Therefore, it is likely that this change may affect the way these individuals relate to one other and behave in a conflict context. Joint experiences, long-term contact, and mutual relationships between people can cause them to regain confidence and trust toward the other side. In this chapter, I described a unique example of a sport-for-peace developmental activity, which utilized a goal-directed and contact-rich sport framework, as well as an extra marginalization variable: disability for changing prejudice. Verbal statements of participants as well as the actions of parents demonstrated substantial direct and extended ripple effects. I believe that the practices used and experiences gained during this experimental activity may be utilized in future large-scale interventions. Regarding the TIBAPA project and the Peace Team, a number of conclusions can be made:

1. First, it could be that the tolerance required between the able-bodied and the disabled, and the choice to enhance ability within a sporting environ-

ment rather than trying to "resist the inability," provide an additional inclusive atmosphere within our contact framework, which also facilitates bilateral national encounters. However, it is crucial that participants, particularly in the Peace Team, be of equal status, rather than of differing performance levels, as has been the case in our experiment.

2. Second, it is imperative to integrate the families and friends of participants through parent meetings, joint workshops, etc., in order to enhance the ripple effect (experiences, knowledge, and attitude change gathered within an in-group can be extended to out-group members if close relationships are fostered with the in-group members). Some meetings were organized at the beginning of the program, and a phenomenon reflecting a potential outcome of such an effect was the fact that the Israeli members of TIBAPA were the first of the twin sport schools to visit the Palestinian venue. Apparently, the prejudice and other attitudinal barriers experienced by the parents of the Israeli children were diminished.

3. Third, it is likely that one of the reasons for the ripple effect may have been the self-marginalized context of the Israeli participants, most of whom were with a disability. Parents of these children have to cope with prejudice within their social and educational frameworks, and might be more sensitive to the marginalization of the other group.

4. Fourth, it is imperative to deliver the message of this project through written and video-based media and to provide educational material to increase the awareness of this activity among the more remote circles of participants. A video report published on YouTube by the "BBC in Arabic" in 2011 and a written report on the Israeli "YNet News" were used to convey this example of good practice to larger audiences.

5. Finally, practices utilized during this experience could be transformed into an educational activity performed at schools on both sides, with participants of the Peace Team acting as peace ambassadors in front of the students and showing both the practice of wheelchair basketball and the peace games, and other students could be invited to participate. Such experiences have been found to be effective during workshops designed to reduce attitudinal barriers toward students with disability in the sport domain.

Putting Social Justice in the Game: Towards a Progressive Coaching Psychology

Ted M. Butryn

Historically, coaching has always had its share of scandals, including the many times when coaches were accused of racism and physical or verbal abuse, among other things. While most coaches, I suspect, have the best interests of their athletes at heart, it only takes a five-minute internet search to find dozens of mainstream media articles describing coaches behaving in ways that run counter to social justice and peace. Obviously, no one expects a coach, at any level, to be Gandhi. But for a profession that can have such a deep, even profound, impact on young athletes, it is somewhat disconcerting that more attention has not been directed at working towards a coaching model that is not simply humanistic or athlete-centered, but is directly aimed at infusing some degree of social consciousness into its practice. The purpose of this chapter, then, is to share some of my own stories related to coach education via my psychology of coaching course at San José State University (SJSU), when issues of social justice and peace came to the forefront. Some of the stories yielded successful pedagogical outcomes, I think, while others, to be frank, failed miserably. Regardless, this chapter hopefully will provide some insight into how coaching can do more for the world than it currently does.

That this chapter was even worth writing speaks to the lack of a solid research foundation on issues related to social justice and coaching. While the past five years have seen a rise in the work in what has come to be known as *cultural sport psychology,* little of this work has dealt specifically with coaching, and it has certainly not led to any kind of substantial increase in research attempting to connect coaching research with issues of social justice, peace, identity politics, or any politics for that matter. So what is an instructor to do when he or she wishes to teach a class in a way that has almost no reference point in the literature? Most textbooks in applied sport psychology in the 21st century have ancillary materials, including PowerPoint files, exam questions, discussion topics, and so on, but no such materials really exist for a university professor trying to infuse the work in cultural sport psychology with the traditional, largely apolitical applied sport psychology or coaching psychology texts.

Indeed, I am currently staring at my bookshelves, full of all sorts of useful and not so useful books. About one-third of the wall is devoted to sport psychology and coaching books; many contain my scrawled comments, my old post-it notes, and perhaps even a few stray hairs that surely were not as grey as the ones I have now. One of the reasons I was hired at my university was because I had an unusual background. I studied cultural studies, a field within which social justice occupies a central position, and sport psychology, which rarely addressed such issues. Throughout my doctoral work, I was determined to connect sport psychology with social identity issues such as race, class, gender, sexual orientation, and disability. At the time I was working on my dissertation, I wrote one of my first academic journal papers on Whiteness and White racial identity in sport psychology.

To move this chapter along, we can fast-forward to the fall of 2000 when I took a position in the department of kinesiology at SJSU. Along with a sociology of sport course and another on diversity, stress, and health, I was also the designated instructor for the psychology of coaching class. I was excited about this because I had never taught the class before, but more importantly because it seemed like a great opportunity to teach the course in a new way, in a manner that connected coaching psychology research with my newfound knowledge and emphasis on cultural studies. I was going to politicize the psychology of coaching! In reality, though, I was also a few days past my 29th birthday, and I had no idea what I would be doing in the classroom.

The psychology of coaching class is offered every spring, so I had the whole fall semester to get my bearings as a new PhD teaching at one of the most culturally diverse institutions in the country. Although I had completed my master's degree here and had taught several physical activity courses as a graduate assistant, the preparation had a whole new level of seriousness. The class was not a mere bowling or weight training class. Gutter balls are no fun, certainly, and neither is figuring out how to handle some meathead who drops a 60-pound dumbbell in weight training. The psychology of coaching course was a "real" class, and importantly, it was required for every teaching education student in the department. In short, the fact that I had a genuine opportunity to influence young and aspiring coaches in a way that spoke to my belief in social justice issues and sport was not lost on me. It was very important that these future teachers, virtually all of whom were already coaching, were schooled in this approach I was preparing.

My own memories of the relationship between coaching and social justice, or politics of any kind, begin in college during the Gulf War. I remember the event distinctly because of the way it was covered, visually, by the media. It was the first time we saw war footage that looked as much like a video game, with green-tinted night vision and flashing tracers, as anything ever had before. I wasn't all that political in 1991 when my roommate and I watched the city of Baghdad come under fire from "Operation Desert Storm," and I had no intention of protesting or supporting anything because I was more concerned about my homework and a tough workout the following day. However, my coach, who had been a member of three Olympic teams, including the 1980 Games that the US boycotted, certainly had an idea that even at a relatively conservative school like the University of Tennessee there might be some sort of student action aimed at either protesting the war, or more likely, supporting the military offensive. At practice he stated that we should not become involved in anything that might go on, because he did not want any of us getting into trouble. I've forgotten his exact words, but I remember thinking, "Okay, I wasn't going to do anything anyway, but can the coach really tell us not to?" Sure enough, there were a few hundred antiwar protesters, and literally a couple thousand pro-war students who marched to the International Student House and protested, even though there were no Iraqi students on campus! The university actually made the national network news, and they showed footage of two drunken guys with huge cups of beer yelling something like, "USA, number 1!" That is when I had some sense that the coach, while perhaps doing it to "protect" us, had effectively dissuaded a group of young college students from being engaged in an important political event in a particular way.

In my first year at SJSU I started thinking about athletes and politics again during the 2000 presidential election campaign. I decided to do a small study on how college athletes saw themselves in relation to social issues and whether their coaches in any way touched on issues related to politics or social issues, or perhaps even worked towards an athlete-as-citizen approach to coaching. I interviewed a dozen or so college athletes, and the results did not bode well for athletes being anything other than. . . athletes. I was not all that surprised, but I did hope that at least one of the coaches would have touched on progressive social issues of any kind. In fact, some athletes were apparently completely disengaged from any sort of social or political issues whatsoever. One athlete, who was actually a co-captain of his team and occupied a central leadership position, summed up the sentiments of most of the athletes when he said, "To be honest, my political stance and issues and stuff weren't at all where I wish they'd be at right now, you know. I'm supposed to vote now, and honestly I haven't voted because. . . I don't know. I'm 21 and I've had three or four years to be capable of voting and I leave it to my mom still." An interesting peripheral finding involved participants' reactions following the interview sessions. Their feelings were often positive, but characterized more by shock that they actually had the opportunity to discuss issues related to politics, agency, and the like. In fact, several expressed that they were apprehensive about even taking part in the study. As one athlete said, "I was like, politics and power? That's all stuff I don't like to mess with." As the rest of the paper will illustrate, helping athletes or coaches see the importance of social justice issues, or the concept of peace, is easier said than done.

STORIES FROM THE FRONT OF THE CLASS

Have you ever looked into the mirror and wondered if you were authentic? Or pondered the question, "Am I really living up to my beliefs, or am I a poseur? A fraud? What kind of person am I?" It is a humbling experience, and one I assume most educators experience from time to time. Over the last 12 years I have done this many times, and I have to admit that many times I have concluded that I have, in fact, stood my philosophical ground in the class, and used difficult moments as the magical teaching moments you hear people talk about. But I'm not going to really talk about those as much as I am going to talk about the times when I, at the very least, felt uncomfortable with the contents of my lectures and the reactions of the students, and at the worst, felt compelled to soft-sell difficult material, and even skip over certain topics in the interest of keeping the peace, as I moved on to less choppy waters.

TESTING THE WATERS

When I teach issues like racism, homophobia, and sexual harassment in the coaching class at San José State University now, I am always careful, yet not apologetic, with how I introduce the topics. It took more than a few years, but I've learned that sometimes how these issues are framed is as important as the content itself. So the first couple of PowerPoint slides are always meant to contextualize what, for some students, might be touchy subjects within the larger philosophy of the class. From the first day, the class takes a humanistic and athlete-centered approach that places overall development and well-being over mere performance. In addition, I frame the coach as an individual who can contribute to social justice and equity, or who can perpetuate things like racism, sexism, homophobia, violence, and so on. I explain that the world of sport has many positive aspects, but that it also has the potential to contribute to very negative outcomes as well, including physical and emotional harm, long-term psychological damage, and regressive social change. At this point, there are always a few students who roll their eyes, smirk, or give looks to the student next to them that seem to say, "What department are we in here, social work?" But for many students, this approach, from the outset, helps to set a tone for the rest of the class. Of course, I make sure to mention my own athletic background and assert that one of the main goals of the course is to ultimately help them become better coaches, although my definition of better certainly diverges at times from their own.

One of the first obstacles I faced when trying to create a coaching class that integrated social justice issues took place even before the class began, and that was. . . the integration. The textbook I used, and have used for over a decade, is an extremely good applied sport psychology textbook. Every chapter, in my view, is highly relevant to young coaches. The problem? The semester is only 15 weeks long, and there is already more material than I have time to cover in one semester. The question I asked myself that first semester was, "What am I going to take out of the course, and essentially deprive the students of, so that I can insert a unit on race, one on gender, one on harassment, and one on homophobia . . . over two weeks worth of course content?"

One focus I was determined to integrate well was racial and ethnic identities in sport, and how they may affect coaching in myriad ways. A couple of times during the semester I integrated into the class some of Kathie Jamieson's work on Latina softball players in an effort to get students to read some of the research, but also because, again, I saw so many Latina/o students in my classroom. It was almost awkward reciting the PowerPoint bullet points as I looked at the class, and I wondered how the research that produced these bullet points generalized to them, whether cultural differences made a difference. The mistake I made, however, was that I went straight through the slides on diversity and coaching for the sake of getting through the testable material for the exam. As I've grown as an instructor, I've come to the conclusion that having facts students can spit back at you is far less important than the rich dialogues that can emerge from class discussions, especially on issues like race and ethnicity that are not mentioned in the more traditional coaching psychology coursework. I usually ask the class if racial, ethnic, or cultural identity had ever played a role in their sport experience, as a player or a coach. While it sometimes takes a while for them to feel comfortable, there are always one or two brave souls who raise their hands and get the ball rolling with often touching, compelling, or maddening stories. That first semester, after the class was over and students were leaving, one Latino student who had been fairly quiet and sat in the back until that day, stopped and said, "That was the first time anyone's ever talked about Latinos ... well, for me, Mexicans ... in any class here in the department. I just appreciate it." It was a connection that continued when he entered the graduate program, and it was actually the first time I realized that I wasn't doing something that was the norm in my relatively new job. It also taught me the importance of understanding that teaching about coaching in the US, with its current demographic shifts, without integrating issues of racial and ethnic diversity into the class is, in itself, a form of injustice.

Another issue related to race and coaching I talk about every semester is what is referred to in the literature as *Whiteness* and the power issues connected to White racial identities. Try telling a group of current and future coaches, who are mostly avid and uncritical sport fans, that White coaches have a wealth of privileges that coaches of color do not and that it has historically been better to be an average White coach with a reasonable record than an African American coach with a good record. As any introductory sociology of sport textbook will tell you, sport is a conservative social institution that more often than not upholds rather than challenges the status quo, even if the status quo involves inequities or injustices.

Whiteness, in my view, is one of the most important topics in coaching psychology, if for no other reason than most coaches in high level sports continue to be White males, and the population of US athletes will continue to become more diverse as the demographics shift over the next several decades. Much as many White coaches were unprepared for the newly politicized Black athletes of the late 1960s, I fear that most White coaches today are similarly and to the same degree ill-equipped to negotiate a culturally diverse athlete population, whether related to race, ethnicity, sexual orientation, or religion.

So what is Whiteness? In short, Whiteness relates to how White racial identity was once accompanied by what scholar Peggy McIntosh called a "knapsack of White privileges." However, while Whiteness was once framed as invisible or transparent, in recent years White ethnic groups have begun to claim Whiteness in ways that they did not in the past. What is important for this chapter is the idea that White coaches have, whether they want to believe it or not, traditionally been dealt a better hand than their minority counterparts. Perhaps not a winning hand outright, but a better hand. In fact, there is ample evidence to support this, and there is research that found, at least in the 1990s, White coaches were more likely than Black coaches to get recycled through the system and to be given multiple opportunities in sports like football. In American pro football, the so-called Rooney Rule was enacted that requires teams to interview a racial minority for coaching vacancies. This, in itself, speaks to the notion that left alone, Whites were going to have some sort of advantage, whether systematic or not.

I always find myself taking the don't-kill-the-messenger approach, even in a classroom where White students wouldn't have the numbers to stage a mutiny. By this, I mean that after explaining what Whiteness and White privilege are, I say something to the effect that, "Now, this isn't some left-wing rhetoric, and I don't hate White men because … well, I don't get off on hating myself." The students generally laugh at that point, and while it might diffuse some of the tension, I am not sure that is it the best teaching technique. Either way, I am pretty sure it confuses some of the more conservative race thinkers in the class, because while they might want to dismiss what I am saying, they cannot do so on the grounds that confronting Whiteness is "my issue." Of course, it is my issue, but in their minds, and from their own comments, they get a bit confused. I can almost see those cartoon bubbles popping out of their heads, with phrases like, "This guy is supposed to be on our side!" Of course, I can imagine that it might be just as uncomfortable for students who are not White. At any rate, my point in teaching the research on Whiteness and relating it to coaching is that White students should, from my perspective, be prompted to confront how their own racial identities affect their coaching and how they interact with other athletes, parents, and administrators.

VIOLENT SPORT AND PEACE: CAN THEY BE RECONCILED?

Part of this book involves the relationship between sport and peace. Throughout the 20th century we can find many examples of times when politicians, for instance, used sport to stimulate civil dialogue with rival nations. Nixon's so-called ping-pong diplomacy would be one example, as would the series of US-Soviet track meets that were held in the 1970s. More recently, I remember reading news stories about how some segments of the Iraqi population rallied around their soccer team after the ouster of Saddaam Hussein. However, when I think about the relationship between coaching, contemporary sport, and peace, I have more trouble coming up with many examples. I have done several studies on the rapidly growing sport of mixed martial arts, including the most prominent brand, the Ultimate Fighting Championship. As I write this section of the chapter, I am struggling to make sense of how sports like mixed martial arts, and the concussion-ridden violent sports of professional football and ice hockey, fit with any sort of peace project.

Despite gender stereotypes, women coaches and athletes are certainly part of the larger culture of violence in sport. In fact, the one group of students who every semester have stories to tell about their coaches telling them—not suggesting but ordering—to commit violent acts against their opponents are the female soccer players. I remember listening to the women talk about how they went onto the field with the intent of putting other players out of the game and being a bit surprised that this sort of thing would be common in the upper-class suburbs of "liberal" California. But then the next semester, and the next, and the next. . . every time women in class raised their hands when I brought up the issue of coaching and athlete violence, I heard similar stories. It really shouldn't be surprising, as we know that violence is as much about socialization as anything else, but for some reason students in my classes have always been taken aback by the stories, not because the coaches told them to go side-tackle someone, but because the female players actually did it! Call it the "Thelma and Louise effect": men committing violence is expected, but when female athletes do it, there is a schism in the time-space continuum, perhaps because we do not have a framework with which to make sense of it.

One form of sport-related violence that has received quite a bit of media attention is hazing. In some cases athletes have been forced to do things like drink until they vomit or run around the track nude, but many of the cases have involved far more humiliating and even sadistic practices, such as forced sodomy with various objects, including in one instance pinecones. When I begin the class, I usually start with the statement, "When I look out that window and see all those pinecones on the ground, I think of them growing up into huge trees hundreds of years from now. I don't think about seeing how far I can cram it up my teammate's rectum to build team cohesion. Maybe I don't get it?" Needless to say, that gets their attention. Although it is certainly offensive to some students, I've never shied away from revealing a view of sport cultures that is not positive, but profoundly deviant. Given the arguably desensitized state of American youth culture, where entire television shows devote time to showing various violent spectacles, I think it takes the graphic but startling pinecone anecdote to get them to really see the impact these deviant rituals have on athletes and how important it is for coaches to intervene at the front end to prevent these episodes from ever happening. For the past several years I have delivered one lecture on hazing every time I teach the psychology of coaching class, with an emphasis on what coaches should do to establish a team culture that simply does not allow hazing to exist.

Should coaches even be involved in peace efforts? Shouldn't they be more concerned about occupying the win column than occupying Wall Street? How can coaches be expected to care about social justice and peace when coaches in the increasing number of elite specialized youth programs face pressures comparable to those in pro sports? Where is the space of benevolence needed for coaches to invest in the kind of projects I've discussed in this chapter? Even more importantly, until recently, athletes themselves have shown little interest in political issues. In the late 1960s, my current school, SJSU, was the epicenter of the Olympic Project for Human Rights that was organized by Dr. Harry Edwards. Since then, the corporate structure of sport has led to more and more athletes sitting idly by while their bank accounts grow, as college coaches and administrators warn them that bad publicity is not something desirable.

My favorite story of how the dominant thinking about effective coaching and aggressive behavior, negative or abusive feedback, and an overall culture of violence can trump an *entire* semester of work involves one student. We will call him Nick, and he was in my coaching class four years ago. He sat in the back, contributed occasionally, and performed adequately on his best day. On the final day of class, we reviewed for the exam and talked about the most important things that the students learned from the class. As this was happening, a senior faculty member performed my peer evaluation, which she had waited until the very last day to do. Everything went well until Nick raised his hand and proudly, even defiantly, said, "You know, I still think you aren't being a good coach unless you scream at them a little. I mean, the good coaches say you need to do it." After a semester of humanistic approaches to coaching and an infusion of positive psychology, this was what his final, closing statement was. The rest of the students shook their heads, though a few nodded. I am not sure exactly what I said, but when I received my evaluation from the senior faculty member, she had written, "WATCH YOUR EVIL EYE! You glared at one student and I think there are more effective ways of dealing with it … maybe take him aside and explain why you were angry. But overall, a great class!" I suppose dialogue is better than intimidation, and her much needed feedback has been useful for other, less flabbergasting student comments.

One final topic I teach in the class is a brief unit on Zen and coaching. Until I started this chapter, I really never thought of how Zen related to coaching and something like peace. It sounds superficial perhaps, but I have tried to use the work on Zen and sport psychology as a way to bring a bit of Eastern philosophy into the class, and to help students to see how some of the common concepts in Zen, like mindfulness, would be very useful in coaching. Numerous consultants and coaches have suggested that by practicing Zen and learning to quiet the mind, athletes may attain higher levels of mastery and even peak performance.

My initial lesson in Zen and sport was very memorable. In my first year at SJSU, I attended a small, regional sport psychology conference in Fresno, and the keynote speaker was Dr. Jerry Lynch, a sport psychologist from Santa Cruz, California, who used a Zen approach in his work with many successful teams and athletes, including top NCAA and professional teams. As odd as it may sound, the most memorable part of his talk involved a sponge. A regular old blue sponge. He was talking about how sometimes sport psychology consultants try to use all of their tools and force too much new information and feedback into the already saturated brains of athletes. As he said this, he poured water into the sponge, and then tossed it on the table. He then exclaimed, "If that sponge is the athlete, why would you try to put *more* into it?" He squeezed the sponge and calmly stated, "Coaches and sport psychology practitioners need to remember to help athletes clear their minds first, before they try to do anything." It was a great teaching moment, and I still use this story, sponge included, every semester to introduce Zen in the coaching class.

Now on the surface, Zen approaches to coaching are not directly related to social justice or peace. In fact, some would say that even using Zen as a tool for performance enhancement goes against what Zen is supposed to be about in the first place. On the other hand, a Zen approach to coaching is also almost incompatible with abusive coaching or coaching styles that center on causing violence to others. In this sense, perhaps an increase in the use of Zen approaches by coaches has the potential to subtly change the entire culture of sport, or at least that of individual teams. The renowned professional coach Phil Jackson has written about how he used some aspects of Zen when he coached the Chicago Bulls and Michael Jordan, but his approach certainly has not become the norm among his peers.

THAT WASN'T IN MY LECTURE! ON (NOT) CONFRONTING COACHES DURING GUEST LECTURES

Hollywood producers would have a potential hit on their hands if they ever invented a game show called "Coaches say the darndest things!" I don't mean this in a demeaning way at all, but I literally cannot count the number of times that coaches have given guest talks in my class and said things that made me cringe and that prompted students to shoot me surprised looks, often in unison. Admittedly, these instances of coaches saying the darndest things have been ripe with teachable moments and full of opportunities for the students to discuss whatever the coaches said that went against most or all of what I'd taught them during the semester. The problem is that for many younger coaches, my lectures and all the research on earth don't carry as much weight as the voice of a Division I coach who has, in their eyes, made it to the big time. Despite my desire to stop the coaches in their tracks when they say something that flies in the face of social justice, peace, or common decency, I have, without exception, allowed them to tell their own stories uninterrupted and unchallenged. I suppose I've always felt that if they were cool enough to give up some of their valuable time, then they didn't deserve to be subjected to an inquisition by someone whose biggest coaching accomplishment was receiving a bronze-level coaching certificate from USA Bowling.

One of my favorite examples of a coach-gone-wild moment was when a former football coach came to the class to talk. It was a great opportunity for the students, since many of them were coaching football at the time. In addition, the coach was one of the few minority head coaches in Division I football and held an advanced degree. It was a perfect … well … Desert Storm. The coach had served in Operation Desert Storm during the Persian Gulf War. He was also a very religious man, and at one point he described a pregame speech during which he yelled to his players, "Go out on the battlefield with the Lord on your wings and beat down the enemy!" That is not a direct quote, but it was pretty close to that; it may have been more over the top. I give him credit for combining militaristic combat-speak with religious imagery. I noticed some students laughing, and others who looked really uncomfortable. It could have been because I had already talked about research that suggests that pregame pep talks are often not worth much. However, I suspect there were other reasons. There were at least two Muslim students in the class, for example, and although I am not sure if any of the students were Jewish, I am sure they did not appreciate him talking about how he forced players to attend church every Sunday. Well, he did add that students who did not attend church could "do their own thing." I have not researched team cohesion, but excluding some students from mandatory team activities because of faith does not seem to be an effective team-building tactic.

At any rate, some students seemed genuinely offended by the violent images he evoked, and maybe others did not like the combination of faith and war and sport. Now I am not coming down too hard on the coach here, because he was simply using his own life experiences and worldview to motivate his team. My point is that much of what he and other coaches have said runs counter to anything resembling a humanistic, social-justice, peace-oriented approach to coaching. Maybe it is too much to expect Division I coaches to think about these issues, but I have often found myself wishing they would have left some parts of their stories out of their guest appearances.

The other issue that male coaches, in particular, have been prone to bringing up during their guest talks involves the supposedly "natural" differences between male and female athletes. Unfortunately, some of the coaches' comments, while not devoid of merit, resulted in some women in the class feeling as though they were an entirely different, and inferior, species. Indeed, one aspect of social justice, gender equity, is among the most pressing issues in sport and has been since the passage of Title IX legislation in 1972. While most women's teams were coached by female coaches at one time, male coaches now hold the majority of coaching positions in most women's sports. Unfortunately, some male coaches carry incorrect and sometimes outright sexist views of gender into their roles as coaches. I am not saying that male coaches are doing any kind of extensive damage to the women they coach. I am stating that I have witnessed, in every single male coach who has guest-lectured in my coaching class, a mindset that women athletes have some sort of fundamental differences from their male counterparts. More importantly, these proposed differences are often framed, intentionally or not, as deficiencies. One coach, for example, mentioned how the "girls" on the team care more about not hurting one another's feelings than they do about competing for a spot on the team. Another told an admittedly funny story about how he met with his team to ask them what they wanted to be called, since someone had told him that calling young, strong female athletes "girls" or "ladies" was inappropriate and perhaps even offensive in the 21st century. Not surprisingly, perhaps, the women on the team eventually said, "Coach, we don't care what you call us. Let's just get to practice!" Importantly, every one of these coaches had coached men before obtaining their current coaching jobs, so they had plenty of "evidence" for believing that some women athletes have some sort of innate personality deficits when it comes to higher-level competition.

A couple of times it was the female students in the class who objected to the coaches' comments, putting the coaches on the defensive. Inevitably, after the coaches left, we would talk further about the research that had been discussed on the known versus perceived differences in how men and women coach, and how athletes react to coaches of different genders. It is encouraging that my teaching experiences have shown me that 40 years after Title IX, many current and future women coaches feel compelled to confront outdated views of gender and gender stereotypes when they see them.

CONCLUSIONS

So what can people take away from this chapter? Since the point of telling these stories was to stimulate critical thinking about the relationship between the coaching profession, social justice, and peace, I hope that readers will find parts of the chapter evocative. One of my favorite things about reading autobiographical writings, whether for professional or personal reasons, is that I can find things in the author's life or in his or her narratives that make me think, "Hmm, I wonder how that applies to my life?" In going through my stories, I think that coaches from the least competitive levels of youth sport up through Division I will see that a number of the issues I raised will come up at one time or another. In addition, I think my stories show that although speaking about sport in terms of its relation to social justice and peace is not always natural or even appropriate, perhaps the choice to do so can transform coaching into a much more benevolent and aware practice.

I have to admit that in transcribing some of my thoughts, I realized I have failed more than I have succeeded in continuing to push the dozens of coaches who take my class each year to take issues of social justice and peace seriously in their coaching. I can think of at least a couple times when I have skipped over the hazing, race, or harassment lectures because of time constraints or because a coach was willing to talk with the class on short notice. I've never neglected motivation, team cohesion, or feedback. In addition, in my work over the past 11 years with university athletes, I have never, even once, talked to the athletes or their coaches about any of the issues I've discussed in this chapter. I am not sure I've had much of a chance to do so, but perhaps it is just because I was more concerned with performance enhancement issues than issues that the young men and women will have to confront for the rest of their lives. I do know that the world of Division I college sport in the US is not really set up in a way that is ready-made for educating athletes on issues of social justice and peace. I wonder if it ever could be, but I'm game for giving it a go.

Of course, not every coach will go about integrating issues of social justice, equity, and peace in the same way, and some may even reject outright the idea of a politicized coaching field. Coaches should coach, not work for any agenda. But my argument is that coaching is always and already politicized. It is never neutral nor has it ever been. When coaches in the late 1960s used racist terms against Black players, it was politicized, and when the late Bill Walsh, the San Francisco 49ers football coach, helped open the doors for African American coaches in the formerly White space of the NFL, it was politicized. Nevertheless, I am not sure what the coaches' role will be, or should be, in confronting issues of social injustice, inequity, and peace.

While I have not really touched on it much, I am less concerned about infusing issues of social justice and peace in elite level coaching than I am in doing so in the younger, nonelite population that comprises the majority of sport participants. In youth sport, little thought is paid to social justice issues because of the changes in youth sport in the US over the past decade or so. It used to make headlines when a father pushed his son too hard and the son eventually flamed out in dramatic fashion. I remember reading stories about former quarterback Todd Marinovich in high school and how his father pushed him in a manner some labeled as abusive. In the second decade of the 21st century, all bets seem to be off, and as I write this chapter, in the midst of deep economic uncertainty, I wonder how much pressure I would be putting on my own child to get a coveted, though rare, full college scholarship.

In conclusion, whenever I hear coaches talk about building character or helping to develop young men and women, my first instinct is to laugh. Of course, I know many coaches do wonderful things, and as the saying goes, you can tell the true nature of a coach by the line at the funeral when they pass on. But I laugh because these trite proclamations are repeated over and over, without much in the way of public critique from the mainstream media, parent groups, or anyone for that matter. Indeed, many polls suggest that parents see sport participation as an overwhelmingly positive thing for children. We know that the athlete-centered approach may dissipate as kids grow into adults and move into the elite levels of competition, but by and large the notion that good coaching builds character and good men and women is taken for granted. This chapter has hopefully challenged that assumption, prompting readers to ask questions like, "What counts as character?" and "What kinds of men and women are coaches helping to develop anyway?" Below are a few final reflections pertaining to this story:

1. Educators should find ways to teach young coaches the importance of social justice to the coaching profession.

2. Coaches should examine their own biases and their reliance on stereotypes when dealing with athletes.

3. The win-at-all-cost mentality is not a necessary component in helping athletes become agents of social change.

4. Coaches have the potential to be a force for tolerance, equity, and social good.

Cases in Sport Development: Our Reflections

Ronnie Lidor and Robert J. Schinke

The cases included in this volume were grouped into three sections: "Remedying Marginalization," "Health and Well-Being," and "Sport for Peace and Social Justice." In each section the authors share with us their experiences, perceptions, and thoughts about how sport can positively contribute to the enhancement of social developmental processes in the individual athlete, the group, and/or the community. Within the section on remedying marginalization we have included a number of contributions about athletes fulfilling their dreams to reach the highest level of proficiency in their sport, in spite of the fact that they lived in countries or regions where inadequate sport systems existed. These cases reveal to us how people can overcome their surroundings by looking within for inspiration. In the section on health and well-being we find stimulating vignettes about the difficulties of two women with body image issues who worked with personal trainers in exercise and obesity control programs. From these writings, we learn about the social stigma of being overweight and navigating through a lack of empathy from others in their exercise contexts. In the section on peace and social justice we learn how the game of soccer can be used to foster relationships between young and adult Jewish and Arab players in nonprofit programs such as Football for Peace (F4P) and Mifalot (an organization in the Middle East that promotes the use of soccer for fostering development and peace). Together, these stories, though featured in separated sections, intersect when the reader considers that distinct pathways were chosen to overcome barriers, opening people up to better lives.

The stories included in our book are narrative; they tell the story of female and male individuals—athletes, coaches, instructors, and researchers—all engaged in the area loosely termed sport development (SD) comprised of both sport *and* physical activity contexts. Each story tells us about the challenges these individuals face in their life, work, or while doing the featured activity. Most of the stories affirm the contribution of sport and physical activity to human development, such as when reaching a high level of proficiency in competitive sport, conceptualizing a more inclusive philosophy of coaching, building more access to sport services for those in need, or promoting research. One may claim that some of the stories are naïve or that they reflect the feelings and thoughts of a small number of storytellers. One might ask, what can be learned from these cases and the images they leave us with? Furthermore, it is worth asking, "How can I benefit from these case studies in my own life journey?"

One of the objectives of this book was to provide individuals who had a positive experience in sport or physical activity with the opportunity to tell us their personal stories about positive experiences, meaning *their* pathway to success. We wanted these individuals to explain why they perceive their involvement in sport or physical activity as positive and stimulating, and what they actually gained through their engagement. The cases featured in this book are told by people from our global SD community, including Africans, Asians, Australians, Europeans, people from the South Pacific, and North Americans. Regardless of their culture, religion, ethnicity, or social-economical status, all continue to feel that their featured context can be used effectively to make a change, either in their personal life or in the community in which they work.

While reading the cases included in the three sections of this book and "listening" to the voices of the contributing authors, the editors derived three observations:

a. Sport and physical activity can serve as a vehicle for the dream of a better life.

b. Sport and physical activity contexts can serve as a mediator in fostering relationships.

c. Sport and physical activity contexts can help individuals cope with barriers within and across parts of their life.

Each of these three aspects is considered directly below.

SPORT AND PHYSICAL ACTIVITY CAN SERVE AS A VEHICLE FOR THE DREAM OF A BETTER LIFE

Some of the individuals who shared their stories with us had distinct dreams that moved them forward in life: playing hockey in a competitive league, losing weight, being more accepted, or engaging others in meaningful physical activity programming. We can learn from these cases that if one works hard, sets appropriate goals, knows how to physically and psychologically face challenges, and above all, believes in his or her ability to achieve and overcome, then these dreams can be fulfilled, leading to personal, group, and/or community advancement. Despite the fact that the roads to fulfilling dreams in sport or physical activity are arduous and complex, as we learned from the cases, these individuals were able to meet their expectations and achieve the goals they set, either for themselves or in support of others. These individuals were proud of their featured achievements. Since the storytellers' experiences were positive and they considered sport or physical activity to be an important contributor to personal development, they decided to share their stories to inspire others to act—mainly those who are young and inexperienced.

SPORT AND PHYSICAL ACTIVITY CONTEXTS
CAN SERVE AS A MEDIATOR IN FOSTERING RELATIONSHIPS

We learn from some of the stories that in regions around the world (e.g., Europe, the Middle East, and in Canadian Aboriginal reserves), individuals perceive sport as a mediator in fostering relationships among people. Individuals who share similar goals, such as athletes playing on the same soccer team, or staff seeking to engage marginalized youth in a physical activity, can use the interactions that exist in practices, competitions, and programmed activities, to learn about and respect each other. The cases offer us a message: that sport and physical activity can help people overcome cultural differences, language barriers, diverging world standpoints, political disagreements, and histories of colonizing practices, for both the colonized and the colonizer. Some of the contributing authors truly believe that sport and physical activity can do for people what other endeavors in life, such as economics, politics, and industry, have often failed to do—break down personal and social barriers. As long as sport and physical activity is perceived as a major cultural-economical-social domain in post-modern society, we should make an effort to use these educational activities in building confidence and trust among people, and in increasing mutual understanding and synergy. Such endeavors could lead to better social integration and the centralizing of many views, shared and understood, contributing to untapped human intersections—feeding peace and social justice.

SPORT AND PHYSICAL ACTIVITY CONTEXTS CAN HELP INDIVIDUALS
COPE WITH BARRIERS WITHIN AND ACROSS PARTS OF THEIR LIFE

We can also learn from this book how the storytellers were able to successfully cope with the obstacles they encountered, both personally and within the contexts that they live. The contributors share the lessons they learned, and provide pathways for those who lack belief in self when faced with barriers and challenges in sport and physical activity. Some of the cases can stimulate the young, and maybe the not so young, to try their best to reach their goals and not to give up when they encounter difficulties. In addition, some of the cases strengthen the belief that participating in sport and physical activity can teach individuals how to excel, beyond a given achievement context. In reality, people need to learn how to encounter obstacles and how to effectively overcome them. We propose, in keeping with the cases featured, that coping can be learned through sport and physical activity, and what is learned can give individuals and groups the "legs" they need to stand on in trying moments. In fact, we learn from the varied cases that one can apply what was learned in and from their chosen context to challenging areas and activities outside of sport, long after one disengages and/or ages out of sport or exercise.

CONCLUDING THOUGHTS

It is our hope that the cases shared in this volume will be read, not only by those involved in sport, such as athletes, parents, coaches, instructors, sport administrators, and researchers, but also by educators at large, policy makers, and politicians. We believe that the authors' accounts reveal the positive side of their chosen contexts, a side that may not be reported in academic journals or observed on the field, perhaps due to the skepticism in each one of us. These cases tell us about the contribution of sport to one's development and character, and help us understand how sport contributes to individuals becoming better people. They also tell us that we need to continue to study the contribution of sport development programs in relation to personal and communal advancement. Above all, these cases are meant to motivate us to seek out the stories of other individuals who have succeeded, in order to benefit from their involvement in sport and physical activity. Perhaps it is also time to consider our very own experiences, and how these, too, can become tales seen through a positive lens, furthering momentum in the way we collectively move through our daily existence. Lessons are there to be learned, promising pathways within!

These cases can help us think out of the box and increase our motivation to act and then realize new initiatives. If some of the readers of this volume adopt a different (i.e., more progressive) view about the contribution of sport and physical activity to our lives as a collective, then the cases did make a difference. That difference must now serve as a catalyst among the readership as we seek to teach others the pathways that have been articulated in this compilation and elsewhere in the form of sport-for-development-and-social-justice cases. However, the reader must also remember that solid SD, in keeping with what the story tellers shared, ought to be derived at the community level, starting with where an SDP opportunity is germane, where a true groundswell can be created, leading to meaningful change among and within each one of us.

Index

About the Editors

Robert J. Schinke, is the Canada Research Chair in Multicultural Sport and Physical Activity and Professor of Sport Psychology in the School of Human Kinetics at Laurentian University. As a Canadian Sport Psychology Association-accredited practitioner, Schinke has extensive experience working with national teams and professional athletes of North America, South America, Europe, Asia, Africa, and the Caribbean. Schinke has authored more than 100 academic and applied articles and co-edited nine textbooks—including *The Cultural Turn in Sport Psychology* (2010) and *Sport for Development, Peace, and Social Justice* (2012), both published by Fitness Information Technology—beyond authoring four books. His research is supported by the Social Sciences and Humanities Research Council of Canada, the Indigenous Health Research Development Program, and the Canadian Foundation for Innovation. In addition, Schinke serves as editor of *Athletic Insight,* associate editor for the *Journal of Sport and Social Issues,* and as an editorial board member for the *Journal of Clinical Sport Psychology.* In addition, a former Canadian Equestrian Team Member and Pan American Games athlete, Schinke enjoys yoga and cross-country running. He, his wife, Erin, and their two sons, Harrison and Pierce, reside in Sudbury, Ontario, Canada.

Ronnie Lidor is a professor and the Director of the Zinman College of Physical Education and Sport Sciences at the Wingate Institute, and he is also on the faculty of education at the University of Haifa (Israel). His main areas of research are cognitive strategies, talent detection, early development in sport, and sport development. Lidor has published over 100 articles, book chapters, and proceedings chapters, in English and in Hebrew. He is the senior editor of several books, among them *Sport Psychology: Linking Theory and Practice* (1999) and *The Psychology of Team Sports* (2003), and served as a co-editor of *Handbook of Research in Applied Sport and Exercise Psychology: International Perspectives* (2006) and *Psychology of Sport Excellence* (2009), all of which were published by Fitness Information Technology. A former basketball coach, Lidor now provides psychological consultation to young and adult elite basketball players. He focuses mainly on attentional techniques used before the execution of free-throw shots. He also consults with athletes from several cultures and writes about these experiences.

About the Authors

Marko Begovic is a former professional tennis player. During his career he was active in local communities across Montenegro and actively involved in the organization of sport-educational camps, various sporting and touristic events, and conducting research regarding gender and sport in Montenegro. He was a member of a Davis Cup team and a captain of University tennis team. Begovic has a bachelor's degree in sports management, a diploma from Sport Academy Field: Tennis, and a diploma from Sport Academy: Sports Management. Working previously as a consultant for the Montenegrin Olympic Committee and Montenegrin Paralympics Committee, he stayed in the field of sport working at the Directorate for Youth and Sports in Montenegro.

Amy T. Blodgett is a doctoral candidate in human studies at Laurentian University in Sudbury, Canada. Her research and practical interests pertain to culturally reflexive approaches in sport psychology and social justice issues within marginalized sport populations. Presently, she is part of a multicultural research team working to develop culturally safe leadership training programs in Wikwemikong Unceded Indian Reserve in order to inspire active lifestyles among Aboriginal youth. Blodgett has presented her research at national and international conferences and has been published in several of the better-established sport psychology and methodological mainstream academic journals.

Ted M. Butryn is an associate professor in the Department of Kinesiology at San José State University. Butryn holds a PhD in cultural studies and sport studies from the University of Tennessee and an MA in human performance (emphasis in sport psychology) from San José State University. His primary research interests involve the intersection of cultural studies and sport, the application of cyborg theory to sport and the body, psychological and sociological aspects of pro wrestling and mixed martial arts, and issues related to Whiteness in sport and exercise. Butryn has published in *The Sport Psychologist,* the *Sociology of Sport Journal,* the *Journal of Sport and Social Issues,* and the *Journal of Sport Behavior.*

Erin Cameron represented Canada at multiple World Championships and major Games events in the sport of cycling. As an athlete and since retiring from sport, Cameron has invested energy, enthusiasm, and passion into promoting sport and active living through public speaking, freelance writing, volunteering, and coaching. She is now working on her PhD at Lakehead University in Thunder Bay, Ontario, where she continues her work in the field of sport for development, physical education, and health.

Kathi A. Cameron has worked in the fitness and health profession for more than 20 years as a fitness instructor, trainer of fitness leaders, and director of fitness and health for various profit and nonprofit agencies. She holds an undergraduate degree in kinesiology, a master's degree in exercise psychology, and is a co-author of *Leading to Lifelong Exercise*. She was a sessional instructor for the University of Victoria for more than six years and continues to facilitate community courses in health and leadership. She is currently Director for Health Promotion at 19 Wing Comox on Vancouver Island.

Tanya Forneris is an associate professor in the School of Human Kinetics at the University of Ottawa. She completed her master's in sport psychology at the University of New Brunswick, in Fredericton, New Brunswick, Canada, and her doctorate in counseling psychology at Virginia Commonwealth University in Richmond, Virginia, USA. Her expertise is in the field of positive youth development and her research focuses on the development, implementation, and evaluation of life skills-based sport and physical activity programs to enhance youth development, particularly with marginalized populations.

Audrey R. Giles is an associate professor in the School of Human Kinetics, Faculty of Health Sciences, University of Ottawa. In general, her research interests include Aboriginal peoples' involvement in physical practices in Canada's north. She is particularly interested in contested understandings of "tradition," crosscultural examinations of understandings of gender and development, and emerging qualitative research methods and methodologies.

Hussain Haleem (locally known as Kuda Husen) is a two-time Olympian (1988, 1992), holds four national records, including the Malé Marathon in 2:45:03 (since 1990). Locally, he has never been beaten in a distance event. In 2010 at the age of 41, he became the national record holder for the half-Ironman. Hussain holds two bachelor's and a master's degree in education (educational psychology) from University of Sydney, Australia, and another master's degree in physical education (sport sociology) from University of Otago, New Zealand. He earned his PhD in sociology of sport coaching from the University of Otago, New Zealand, in 2005. Haleem has also written articles and chapters for several publications and, currently, is in the process of publishing three books of his own. He is a Lieutenant Colonel at Maldives National Defence Force (MNDF) and also the Vice President of Maldives Olympic Committee (2009-2013). He lives in Malé, the capital of Maldives, with his two children—Humam and Hanan. At present, his most ardent goal is to become the first Maldivian to complete an Ironman Triathlon.

Stephanie J. Hanrahan is an associate professor in the Schools of Human Movement Studies and Psychology and the convenor of the sport and exercise psychology program at The University of Queensland in Brisbane, Australia. As an author and researcher, Hanrahan has obtained 22 grants and published eight books, 33 book chapters, and over 100 articles. She has made hundreds of presentations at professional meetings and to community clubs and organizations. Hanrahan, the former editor for the *Journal of Applied Sport Psychology,* is a fellow of the Australian Sports Medicine Federation and the Association for Applied Sport Psychology. She is a member of the Australian Psychological Society, Sports Medicine Australia, and the International Society of Sport Psychology. As a registered psychologist, she has worked with individuals and teams from all levels of sport (both with and without disabilities), Aboriginal performing artists, Mexican orphans, teenagers living in poverty, and former gang members. Hanrahan resides in Queensland and enjoys traveling within Australia and abroad.

Yeshayahu "Shayke" Hutzler currently serves as senior lecturer at the Zinman College for Physical Education and Sport Sciences, development officer at the Israeli Sport Center for the Disabled, Past President of the International Federation of Adapted Physical Activity (IFAPA), and associate editor of *Adapted Physical Activity Quarterly* (APAQ). Hutzler's main scholarly interests are multidisciplinary research focusing on physiological and psychosocial aspects of movement performance in persons with disabilities. He has published books on adapted physical activity and motor learning and control, and more than 60 articles in international and national peer reviewed journals, and has been involved in many European Projects, where he has also served as a guest professor at the European Master Mundus Program.

Kerry R. McGannon received her PhD (health and exercise psychology) from the University of Alberta after receiving a BA (psychology) and an MA (sport and exercise psychology) from the University of Victoria. She is an assistant professor in the School of Human Kinetics at Laurentian University. Her research bridges traditional epidemiological approaches and cultural studies approaches to understand physical activity participation. Her specific interest is in the social construction of the self and critical interpretations of physical activity and fitness using social theory and qualitative methodologies (e.g., narrative, discourse analysis). The journals in which her work is published, such as *Quest,*

Sociology of Sport Journal, and *Journal of Sport and Exercise Psychology,* underscore the inter-disciplinary nature of her research.

Carole A. Oglesby is professor emeritus at Temple University following 49 years in the professoriate. She serves as vice president of Women Sport International and formerly was on the executive committee of the International Working Group for Women and Sport. She is the author of *Women and Sport: From Myth to Reality* (1978) and editor of the *Encyclopedia of Women and Sport in America* (1998). She is the recipient of many awards including the Noel-Baker Research Award from ICSSPE; Distinguished Alumni Awards from Temple University and Purdue University; National Association of Girls and Women in Sport Honor Fellow; the Association of Intercollegiate Athletics for Women Award of Merit; Women's Sports Foundation USA Billie Jean King Contribution Award; American Alliance of Health, Physical Education, Recreation and Dance Honor Award; R. Tait McKinzie Award; and Alliance C.D. Henry Award for contributions to African American professional advancement.

William D. Parham is the Director of the Counseling Program in the School of Education at Loyola Marymount University in Los Angeles, California. He has devoted 28 years of professional service to clinical, educational, training, administrative, and organizational consultation venues. The interplay between sport psychology, multicultural psychology/diversity and health psychology represents the three areas of professional emphases with which he has been most associated. His emphases on personal empowerment, discovering, and cultivating innate talents and looking for hidden opportunities in every situation represent trademark foci. He is a licensed psychologist, Board Certified in Counseling Psychology by the American Board of Professional Psychology (ABPP), and Past-President of the Society of Counseling Psychology of the American Psychological Association, where he is also a Fellow in Divisions 17 (Society of Counseling Psychology), 45 (Society for the Psychological Study of Ethnic Minority Issues), and 47 (Exercise and Sport Psychology).

Ann Peel has been active in sport for community throughout her life—competing as an athlete for Canada on the national track and field team in the racewalk. She won medals in World Championships and the Pan Am Games, while also representing Canada at the Commonwealth Games. Shee was an active volunteer in sports administration during her career, and was the founding co-chair of Athletes CAN, the first independent association of national team athletes in the world. On leaving the practice of law, she designed the original programs of Right to Play, (then Olympic Aid), and was active in building the field of sport for development. She continues to coach children in her home of Toronto, and is the director of the AIM Jumpstart camp that connects children in priority neighborhoods with high school students and national team athletes in a multi-sport, inclusive camp experience. She creates, writes, and speaks on the subject of sport for development, working to connect theory with practice.

Duke Peltier is the elected Chief of the Wikwemikong Unceded Indian Reserve. A former NCAA Division I athletic scholarship recipient and CIS ice hockey player, Peltier has coached elite ice hockey for several years in Northern Ontario, Canada. As the former Director of Recreation, he oversaw the sport programming for Wikwemikong. In addition to his professional capacities, Peltier has also collaborated on two successive SSHRC-funded research projects with Robert Schinke and his colleagues from Laurentian University. The articles resulting from such work have been published in *The Sport Psychologist*, the *International Journal of Sport and Exercise Psychology, Quest, The Journal of Sport and Social Issues,* the *Journal of Physical Activity and Health,* and the *International Journal of Sport Psychology.* Peltier has also co-authored several academic book chapters.

Barbara Ravel is an assistant professor in the School of Human Kinetics at Laurentian University in Canada. She received her MSc (sport psychology) and PhD (sport sociology) from the Université de Montréal after receiving a BA (psychology) and an MA (social psychology) from the Université Lyon 2 Lumière (France). Her research interests focus on nonconventional genders and sexualities in sport using queer theory, feminist post-structuralism, and qualitative methodologies (e.g., conversations, discourse analysis). She has co-authored publications in *Sociology of Sport Journal, International Review for the Sociology of Sport,* and *Journal of Sport and Social Issues.*

Scott Sandison has development through sport experience in Africa, North America, Europe, and the Caribbean. Sandison has been involved as a trustee for the athlete organization AthletesCAN, as well as Field Hockey Canada. His involvement with Commonwealth Games Canada's International Development through Sport Unit has been ongoing since 2004 and he has worked with Right to Play, World at Play, and the Kicking AIDS Out! International network. In addition to his development through sport background, Sandison also competes for Canada in the sport of field hockey. He participated in two Commonwealth Games, three World Cups, and the Beijing Olympics.

Tamar Z. Semerjian is a professor of sport psychology in the Department of Kinesiology at San José State University. She received her bachelor's degree in psychology and human biodynamics at the University of California, Berkeley, and her master's and doctoral degrees in sport psychology at The University of Iowa. Her research focuses on marginalized populations and their sport and exercise experiences, incorporating theoretical perspectives from both social psychology of sport and cultural studies. She has published work based on her research with older adults, individuals with spinal cord injuries, and transgender athletes.

John Sugden is Academic Leader of the Sport and Leisure Cultures subject group and Director of the University of Brighton's flagship international community relations project in Israel, Football for Peace. He has researched and written widely around topics concerned with the politics and sociology of sport, and his books on international boxing and on sport in Northern Ireland have won national and international awards. Sugden is well known for his work on sport and peace building in divided societies; his studies, with Alan Tomlinson, of the world governing body for football, Fifa; and his investigative research into football's underground economy. He earned a Doctorate in the Sociology of Sport from the University of Connecticut.